THE LH7 RANCH
IN HOUSTON'S SHADOW

The E.H. Marks' Legacy
From Longhorns to the Salt Grass Trail

THE LH7 RANCH
IN HOUSTON'S SHADOW

The E.H. Marks' Legacy
From Longhorns to the Salt Grass Trail

DEBORAH LIGHTFOOT SIZEMORE

UNIVERSITY OF NORTH TEXAS PRESS

Excerpts from this book have appeared in "The LH7 Ranch: Remembering How It Was With Jeanne and Travis Marks," by Deborah Sizemore, *The Longhorn Scene*, April 1983, 6–13; and "You Think Things Are Tough Now," by Deborah Lightfoot Sizemore, *Simbrah World*, March 1985, 26–32.

Grateful acknowledgment is made to the following for permission to reprint previously published material:

Horseman magazine: excerpts from the article "Toughest Horse I Ever Rode!" by Emil Marks as told to Bob Gray. Copyright 1965 by *The Texas and Southwestern Horseman*. Reprinted by permission of David T. Gaines, publisher, *Horseman* magazine.

The *Houston Post*: portions of George Fuermann's "Post Card" column of 28 August 1958. Reprinted by permission of the *Houston Post*.

S. Omar Barker: "Code of the Cow Country." Copyright 1954 by S. Omar Barker in *Songs of the Saddlemen*, Sage Books, Denver, Colorado. Reprinted by permission of Robert E. Phillips, executor of the Barker estate.

Copyright © 1991 Deborah Lightfoot Sizemore
All rights reserved
Manufactured in the United States of America

Library of Congress Cataloging-in-Publication Data

Sizemore, Deborah Lightfoot
The LH7 Ranch in Houston's shadow : from longhorns to the Salt Grass Trail / Deborah Lightfoot Sizemore.
    p.   cm.
Includes bibliographical references.
ISBN 1-57441-111-X (paper)
1. LH7 Ranch (Tex.)—History. 2. Marks family. I. Title.
SF 196.U5S58 1991
63S.2'13'09764141—dc20
[B]   91-20920
                                        CIP

To Gene
Who knows where the center of the world is.

Contents

Preface   ix
1 August Texas   1
2 Prairie Poetry   13
3 The Addicks Years   31
4 Barker Rancher   49
5 Brauhauser and Henry Ford   67
6 Maud   85
7 Real Cowboys and Rodeos   103
8 Danger on the Range   121
9 Delirium and Depression   137
10 LH7 Longhorns   153
11 In the City's Shadow: A Clash of Two Cultures   171
12 The Last Trail   179
Epilogue   193
Notes   197
Bibliography   213
Index   217

E.H. Marks hand feeding one of his favorite longhorns. (*Photo courtesy E. M. Marks.*)

Preface

I was introduced to the Marks family and the LH7 Ranch in September 1982 when I interviewed sixty-six-year-old Travis S. Marks, owner of the LH7 Fannin Ranch, on assignment for the *Longhorn Scene* magazine then being published at Fort Worth. In an easy South Texas drawl, Travis told me of his father, E. H. Marks, their Texas Longhorn cattle, the rodeos and barbecues that had attracted thousands to the original LH7 near Houston, and the parade of colorful characters sprinkled through the ranch's eighty-year history. I was captivated.

So had been many other writers over the past half century. News items about the ranch had appeared regularly in the Houston papers since at least 1930, and the LH7 was featured in several farm and ranch magazines and other publications. Yet the story of Emil Henry Marks and the ranch he founded early in the twentieth century had not been told in anything approaching its entirety. To do so would be to record not only the history of a unique family but also to tell something of the cattle business on the coastal prairies of Texas when ranching was the principal industry of the region and to describe some of the changes imposed by the great industrial and petrochemical development since World War II.

To go beyond the news reports and get a more complete story, I relied largely on those who had lived it: the fourth generation of Markses in Harris County, Texas—the four children of E. H. and Maud Marks born between 1908 and 1918.

At Travis's suggestion I visited his sister Maudeen Marks, youngest of her generation and heir to the original LH7 Ranch at Barker. Maudeen's collection of newspaper clippings and family papers traces the Markses back to 1840s' Prussia and provides a wealth of detail about family members and the times in which they lived. From the ranch archives I gleaned documentary evidence that helps make this book not just a family history but a more extensive account of a region and an era.

Initial interviews with Travis and Maudeen led to lengthy visits with their elder brother and sister, Emory and Atha. Skillful storytellers, with a deep sense of place and family, Emory and Atha reached back through seventy years of memories to describe ranch life on the fringes of Houston in the 1910s, 1920s, and 1930s. No researcher could ask for more eloquent, thoughtful, or candid answers to questions.

The four siblings spent many hours digging for obscure particulars of LH7 history, verifying names and dates, and reading preliminary drafts for accuracy and completeness. Their conscientious work and unflagging interest in this project is much appreciated.

Others deserve credit for helping with the detail work necessary to produce a book of this kind. Hugh Berry of the Real Estate Office, U.S. Army Corps of Engineers, Galveston District, provided information about the Barker-Addicks flood control reservoirs; P. Ann Kaupp, information specialist with the Department of Anthropology, Smithsonian Institution, Washington, D.C., described the Smithsonian's excavations in the flood control area; William Pohl of the Department of Modern Languages, Texas Christian University, Fort Worth, and Dr. Ida K. Walton of Houston helped translate German phrases; and the reference staff of the Fort Worth Public Library produced needed information about books published eighty to ninety-five years ago.

Dairymen's Digest editor Phil Porter, now retired, and the staff of the Boy Scouts of America national office Editorial Service, especially Jimmye Anderson and Raymond F. "Ray" Sleater, alternately kept me in enough work to provide an income and refrained from calling me when I needed time to finish the manuscript. They and others encouraged me to persevere through several years of stop-and-start work on this book. My husband, Gene Sizemore, came through time and again with moral support and constructive criticisms. Although my own instincts may sometimes fail, I can always trust his.

Though he died in 1969, E. H. Marks contributes immeasurably to this book. The quotations that begin each chapter are his words, as recorded by various interviewers over the years and verified by his children. They tell a little of this old-time cowman's homespun philosophy, rich experiences, and enormous knowledge of the cow business. I am indebted to the group of Houston-area journalists who came to the ranch in 1967 to talk with E. H. at length. The forty-page transcript of that interview shows E. H. in top storytelling form. In this book I have drawn from that transcript extensively, letting Mr. Marks tell his own story wherever possible. Special recognition also is due E. H.'s first daughter, Atha Marks Dimon, for taking her dad to a recording session in Houston in December 1968. The resulting record album, *Ranch Poetry and Stories*, is an irreplaceable archive of E. H.'s favorite cowboy verses and reminiscences.

People say that no one who knew E. H. Marks ever forgot him. I was not privileged to know him in life, but through his children and the records that remain of his old-time tales and cowboy poems, I feel we did meet. I'll not forget him either.

Sophie and Johann Joachim Friedrich Schulz, grandparents of E. H. Marks. Sophie was killed during the Great Galveston Storm 8 September 1900; Johann died the following day. *(Photo courtesy Atha Marks Dimon.)*

Albert and Minnie (Mina Walter) Marks in front of their home south of Addicks. The land now is in the Addicks Reservoir. *(Photo courtesy Atha Marks Dimon.)*

1

August Texas

"My folks came to this country on a sailboat. My father was born on that boat . . . born on the way to Texas."[1]

In the cramped and airless passengers' quarters of the old wooden sailing ship, in the Gulf of Mexico six thousand miles from home, Sophia Marks gave birth to her third son. It was the 15th of August, 1843. The ship lay off the Texas coast, barred from its destination by a plague, blown from its course by a storm, and now approaching Galveston harbor for a last-chance landing. Among the anxious passengers were Sophia's husband Godhilf Marks, their sons 'Hilf and Albert, and Godhilf's five brothers. The Meyers, Brandts, and Groeschkes also had made the voyage from Germany. While the women stayed below to attend Sophia in childbirth, their families crowded on deck for a glimpse of the strange land that both threatened and beckoned the new settlers.[2]

It had been a trip beset by near disasters. When Godhilf Marks and family left Querfurt, Prussia, in the early 1840s, they sailed for old Indianola in the Republic of Texas. But there, epidemics of smallpox and yellow fever forced their ship to stand off. It was the season for Gulf storms; high winds lashed the tiny vessel as it struggled on to Galveston, 130 miles up the coast. At Galveston, too, they found yellow fever. With Sophia cradling the newborn in her arms, the immigrants hurriedly disembarked, loaded their few belongings on a two-wheeled cart, and walked inland to escape the contagion, scarcely pausing to rest after the long and difficult Atlantic crossing. They traveled on foot seventy miles north and west, making for a small German community near the young city of Houston. The trail led through the mosquito- and snake-infested salt grass country, a marshy lowland extending about fifteen miles inland from the Gulf. With grim determination the family trudged through the tall, bunchy salt grass, sweltering in the August heat.[3]

Sophia and Godhilf named their new son, born on the way to a new world, August Texas Marks. The boy's name celebrated the time and place both of his birth and of the new life that was beginning for his family. Before them, on the vast coastal prairies of Texas, lay the opportunity to start again. The Germany the Marks family had left behind was split by the two great powers of Austria and Prussia and squeezed by population and economic pressures. The crowning of Frederick William IV as king of Prussia in 1840 had opened an era of repression. The German press was severely censored and individual freedoms denied. Poor economic conditions created widespread unemployment and sent prices soaring, forcing many of the working class to emigrate. The United States and the Texas Republic held the promise of freedom and prosperity for those who, like Godhilf and Sophia, would risk everything to make the journey.

The Markses joined other German families at a settlement in Harris County about fifteen miles west of Houston. The town was variously known over the years as Bear Creek, Letitia, Rawhide and, finally, Addicks. Buffalo Bayou, about a mile to the south, was the border between the German Methodist farming community and the unfamiliar world that lay beyond. In this little bit of Deutschland recreated, the immigrants built homes, tended cattle and crops, and kept the comfortable traditions of the old country. Roads and landmarks in the western part of Harris County still carry their solid German names—Groeschke, Brandt, Habermacher.

The settlers had their freedom on the bald prairies, but little else. Money was scarce. In Germany the Marks brothers had been piano makers, but only two lived to follow their trade in America. Carl and Adolf made their way from Galveston to New York, where they are believed to have started that city's first pipe organ factory. Two of their brothers fell victim to thieves within hours of arriving in Texas, killed for their money after leaving the ship in Galveston. Another Marks brother who came to Texas on the same ship drowned in Cypress Creek while traveling cross-country to repair a piano, perhaps caught in a flash flood as he used the creek bed for a road through the brush, a common practice.[4]

Settling on the wide, flat land, Godhilf revealed ambitions to be a cattleman, tempted by the open range's thousands of acres of free grass and the potential of the nearby Houston market for beef, tallow, and hides. He recorded the "Wet Hat" brand in Harris County in 1851.[5]

Ranching in the Gulf prairies and marshes meant summer-long battles against heat, humidity, tenacious cattle parasites, and disease. Setbacks were inevitable as the Marks family tried to wrest a livelihood from the land. To finance his cattle venture, or simply to feed and clothe his children, Godhilf left the family on Bear Creek and returned to Galveston to find work at the du Pont gunpowder factory. He disappeared. No word ever reached Sophia Marks of her husband's fate, though some people speculated he had met death in Galveston, like his two brothers, at the hands of cutthroats. It seemed unlikely Godhilf would abandon his wife and children; Sophia could only assume him lost to an accident, or murder.[6]

A woman alone had scant chance of running a farm and raising a family on the unforgiving prairies. Sophia soon remarried, though her match to Christian Striepe may have been largely a marriage of convenience. In the spring of 1853 Striepe purchased one hundred acres on Coon's Bayou, paying William Anders a dollar an acre plus interest at the rate of 12 percent per annum.⁷ Then Striepe, too, disappeared, at least from the record of Sophia's life. It was rumored she ran him off. For a time she signed her name Sophia Striepe, then married again, to a John Rinkel. But her tombstone was to bear the legend *Hier Ruht* ("Here lies in peace") *Sophia Marks*, evidence that she never wholly cast off her bonds to the absent Godhilf.

When Texas seceded from the Union in 1861, all three of Sophia's boys joined the Confederate Army. Only Albert and August Texas Marks survived the war. Their elder brother, 'Hilf, was missing and presumed killed in the Vicksburg campaign.⁸

The sacrifice of her firstborn son may have moved Sophia to contribute to the war effort in yet another way. Ninety-three years after the siege of Vicksburg, her grandson E. H. Marks came home from hunting trips in Colorado and West Texas to discover the theft of a single-barreled muzzle-loader that had belonged to his grandmother. Part of the gun's stock had been whittled away on the left side so she could more easily sight the weapon. Sophia was said to have shot the gun for the South during the Civil War, reportedly to great effect: "There were seven notches on the stock, and she never would tell us what they were for," Marks related. "But if they had been for deer, I'm sure she would have told us."⁹

In 1862 Sophia received a homestead grant from the State of Texas for 160 acres two miles north of Addicks on Bear Creek, a tributary of Buffalo Bayou. The document was patented by Governor Francis R. Lubbock, whose administration covered much of the period of the Confederacy. As the oldest son to survive the war, Albert Marks had first claim to the family homestead. After he came home from the fighting, he purchased his mother's Bear Creek land for $350 in coin and a lifetime supply of corn. From 1874 until Sophia's death in 1882, Albert was legally bound to furnish his mother twenty-five barrels of corn annually; furthermore, stated their agreement: "The Twenty Five Brls. of Corn to be given yearly to Mrs. Sophia Striepe by Albert Marks, during her life until her death, must be of a good sound and merchantable Quality and deliverable in the proper season of the year...." The contract stipulated that, should Albert fail to deliver to his mother the specified amount of good quality corn, "at the time of the general and usual harvesting of corn in Harris County," he must pay Sophia one silver dollar for every barrel of corn owed.[10]

Albert accepted his mother's terms, signed the agreement, and took over the farm. In 1875 he married eighteen-year-old Mina S. Walter, and together they raised seven children on the Marks homestead: Adolph, Albert Jr., Hilf, Laura, Hattie, Clara, and Minnie. Albert Sr. worked as a carpenter and wagonmaker. One of his unusual creations was a desert-going water wagon built in 1885. Made of three-inch cypress boards and hand-hammered iron, with wooden wheels on iron axles, the mule-drawn wagon's only purpose was to haul water. It was built for a wagon train going from Harris County to California, across the deserts of the Southwest. But the train never got off, so the water wagon remained in the Marks family to be used by future generations to water potatoes and serve lemonade at barbecues and church picnics.[11]

In taking the family land on Bear Creek, Albert little harmed the cattle interests of his younger brother, August Texas Marks. Cattle raisers on the coast prairies had access to a nearly limitless open range with knee-high grass. A man could ride from the Gulf to the Colorado River and never see a fence.[12] Cattle of many brands grazed the free grass, the herds mingling undisturbed until at periodic roundups each cowman cut out the beeves carrying his own mark and drove his stock to market.

Before the Civil War, cattlemen on the Texas coast had shipped livestock from Galveston, Indianola, and Corpus Christi to the Port of New Orleans. When the coast was blockaded during the war, the Gulf area cattle markets dried up. The loss proved disastrous for ranchers. Cattle prices in the war years fell to one or two dollars a head. Thousands of cattle were killed for their hides and tallow, and buttons were made from their horns, but the meat was largely wasted.[13]

After 1865, with the nation's appetite for beef whetted by wartime shortages, cattle were selling in the north for thirty to forty dollars a head. Penniless soldiers who returned from the war to find their homes and farms ravaged by marauders or rotting in neglect rebuilt on the backs of tough Texas cattle.

Long-legged and long-horned, the wild cattle were products of the wilderness. Descended from Spanish stock brought by conquistadors and missionaries centuries earlier, the rangy Texas Longhorn provided the foundation on which Texas based its economy in the three decades after the Civil War. Money from the sale of cattle in Kansas established fortunes in Texas.[14]

"The Longhorn was the salvation of Texas," E. H. Marks would say many years later. "In the Civil War when all the men went to the army, the womenfolks couldn't find any cattle. They ran off and they didn't have a brand on them. The women couldn't take care of them. But the Longhorns could take care of themselves. Then when the men came back, why, there was a lot of wild cattle. Everybody that had cattle when they went to the army could brand all the unbranded cattle they could find."[15]

The story is told of one former Confederate soldier from the salt grass country, Fritz Koennecke, who could not decide whether he was eligible to claim a herd by virtue of prewar ownership. He talked to his major about it.

"Did you have any cattle?" asked the old major.

"I had two yoke of oxen when I went," Koennecke replied.

"That's cattle," declared the major. "Go to branding."

The war veteran put his mark on thirty-six head. His two pair of oxen had effectively multiplied ninefold during their master's absence—quite a reproductive feat for steers.[16]

Across South and Central Texas, stockmen took similar advantage of the chaos of war's aftermath to build their herds, gathering wild cattle from prairie, thicket, and creek bottom and setting off on the road to fortune. Northward, those cattle meant cash.

The way to get beef to northern markets was to walk it there. Texas drovers pushed an estimated ten million Longhorns across plains, rivers, and Indian territory to meet the railroads in Kansas and Missouri. The great trail drives lasted only twenty-eight years but delivered some two hundred million dollars into the hands of Texas cattlemen.[17]

"Nothing but the Longhorn could have stood the trail drives to the rail heads of the Midwest," maintained E. H. Marks, youngest son of August Texas. "In those days, they had to walk all the way to Kansas or beyond. No railroads down around here."[18]

August Texas Marks, in his twenties and just beginning a family, was among the cowboys who took to the trails after the Civil War. When he was home, the fiddle-playing drover entertained his children with stories of adventure on the long northern drives.

"My daddy told me about how during a trail drive back in the '80s, a rattler struck a Longhorn steer by the jaw," E. H. recalled. "The snake really dug in. The steer whipped his head around and the snake held on. Oh, the steer's eye swelled up, but he was OK after a few days. Anything else, a horse or any other kind of steer, would have been dead for sure."[19]

On one trip, Marks said, Indians confronted the drovers between Addicks and Houston and demanded a beef. He offered no resistance and let them take a steer from the herd. That was the surest way to avoid trouble.[20]

The cattle business made A. T. Marks a man of property and position in the community. Married on Christmas Eve 1870 to Anna Marie Elizabeth Schulz, eighteen-year-old daughter of a neighboring German family, by 1871 Marks owned 260 acres at Addicks. A joint purchase in 1888 with his brother-in-law, Wilhelm "Uncle Billy" Schulz, gave him an interest in another 120 acres, bought from Adolph and Emma Brandt for $650.[21]

At one point Marks owned sixteen hundred acres and a stagecoach inn on the banks of Buffalo Bayou. The inn had been a landmark in the area since well before the Civil War, providing a stopping place for coaches and ox teams crossing the bayou. Before the war, a Mrs. Silliman operated a tavern there.

"I wish I could sell this old flak land. I'd take eight hundred dollars for it," Marks reportedly said. It may have been a remark made in haste. The grasslands of West Harris County brought upwards of five dollars an acre. At fifty cents a measure, Marks's offer apparently sounded like a bargain to W. J. Habermacher, Sr., even for "old flak land." Habermacher made a down payment of one hundred dollars and sold cattle inherited from his father to cover the balance. In 1871 he moved his family to the old inn, known thereafter as Habermacher House. According to the Habermacher children's grandmother, Henrietta Bleick, "The Indians came in large numbers and camped near Buffalo Bayou near the Habermacher Crossing. In 1875 they suffered from a severe winter and many died. This was the last time that a large tribe ever came."[22]

About three miles south of Buffalo Bayou ran the East-West Narrow Gauge Railroad, the earliest rail transportation in the territory. A horse could easily outrun it. Thirsty cowboys could ride up alongside the engine and ask the fireman for a cup of water. On its cross-country run from Houston to San Felipe, before its demise in the late 1890s, the Narrow Gauge made scheduled stops at Habermacher Station and elsewhere along the route, but anyone wanting to board the train could simply wait by the track and flag it down anywhere on the prairie.[23]

A. T. Marks used the Narrow Gauge when he hunted in Bray's Bayou Slough. That was good land, E. H. remembered: "It was rich. They used to say you could raise a bale of cotton an acre and two ears to the stalk and a peck of shelled corn in the shoot. But they've cut ditches through there now and drained it off.

"When I was a boy in the '90s, my father used to go down there and shoot deer. Then he'd flag the train... and he'd throw his deer on a flat car and go into Houston and sell 'em. Used to get [$2.50 or] $3 a head for the big ones."[24]

Deer and other wild game were so plentiful in the bayou country that even the most cash-poor farmer could be choosy about what went on his family's table. E. H. recalled that as a boy he never had to eat raccoon, opossum, or even rabbit:

> We had too much turkey, prairie chicken, deer, ducks, and geese in my days. We always had plenty of wild game. My folks never would eat a rabbit or a 'coon or a 'possum. We never had that on the table in all my days, from the time I was a boy. We raised our sweet potatoes and killed our meat. We had plenty of meat in the summer and pork in the winter. We had wild hogs running in the woods, and the acorn crop was lots better than it is now, you know.
>
> We raised our potatoes and we always had lots of turnips and we ground our own corn and made our own molasses, so we didn't have much to buy, just flour and sugar. We had cornbread all week. We didn't make flour bread, but we had

cornbread for breakfast every morning and good homemade syrup. We raised peaches and plums and apples by the bushels. We had five acres in an orchard when I was a boy.[25]

Besides the cultivated crops, dewberries and blackberries grew wild and bountiful in the spring. The countryfolk needed to buy only flour, sugar, coffee, tea, extracts, and spices, which were purchased in large amounts to last the year. If a family had more meat, grain, or garden produce than it could use, the surplus was traded with friends and neighbors. Sharing the bounty of the land assured that no food would go to waste and also put some variety into the daily fare.[26]

"Before my father passed away, we would go across the prairie with wagons and go up to my aunt and uncle's on the Brazos River," E. H. recalled. "We had a lot of hogs down here [but] we didn't raise much corn. They didn't raise any hogs, so we would take them some hogs and bring back a load of corn."[27]

E. H.'s aunt and uncle on the Brazos were Louise and Rufus Muske. Louise—"Lula"—was a Schulz and a sister to Elizabeth, E. H.'s mother. Lula and Elizabeth were the youngest daughters of a large German family that had arrived on Bear Creek shortly after the Civil War. The Schulzes, including E. H.'s Aunt Lula, Uncle Billy, and grandparents Johann and Sophie, were to be the youngster's only comfort after the loss of both parents.

In the first eleven years of her marriage to A. T. Marks, Elizabeth bore five children; the youngest, Emil Henry, arrived 26 October 1881. Pregnant again in 1887 at age thirty-five, Elizabeth died in childbirth.[28]

A. T. Marks soon followed his wife to the grave. In January 1891 he died of smallpox, which he contracted while removing his youngest daughter from a pesthouse. Marks climbed in through a window and stole little Sophie from the isolation "hospital" where health officers confined smallpox victims. Breaking quarantine rules, he hauled the child home in a wagon on featherbeds. Sophie recovered, but her father succumbed to the disease, leaving his children parentless.[29]

By order of the Harris County Court, 5 March 1891, Uncle Billy Schulz became the guardian of the five orphans. The oldest were Hulda, Sophie and Willie, listed in court records as over the age of fourteen; August E. was eleven years old. Little Emil Henry was nine. Faced with making their way in the world so young, the children grew up fast. The two girls soon married. Sophie's first husband was Mason Baker; later she married Judd Simpson. Hulda, young wife of Willibald Hillendahl, died in childbirth in 1895.[30]

The three boys continued to live at home in Addicks, looked after by their grandparents, Johann Joachim Friedrich Schulz and Sophie Schulz. August got a job as a mule harnesser for Ed Barker, a contractor for the Missouri-Kansas-Texas Railroad. During track construction in the Addicks area in 1892, when he was twelve, August worked for the Katy Railroad lighting lanterns for twenty-five cents a night.[31]

The old couple found the care of all three grandsons too much, so after a time young Emil went to live with Uncle Billy Schulz. He worked in Schulz's combination general store and saloon in Addicks, sweeping floors, running errands, seeing after cowboys' horses, setting up tenpins, tending bar, selling whiskey from a barrel at a dime a drink, and occasionally dodging bullets when cowboys emboldened by the whiskey decided to shoot out the lights. The walls of the saloon were peppered with bullet holes.[32]

Schulz had started in business on Bear Creek after the Civil War when the area was thickly populated with wildlife and little else. In 1893, when the Katy Railroad laid tracks north from Houston to Waco, Uncle Billy moved over near the flagstop and built a new general store and cotton gin. His store housed the United States Post Office at Addicks; his saloon did double-duty as courtroom for the justice of the peace, with Uncle Billy himself presiding. He was postmaster, notary public, banker, and, said the old-timers, the real law in the bayou country.[33]

He did not stand for much nonsense. One saloon patron, looking for a fight, taunted that he had never seen Schulz use his pistol. Uncle Billy shot the man's hat off his head, silencing the fellow's insults.[34]

Exciting as life was with Uncle Billy, Emil Henry soon had a better offer. Aunt Lula and her husband Rufus Muske—affectionately known as "Tanta" Lula and Uncle Rufe—owned a big cattle spread on the Brazos River at Pattison, northwest of Addicks. The Muskes had no youngsters of their own; their only child had died in infancy.[35] So they sent word to Addicks: young Emil was to come live with them.

With all he owned packed in a small wooden trunk inscribed EMIL MARKS—LETITIA, TEXAS, the boy boarded the train for Pattison. Uncle Rufe and Tanta Lula gave him a home filled with love, strict discipline, and high moral principles and put him to work as a ranch hand. For fifteen dollars a month Emil rode bucking horses, slept under wagons, and studied cows. The years he spent with the Muskes shaped the course of his life, for there on the Brazos River, E. H. began his cattleman's career. Nearly eighty years later he recalled his first days on the range:

> That's when I started to follow the chuckwagon and I finally got to be a fairly good cowhand. I finally got big enough and I went to a roundup. Those days we didn't have these fancy bedrolls we've got now. We followed the chuckwagon and it didn't make any difference. A chuckwagon is a provision wagon for a bunch of cowboys, and wherever night overtook us that's where we camped.
>
> That's all I knew, because my people passed away when I was small, and my grandfather and grandmother came and lived with us and we were just too many boys around there, so they sent me up here on the Brazos River about thirty miles to my aunt and uncle's, and they were big cattle people and that's where I learned the cow business.[36]

CODE OF THE COW COUNTRY

It don't take such a lot o' laws to keep the rangeland straight,
Nor books to write them in, because there are only six or eight.
The first one is the Welcome sign written deep in Western hearts—
My camp is yours and yours is mine in all cow country parts.
Treat with respect all womankind, same as you would your sister.
Take care of neighbors' strays you find, and don't call cowboys "mister."
Shut the pasture gates when passin' thru and takin' all in all,
Be jest as rough as pleases you but never mean nor small.
Talk straight, shoot straight, an' never break your word to man nor boss.
Plumb always kill a rattlesnake; don't ride a sore-backed hoss.
It don't take law nor pedigree to live the best you can;
These few is all it takes to be a cowboy an'—a Man!

—S. OMAR BARKER

PRESENTED BY

E. H. Marks, LH 7 Ranch, Barker, Texas

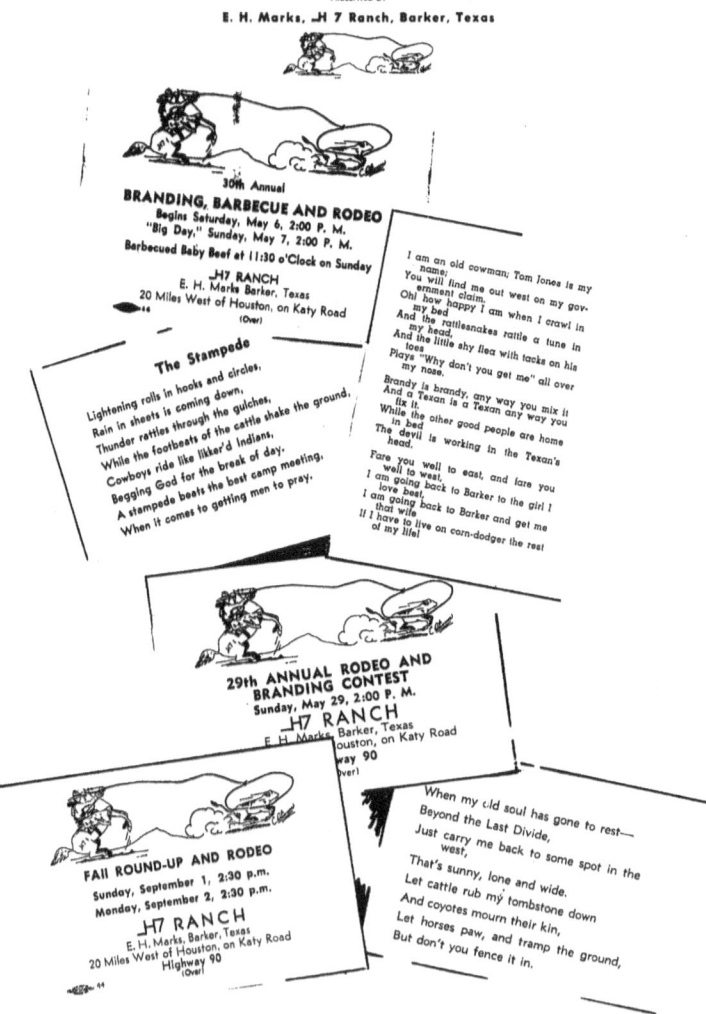

LH7 Ranch Rodeo advertising cards with poems on backs

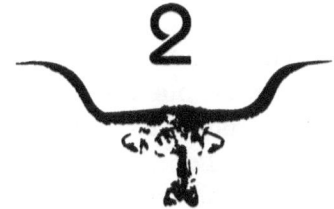

Prairie Poetry

"I lived in the days when Texas was young. I followed the chuckwagon and rode bucking horses from ranch to ranch. But that was in those early days, in the nineties, when I was young."[1]

Wild horses, wily Longhorns, and rattlesnakes can teach a twelve-year-old cowhand things not found in any book. After he went to live with the Muskes at Pattison, E. H. got most of his education on the prairie, riding range first for Uncle Rufe and later for other ranchers. The youngster had time for only a smattering of formal schooling between roundups and ranch jobs.

"I never did get out of the third reader in school," E. H. admitted. "We didn't have any schools in this country in the early days. We just went to a private home and paid a dollar and a half a month. Half the time we didn't get there—we went swimming and ran horse races, and the folks wouldn't find it out, maybe never. The teachers, of course, didn't miss us. They didn't know what we had to do at home—maybe the folks just didn't send us. Anyhow, we didn't get much education."

One highlight of E. H.'s brief hitch as a schoolboy was a classroom visit by the county superintendent. The teacher, Miss Eva, was eager for her pupils to perform well for the visiting official, so she coached them in the proper responses to the superintendent's predictable questions. Dick Sauer, at the head of the class, would answer first, and so on down the line.

"The first question in the book is, 'Who made you?'" Miss Eva told Dick. "You say, 'God made me.'"

Emil Henry had the next question: "Who discovered America?" He was ordered to commit his answer to memory—"Yours is Christopher Columbus, just remember that, Christopher Columbus."

> So I kept saying "Christopher Columbus, Christopher Columbus." I went home and studied that thing. I didn't know nothin' about the question but I knew the answer.
>
> The next day when I got to school, Dick told me, "I'm not going to school tomorrow, I'm going to the cotton gin with my daddy." Well, I never paid any attention to that, but that threw me at the head of the class. And, of course, when the superintendent got open the book and asked, "Who made you?" I said, "Christopher Columbus."
>
> He said, "Why, God made you!"
>
> And I said, "No, come to think about it, that boy God made went to the cotton gin with his daddy."

No book could compete with cowboying for E. H.'s attention unless it told a tale of Texas cattle or Wild West days: "Anything that pertains to a cowman's life, I enjoy. People tell you that the fellow with the covered wagon conquered the wilderness. Listen, before he got in there, some old boy went in there a-horseback. He blazed the trail into the wilderness so that those that came after might come along a safer trail and know where there was water. He had to do those things in order to establish a country. I know my daddy said they'd always send a man ahead thirty, forty miles and see where the water holes were before they drifted the cattle on."

E. H.'s education might have had its weak spots, but his grasp of Western history was strong. His father's tales of the trail and the stories told by the cowpokes E. H. rode with as a boy brought the past to vibrant life in his imagination. "When I got in second reader I got pretty good at history," he said. "Guess I learned to read out of a Texas history book. We didn't have any newspapers or magazines then. A man learned most of what he knew around a campfire."[2]

The lessons of the campfire touched on everything from cowboy etiquette to the many uses of an old Stetson hat. When night fell on the prairie and men gathered around the fire to fill the evening with tall tales and song, E. H. listened intently to the older riders' poems and stories. Flickering light pushed back the shadows as rough voices and off-key melodies drifted across the range, with no one to hear beyond the firelit circle except dozing cattle and the night riders who herded them. In verse and song, the cowboys told of starry night skies, baking powder biscuits, and riding a flat, wide land where a man could stretch out a horse. When supper was done and the fire burnt low, E. H. heard rhymes of rodeos, outlaw steers, prairie fires, and thunderstorms:

"On the open range, almost every old cowboy made him a piece of poetry, and later on he'd make a song out of it. That's what we did at night. We didn't have anything to read, and no lamp to read it by if we had. There wasn't but one or two lanterns and they belonged to the cook. You better not fool with them unless you wanted to get hit over the head with a skillet. So we just sat around the campfire, and first one would recite a poem he'd made or learned, and then another would take a turn."[3]

Cowcamp poems were rough and rangy and real, strung together in men's heads as they rode for miles following a drifting herd. These unpolished stanzas and simple melodies served a purpose beyond the cowboy's need to while away long hours in the saddle. Poetry and song were tools of the trade, useful in handling a herd. At night, E. H. explained, improvised tunes lulled the half-wild range cattle and helped keep them from straying:

"When we made a roundup on those open ranges, we branded calves on the open range, and if we didn't get through we had to herd the cattle at night. There'd be a man on the north, east, west and south side. They'd ride to and fro, and they'd have to sing to let the cattle know there's somebody on duty. There would be four men herd till twelve, and then at twelve o'clock four more men would go out there and relieve them, and sing till daylight. They would sing all night long. If you didn't sing the cattle didn't know you were on duty. Every man had his own song, and you could keep track of every man by his song. That is one of the biggest things that will never come back, because our land is all fenced now, and we don't brand on the open range."[4]

The night herder's song was a gentle lullaby, a soft and soothing tune for quieting a restless herd. "You could sing a cow to sleep just like you can a baby," E. H. said. "Of course, you couldn't sing a rock 'n' roll and a boom-de-ay and a hot time, your baby would crawl out of the cradle with that kind of stuff. There's two different kinds of songs, a night song and a driving, moving song. The night song that those old cowboys would sing would go something like this," and E. H. recited:

> I'm a lonely cowboy, I'm far away from home.
> If I ever get back to Texas, I never again will roam.
>   Hey, hey little dogie,
>   Go to sleep, oh, won't you go.
>   Hey, hey little dogies,
>   Hey, hey, oh, ho, ho.
> Montana is too cold for me, the winters are too long;
> Before the roundups do begin my money is all gone.[5]

"There's about fifty verses to that darn thing. They could sing it all night long, and that would calm cattle down. Then tomorrow morning, when we wanted to move that herd on up the trail, we would sing entirely a different song. Those old cowboys would say:

> Foot in the stirrup, hand on the horn,
> Best old cowboy that ever was born.
>   Come-a ti yi youpy, youpy yea, youpy yea,
>   Come-a ti yi youpy, youpy yea.
> Foot in the stirrup, sittin' in the saddle,
> Going up the trail with the Longhorn cattle.
>   Come-a ti yi youpy, youpy yea.[6]

"Now that would make 'em move on. You couldn't sing 'em to sleep with that kind of song, and you couldn't move 'em along with the other one."

Night riders passing slowly in the moonlight, their soft serenades carried on the breeze, the occasional click of cattle horns blending gently with the cricket's chirp—for a boy just entering his teens, these were irresistible images. "There is nothing that would ever take the place of a bunch of cowboys out singing at night," E. H. declared. "The moon would be shining, and the stars, and you'd hear the yelping of a coyote and maybe an old owl hootin'. I laid . . . a-many a-night around the chuckwagon and listened to those night herders, and I finally got to be a night herder myself. They wouldn't take a greenhorn. I've herded cattle when it was thundering and lightning and pouring down rain—that was what could cause a stampede. 'It is a-thundering and a-lightning and a-pouring down rain / The darned old slicker's in the wagon again.'"

In poetry and song, the cowboys of E. H.'s youth told of their lives and their work and their pride in a job well done. Some boasted of their skill in the saddle and their talent with a rope. "I remember one time an old boy rode in and the boss asked him where he was from," E. H. said. "That was a thing they didn't much want to tell in the early days, where they were from. He said, 'I'm lookin' for a job.'

"Old Butler said, 'Can you rope? Can you ride?'

"He said, 'Listen—

> When my rope takes a-hold of a four-year-old
> By the foot, by the neck or the horn,
> He can flounce and fight till his eyes grow white,
> But I'll throw him as sure as you're born.
>
> Though the taut rope sing like a banjo string,
> And the latigo squeak and strain,
> Yet I have no fear of an outlaw steer,
> I'll throw him on the plain.
>
> A man is a man and a steer is a beast,
> And a man is the boss of the herd.
> From the biggest to the least
> They must all come down when he says the word.

> When my leg swings across an outlaw horse
> And the spurs cling into his hide,
> He can rear and pitch over hill and ditch,
> But wherever he goes, I'll ride.
>
> He can flip and flop like a crazy top
> And twist like wind-whipped smoke,
> But with the feel of my roweling heel
> He'll be happy to own he's broke.
>
> A man is a man and a horse is a brute,
> Still, a horse is the boss of his clan.
> But he'll bow to the bits and the steel-shod boots,
> And he'll admit that his boss is a man."[7]

Presumably, Boss Butler gave this unnamed cowboy a job, if for no other reason than to tell fanciful tales around an evening campfire. Only the men there that day ever learned if the cowboy could bulldog as well as he could boast.

"Along in the nineties," E. H. continued his narrative, "we had an old geezer ride in one night to the cow camp, he had whiskers about two inches long, and he was leading his pack horse where he had his bedroll and cooking utensils. He gave this piece of poetry and I remembered it. He said:

> When I reached the age of sixteen I joined the jolly band.
> I followed the chuckwagon plumb out to the wild land.
> Our boss man, he was with us, he was sober, brave and true,
> He said, "Where we'll camp tonight we may have some fighting to do."
>
> That night when our boss man hollered he give us all a fright,
> He said, "Come on, boys, git ready, we're all going to have to fight."
> Below I saw the Indians' campfire and the smoke seemed to reach the sky.
> I thought at that moment that my time had come to die.
>
> The Indians came at us and the arrows about me fell,
> My thoughts at that moment no tongue would ever tell.
>
> We fought for nine hours before that fight was over,
> And the like of blood and wounds I never saw before.
> When the sun was rising and the Indians had fled,
> We loaded up our rifles and we counted up our dead.

All of us were wounded and our old boss man was slain,
And the sun was shining sadly down across that bloody
   plain.
Sixteen as brave as cowboys that ever rode the West
Were buried by that plain with arrows in their breast.

It was then I thought of my mother, to me what she did say,
"To you they're all strangers, at home you'd better stay."
But I thought that she was childish, and the best she did not
   know.
My heart was set on rambling, yes, I was bound to go.

Boys, I rode the range, north, south, east, and west.
I stood at the head of graves where they buried the sorriest
   and the best.
But I headed back for the old home ranch, and there shall
   ever stay,
So let this be an advice to you strangers, is all I have to say.[8]

"That old boy's name was Jack Owens. He recited that about three times and I had it," E. H. remembered. "Now, it may not be just exactly, and I've never seen it in print. But I used to love that kind. If it didn't have something in it about a cowboy or a horse or something, I wouldn't try to memorize it.

"Old Jack, he could really sing some songs. He sang a song about the killycure—the killycure for whiskey-drinking, you know. It'll either kill you or cure you.

"And Sam Ward [one of E. H.'s employees in later years] used to sing a song, it said:

> Here's to old Texas,
> Where they never have the blues.
> Where the cowboys work cattle
> And some of 'em drink a little booze.
>
> Where hospitality flows like water,
> Bullets fly like hail,
> Every pocket has a pistol,
> Every coat has a tail.
>
> Where you start out in the morning
> To give your health a chance,
> Where you might come home at midnight
> With buckshot in your pants.

> Where the owls is scared to holler,
> Where the birds are afraid to sing.
> It's heck down there in Texas
> Where you shoot 'em on the wing.
>
> Brandy is brandy any way you mix it,
> A Texan is a Texan anyway you fix it.
> While the other good people are home in bed,
> The devil is a-workin' in the Texan's head.
>
> But fare ye well to the east
> And fare ye well to the west,
> I'm going back to Texas
> To the girl I love best.
>
> I'm going back to Texas
> And git me a wife,
> If I have to live on corn dodgers
> The rest of my life.[9]

"There were so many of those little old poems that they added together," E. H. reminisced. "Each fellow would add something on, one would start a song and another fellow would make another verse. Any old cowboy would make a piece of poetry and sing a song around the campfire. All my poems are what we call campfire memories. They are things that were just gotten together and I've picked all these up around the campfire."

Some poems revealed an introspection born of long hours alone on the prairie, when a man had no company but his thoughts. To E. H.'s bottomless store of cowboy verse, he added this tribute to wide-open spaces learned from some wandering buckaroo:

> When my old soul goes to rest
> Beyond the last divide,
> Just carry me back to some spot out West
> That's sunny, lone, and wide.
>
> Let cattle rub my tombstone down,
> Let coyotes mourn like kin,
> Let horses paw and tromp the ground,
> But don't you fence it in.[10]

Remarked E. H., "I believe he meant it, out on the open range."

The poetry, the tall tales, the rough-edged tunes young Emil Henry heard around the campfire were stamped indelibly on his memory. From an early age he could recite cowboy poems by the dozens, one behind the other without pause or lapse for an hour at a time.[11] "I believe that I can recite fifty poems and I doubt that half of them have ever been published," he said. "I find some once in a while in a book, but they're not the way I got 'em."

When people marveled at his incredible memory, which would still be serving him well at age eighty-seven, E. H. said he could recall those old songs because he learned them by ear: "I never did get out of the third reader, but I could always memorize. I could hear an old cowboy sing a song two or three times, and then I'd have it. It would rhyme, anyhow."[12]

And so the boy grew up, learning the cow business and cowboy poetry, studying steers from the back of a horse, and memorizing Western ballads at night around a campfire. He became a first-rate cowhand and often rode night herd, a job trusted only to experienced men. He was a light rider, something ranchers looked for. It took a good horse to carry a grown man all day across the prairie; as E. H. said, "those little old pestle-tail ponies we used to have" would play out, though after a rest they were ready for another run. Ranchers wanted a bantam-weight boy like Emil who could rope and ride and spend a day in the saddle without putting his cowpony in the dirt.

For fifteen years E. H. worked as a cowhand on Southeast Texas ranches—"I could name you a dozen different"—from the Colorado River to the Big Thicket: "I worked for a lot of cow outfits, and going from one ranch to another learned me how the people did their business. If there was a bunch of cow work going on and I didn't have a job, I'd saddle up and go there and it wouldn't be long I'd get something to do. I'd make a dollar because that was my life and I loved it, that was all I knew."

Young Emil's reputation as a cowhand was such that legendary rancher "Shanghai" Pierce and Houston philanthropist George Hermann sent for him when there was work to do. Hermann paid him four bits a day to herd horses on the grounds of what would become Hermann Park, near where the fashionable Warwick Hotel later would stand on Houston's Main Street. That part of the city was open pasture when E. H. was a teenaged cowpuncher. He put Hermann's horses with a few head of cattle that he herded for another rancher and doubled his wages for the same day's work.[13]

Occasionally, he was sent on train trips to tend the cattle his employers shipped by rail. There was little opportunity for sightseeing on these trips: "The cattle was in those cars pretty snug and sometimes they'd get a front leg or a hind leg hooked over a horn. Then you had to get down in there and punch 'em loose."[14]

One of E. H.'s most difficult jobs was gathering cattle for the Stafford Smith outfit in the tangled brush and dense thickets of East Texas. A big buyer of East Texas cattle, Stafford had to contend with the beasts' tendencies to head for home every chance they got. Once pastured on the bald prairies west of Houston, the cattle often showed a remarkable homing instinct for the brush and woods they had left behind. When Stafford cattle strayed, E. H.'s assignment was to round them up: "Stafford in those days didn't ship cattle [by rail]. They drove 'em, and when they'd drive 'em over here from East Texas they'd get out and drift back. Old man Stafford—he branded horseshoe on hip—he sent me and another fellow down there to gather these cattle wherever we could find them."

Stafford gave E. H. enough cash to pay his own and the other cowboy's wages. "I paid him ten dollars a day," E. H. said. "He was a good brush man. He had a bunch of dogs that the wolves couldn't get. We roped those cattle and propped their eyes open with sticks. A cow will not go into the brush with eyes open, so he propped them open with sticks but he rounded the stick off so it wouldn't hurt them. He just fixed it so that their eyes popped open. Well, when you got those old cows in the trail they wouldn't run in the brush, they couldn't shut their eyes. 'Watch,' he'd say, 'they'll stay right in that trail.'"

Another trick young Emil picked up from his cow-wise companion was how to swim cattle across a river. "We had about thirty head of cattle we were driving across the San Jacinto River, and he said, 'We can't cross it, we'll have to wait till morning. You can't swim cattle against the sun. The water blinds them, it's just like a mirror. Cattle will turn around and look and wherever they see land, that's where they go. They'll mill around and come out right where they went in. The sun has got to be behind their back. You can't swim 'em east in the morning; you can't swim 'em west in the evening.'"

Getting horses across creeks that could be two hundred feet wide at flood stage also required a bit of animal psychology. E. H. learned to use a small boat and a haltered horse as a decoy to lead the others across. First the saddles went into the boat to keep dry during the crossing. Then a cowboy got in the back of the craft, took hold of the decoy horse's head, and steadied it as the boat was rowed across. The lead animal had no choice but to swim behind the boat; reassured, the other horses would follow the decoy.[15]

E. H. generally had some time off in December, when there was not much "cow work" to do. Occasionally in wintertime, however, a flood would threaten herds on low-lying ranges. Then the cowboys had a grueling, dangerous job of it, getting cattle out of flooded creek bottoms.

In springtime the pace of the work quickened to tax the stamina of man and beast. During an open range roundup, horses as well as their riders deserved a good rest when night fell across the prairie. Before a cowboy headed for supper and an evening around the campfire, he first unsaddled his pony, hobbled it with rawhide, and turned it out to graze the prairie bluestem under the watchful eye of a wrangler. E. H. spent many twilights in the saddle riding herd on the remuda.

"I've worked high as fifty, sixty horses, and that's one of the prettiest sights you ever saw." He recalled a prairie scene of half a hundred cowponies grazing in the moonlight. "I'd herd them till they'd go to lying down, and when the moon was shining on fifty, sixty horses, it was a beautiful sight. I don't suppose anybody could have ever got a picture of it because it was night. Those horses will lie down about twelve [midnight] and they won't sleep over about two and a half hours before they're up. That's when you've got to be watching them."

Some larger ranches had remudas of up to five hundred horses and needed twenty or thirty replacements broke to work the spring roundups. Many of these were roped out of the thousands of branded but wild horses that ran loose on the prairie. The outlaws were tamed by enterprising broncbusters like E. H. who rounded them up and put them under saddle, earning $2.50 for every bronc gentled.[16]

"In 1900 we had thousands of wild horses—broomtails, we called them," E. H. said. "That was the only transportation they had in those days. Everybody had a bunch of horses with his brand on them. We'd round those horses up and rope them by the front feet. I've roped thousands of 'em by the front feet. We'd throw them and when they hit the ground we'd trim their mane and tail like a mule."

Cowboys sheared their horses to keep "witch knots" from forming. Left long, the mane and tail would mat with dry grass, weeds, and dirt. The tangled knots of hair could grow so heavy with dried mud they would have to be chopped apart.

Sheared hair from manes and tails was worked into many useful items of cowboy gear: hair girths and bridle reins from the mane; lariats from the coarse, twisting hair of the tail. The horsehair rope was every man's standard defense against a rattlesnake crawling into bed with him. Laid in a circle around the spot where he slept, a horsehair lariat kept a man safe from snakebite, so the cowboys believed. "A snake won't cross a hair rope, y' know," E. H. insisted.[17]

The pay for cowboying generally ranged from fifty cents a day to a top wage of twenty-five dollars a month, plus board. "We had beans and plenty of beef," E. H. recalled of a typical range meal. "We would kill a good fat yearling every three days, as long as it was early in the spring and it was cool. In the hot weather, we would try to kill one every other day, according to the [number of] cowboys you had on the roundup. There would be a lot of people on these roundups. A bunch would work anywhere from Pattison on up to Hempstead in that big prairie and we'd work on down and work on down.

"They'd kill a good fat yearling. It didn't make a difference whose it was—that was the law in those days. If a man needed beef, if he needed something to eat, that wasn't considered stealing. You just got one of them. Of course, if they had plenty of cows then they would generally kill one of their own. If we'd kill a steer that was pretty heavy and we didn't have but ten to twelve men on the trail, we would send [the owner] a hindquarter or maybe a half a beef."

Not all cowpunchers were so conscientious, however. "Some of them old cowboys, when they'd kill a fat animal, they'd say, 'I want a hobble out of that hide.' I finally found out that they always split the hide all to pieces [ostensibly to make horse hobbles] so nobody could find the brand," E. H. confided. "They would generally kill one that didn't belong to anybody in that crowd."

Sourdough biscuits were usually on the menu to round out a meal of beef, beans, and black coffee. E. H. said the "sour" would bake out of sourdough so that the end result was almost like soda biscuits. Good sourdough began with a well-fermented starter, he noted: "A lot of people think it's a hard thing to make sourdough biscuits, but that's easy. If you didn't have a starter you'd just take some Irish potatoes and boil 'em half done and mash 'em all to pieces, and put 'em in a herring keg or any kind of wood keg because that wouldn't break. A stone crock would break on a trail, in the chuckwagon.

"In forty-eight hours or three days it would go sour and then they'd mix that with some flour, and pinch off a chunk about twice as big as your fist and throw it back in that old keg. That was another starter. The next day they'd mix [flour] with that chunk and make as many sourdough biscuits as you'd want to make."

If cooks had more cowboys at supper than they had sourdough biscuits, they would hurriedly pan-fry a few dozen "rush cakes," E. H. recalled. "They'd mix up a batch of cornmeal with about a fourth or a third flour, and grease one of these long-handled skillets and pour it almost full. When it'd get brown they'd shovel it around and lay it out there. They'd make thirty or forty [at a time]. That's what they called rush cakes."

Vinegar as a preservative or flavoring for use at home and on the trail was generally homemade. E. H. praised it for economy and quality: "You can make vinegar out of anything, any old molasses or sweet syrup. You'd pour it in a hot crock to get a starter. This is what they called mother of vinegar. You'd start it and it'd make its own vinegar. Drain it off and strain it and I guess it was better vinegar than they make now."

Fresh vegetables and greens were so uncommon on the range that if some kindhearted farmer should share the fruits of his garden, the men were unsure how to treat the gift, E. H. recalled. "You didn't get any vegetables a-tall. Sometimes some old boy would have a patch of turnips and he'd give a cowboy a sack full, and the cowboys wouldn't hardly eat 'em. They weren't used to them. There wasn't any kind of vegetable but potatoes, and they were sweet potatoes. We didn't have Irish potatoes in this country like we have now, but we had good sweet potatoes. They'd bake them in a Dutch oven and they were good food. They'd boil them sometimes and peel them, and then fry 'em brown in bacon grease. Bacon grease in those days never hurt anybody."

For lonely, weary cowboys, a chuckwagon on the range promised hot meals and company. It was the equivalent of a roadside diner without the road. As E. H. described it, any man passing through was welcome to take his meals at the wagon: "In those days if you'd see a chuckwagon you could go there and get something to eat and stay there two or three days for your grub."

Except for what wild game they could catch, cowboys were almost wholly dependent on their outfit's chuckwagon for food. Houses were widely spaced on the bald landscape, and farmers seldom had an abundance to share with transient cowhands. "There were a few houses between home and Hempstead but there were very few," E. H. said. "We'd go over and maybe get a couple dozen eggs, and half of them were good, anyhow."

Fresh fish was a treat and a welcome change from the monotonous diet of beef, beans, and biscuits, but during a roundup there seldom was time to fish with line and hook. E. H. and company resorted to less sporting but more effective methods: "We took a seine and got a tub full. We didn't have time to wait for the cork to go under. Where there was a good water hole and we had time, we might drain it. We'd shoot fish, and we speared fish. In the early days we had lakes and there were lots of fish in the lakes. We didn't have the drainage we have now. More water would accumulate and these big ponds would get deeper and deeper because the cows would go in there and drink and every cow would carry out a little mud on each foot. I've seen ponds four or five feet deep and they weren't dug by anybody."

Riding the prairies north and west of Houston for most of his teen years, E. H. came to know the land in all seasons and conditions, in times of drought and flood, good weather and bad. By age seventeen he was an old hand at cross-country travel, alone on horseback for miles across the grasslands. After weeks of riding the empty landscape, no trip seemed too lengthy to have the company of others:

"I worked up at my uncle's in those days and I used to ride twenty-seven miles across that prairie and come home about every two weeks to our old home where my brother and sister and my grandfather and grandma lived. I wasn't but seventeen years old and I rode across that prairie. I'd have my boots on and I'd take my dancing pumps—we used to have dancing pumps in those days. We'd tie them behind the saddle, rolled up in a slicker, and go to the dances."

E. H. wore a six-shooter from the time he was fourteen. Wolves, coyotes, rattlesnakes, and chicken-stealing dogs all felt the bite of his .45 Colt. Other common varmints—cattle rustlers and horsethieves—might be dispatched nearly as unceremoniously. If caught in the act, thieves could expect justice to be quick and unequivocal: "When they caught them red-handed they had a rope for that purpose," E. H. explained. "My daddy always said that the rope was worth more than what was hanging on it."

E. H. had a favorite joke about his father and a horsethief named Emerson. Like Aesop's fables, the parable likely grew from a seed of truth: "Emerson stole a horse. He was caught by the owner, Crawford, and my father. Crawford wanted Dad and Leiber Coon to hang him. They asked Emerson if he had anything to say before they put the rope around his neck. Emerson read from a book that looked like a Bible and said, 'Let he who throws the first stone be without sin and never stole a horse, cow or yearling.' Dad and Leiber Coon said they knew nothing about hanging a snake. Boss Crawford said, 'Well, get going. I'll take care of him.'

"In about fifteen minutes Crawford overtook Dad and Coon. They asked what he had done with Emerson. Crawford said, 'I just give him that horse. He wasn't much good anyhow.'"[18]

Emil and Maud Marks with baby Emory in Maud's lap, 1908. The buggy horse, "Lou," has brought them to the home of Maud's father, Fred H. Smith, at Fairbanks, Texas. (*Photo courtesy E. M. Marks.*)

Maud, Atha, Emory, E. H., and horse "Billy" (left to right) in front of the family's second home at Addicks, built in 1914. Second son Travis was born in 1915 in the room with the window at left front. (*Photo courtesy E. M. Marks.*)

3

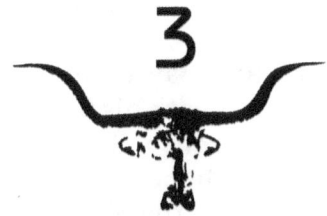

THE ADDICKS YEARS

"The cowboy, you know, has got a tender heart. He'll pick up a baby calf that can't make it and carry it in front of his saddle and the old cow will sure follow. Wherever he finds a water hole he dumps that calf off and leaves that cow and calf. That's what we always did."[1]

Never in E. H.'s life did cow work lose its appeal or the spring roundup its thrill. He was first and last a cowboy. He also was an ambitious young man determined to be a success. Anticipating the day he would become a rancher in his own right, E. H. registered the LH7 brand in Harris County in 1898 when he was seventeen. He wanted 7HL-connected but it was already recorded, so he settled for LH7 with the *L* reversed and connected to the *H*: ⌐H7.

It seemed an offhand choice for what would be his lifelong trademark, but as E. H. explained: "I was a green country boy. I went to town to get me a brand. I wanted a seven on there because I knew there were seven in our family. A fellow said to me, 'You want an H on there and a seven, why don't you just put the L backwards?' Well, not having much education, that's what I did. I just wanted a brand. They saddled this LH7 off on me and I took it." E. H.'s holdings then consisted of a cow with calf worth twenty-five dollars.[2]

It would take more than a pair of cattle and pocket change to build a herd. As a teenager with his future in mind, E. H. did anything he could to make money. So much the better if a job promised a little variety or a chance to travel. When ranch work played out or the pay fell short, the cowhand hired out as an oil field worker in Southeast Texas. The wages were a handsome three dollars a day. At the turn of the century, E. H. drove mules at the building site of earthen storage tanks at the Spindletop Field near Beaumont. He also worked in the nearby Sour Lake oil field. He helped lay a pipeline through the wild and remote Big Thicket of East Texas. Each morning, in the freshly turned earth, the workers saw bear tracks. He helped plant the trees that grace the campus of Rice University in Houston. E. H. and Henry Groeschke, a friend and fellow adventurer from Addicks, were in the gang manning the floating pile driver that built the Texas City docks. When they wanted eggs, Henry and Emil stole them from gulls' and pelicans' nests.[3]

Slim, wiry, standing about five-feet-seven-inches tall, E. H. was never afraid of a fight. When his wits alone failed to win the battle, he had no objection to a brawl, though he early learned not to push his luck. In recalling his father's roughneck days, E. H.'s youngest son, Travis Marks, described one episode that taught a lesson in prudence: "E. H. did not mind mixing it up with someone if he had a reason to. One time in the oil field, words led to a fist fight. He got the best of his opponent and put him on the run. Thinking he was pretty good with his fists, he thought he should catch him and give him a little more. The man he put on the run saw him coming, turned around just when he arrived, and delivered a haymaker that made E. H. wish he had not caught him. After that his advice to himself and others was: 'If you get someone going, let him go.'"[4]

As good fortune would have it, in the early autumn of 1900 E. H. was not working at his usual assortment of odd jobs around Galveston Bay. He was home in Addicks when the Great Galveston Storm broke over the island on the morning of 8 September, drowning Galveston in a tidal wave. The worst natural disaster in Gulf Coast history, the hurricane left destruction in its wake for many miles inland. When the winds abated at Addicks, E. H. and his brother August hurried to the home of their grandparents, Johann and Sophie Schulz. They found the house in ruins, the roof taken off by the storm, and their seventy-five-year-old grandfather pinned beneath it. He was holding his wife's head in his lap. Sophie, seventy-four, was dead. The boys' Aunt Marie Emilie, who had been staying with her elderly parents, also was badly injured and not expected to live. Johann's injuries were not fatal in themselves, but the shock of Sophie's death and the ill effects of exposure to wind and rain were more than he could stand. He died the next day.[5]

That deadly storm haunted E. H. for years. In later life, as a married man and the father of four, he would insist that everyone be up and ready to evacuate if the weather turned threatening during the night. "Mother wanted to go to bed and go to sleep," recalled his oldest daughter, Atha. "But Daddy wanted everybody dressed. We grew up with the thought that we should be dressed during a storm, and I guess we always will be."[6]

Single still in 1904, E. H. was a footloose cowboy, twenty-three years old, and bound to see the world. He and Henry Groeschke saved up from their cattle and oil field work and went to St. Louis for the Louisiana Purchase Exposition. As they were buying their train tickets, the pair told the agent they wanted "the longest ride for the money." Boarding the train in Houston, the boys awoke next morning in Sugar Land—a twenty-mile trip as the crow flies, but an all-night journey on the circuitous route they were traveling.

On the way to Missouri the train stopped to take on water, so E. H. and Henry got off to buy boiled eggs for lunch. Unexpectedly, the train took off without them. Down the tracks they ran to catch up, sending boiled eggs flying in all directions.[7]

For the trip, each of the cowboys had bought a ten-dollar hat, ten-dollar shop-made boots, and six-dollar suit. Arriving in the

Show-Me State, they turned a few heads. "'Are you'uns from Texas?' the people would ask. We'd say, 'Sure are!'" E. H. remembered. "And we wondered how they knew!"[8]

To smooth their way in St. Louis society, the two young gentlemen carried a letter of character obtained somehow from the mayor of Houston. The boys soon had occasion to use the document. The trouble started at an Indian camp on the fairgrounds where Henry was having a pair of moccasins made. As Henry leaned over to watch the squaw sew them, E. H. goosed him, setting off a chain of events that might have played in a future Laurel and Hardy film. Henry jumped into the tepee and fell on the squaw, startling them both into screams and shouts and raising a ruckus in the camp. With a band of infuriated Indians close behind, the offenders bolted for safety.

Once out of sight, E. H. and Henry changed coats and hats but soon were spotted on the fairgrounds by the Indians, who pointed them out to a U.S. marshal. Arrested for stomping on the Indian matron, the rambunctious Texans were hauled before a federal judge. E. H. pulled out the Houston mayor's letter and launched into an animated explanation of the affair, but the Indians pushed him back and pointed to Henry—he was the culprit. On the advice of a lawyer, E. H. produced five silver dollars and held them out to the outraged moccasin maker. She took the money and ran, and the case was dismissed.[9]

Life at home in tiny Addicks might have seemed dreary after E. H.'s high adventures except for one thing: the young man was in love. The girl was sixteen-year-old Maud May Smith, a raven-haired beauty from the nearby Fairbanks community. E. H. saw her at a dance and was attracted to her long, shiny, coal-black hair. He found out where she lived and would ride out of his way to get a drink of water at her house and press his suit.[10]

The four-year courtship seemed certain to lead to matrimony. But then there was a tiff, a little quarrel, and they broke the engagement. Emil rode to Maud's house to return a large packet of letters he had received from her during the long romance. Miss Smith walked to the gate to meet him. "Maud"—E. H. took a deep breath and said what was really on his mind—"let's cut out all this foolishness and go get married." Parson John Wesley

Anderson, author of *From the Plains to the Pulpit* (Goose Creek, Texas, 1907), performed the ceremony the next day, the 17th of April, 1907, as the couple sat in a horse-drawn buggy. Willie Marks, E. H.'s eldest brother, hosted the wedding dinner at the old Schulz family homestead at Addicks.[11]

Emil and Maud's first home was a modest affair east of Addicks that dated from the era of the Texas Revolution. A small, plain house that looked as if it never knew a coat of paint, it was shiplap on the north (kitchen) end and log cabin in the middle, with logs up about halfway on the south (front) end. It was built shotgun style: If you fired a shotgun through the front door it would go straight through and out the back. Old-timers in the area claimed that General Sam Houston had spent the night in the house during the Texas campaign for independence. Mrs. Bleik, an elderly widow, sold the celebrated little structure to the newlyweds together with sixty-three acres of land for six dollars an acre. With that patch of grassland and a few head of Longhorn cattle, E. H. established the LH7 Ranch in 1907.[12]

Emory Myron Marks, E. H. and Maud's first child, was born in Addicks 10 June 1908. As soon as Emory was walking, E. H. took the boy with him on periodic wagon trips into Houston to pick up supplies. They left home well before sunup and during the twenty-mile ride downtown were lucky to meet another traveler.

E. H. always tied a saddled horse to the tailgate of the mule-drawn wagon so he could round up any stray cattle they saw on the way. On one trip, as they passed a patch of woods, E. H. spotted a lost yearling. Leaving little Emory in the wagon, he tied the mules to a tree, got his horse, and gave chase. Dodging a tangle of low-hanging limbs, he roped the yearling and dragged it to the wagon, only to find he had nothing to tie the calf with except his big roping lariat. Reluctant to leave his rope behind, he tried using a string cut from his saddle, but it was not strong enough. Unwilling to free the calf after all that work, E. H. made a pigging string out of his belt, a wide, heavy strap with a big mother-of-pearl buckle. He tied the yearling's legs together with the belt, wrapped it twice and fastened the buckle, and told Emory they would get the calf on their way home.

In town, E. H. drove to the Henke and Pillot store downtown and stocked up on barbed wire and hardware. The store had a wagon yard where out-of-town customers could spend the night. It was a combination parking lot and campground with spaces large enough to accommodate a buckboard and team. Once the mules had been given their feed bags, some visitors left their teams at Henke's and took rooms for themselves; others, like E. H. and Emory, built campfires and stayed the night in the yard, sleeping under or in their wagons. E. H. often said, "Don't leave home without a wagon sheet," a tough, waterproof tarpaulin useful for pulling over the back of a wagon to make snug sleeping quarters. As a fifteen-year veteran of the open range roundup, he had little use for hotels.

Father and son left the yard early next morning and started home, intending to pick up the wayward yearling en route. When they got to the patch of woods where E. H. had left the calf trussed up with his great belt, pearly shards from the heavy buckle were scattered all over, and the yearling was nowhere to be seen.[13]

Emory was a well-traveled youngster. Before her other children were born, Maud would occasionally hitch the buggy to her horse Lou and take the boy to visit her family, the Smiths at Fairbanks. Mother and son were on their own for the fifteen miles there and back. The way from Addicks led around a turn at the old Hillendahl place on Long Point Road, through Spring Branch, and past a towering oak tree where the Snakeys lived. "One of them was Mabel Snakey and she was crazy," Emory later decided. "The Snakeys would be sitting under the tree, and Mabel would run out and try to get in the buggy. Everytime we'd go around by there Mother would hit old Lou and we'd really fly to get away from there."

A dependable horse was a must for anyone who traveled the open prairie north and west of Houston, a country still largely unfettered by fences in the early 1900s. Maud had solid, reliable Lou; E. H. had big-hearted Billy. A good working horse possessed of strength, stamina, and smarts, Billy was highly prized. E. H. bought the bay gelding about the time he married and started ranching on his own. Strong-backed, deep-chested, and game for anything, Billy gave E. H. some of his most memorable moments on horseback. The bay's extraordinary stamina enabled E. H. to do what few could boast of: rope a running wolf. Years later, E. H. would describe the experience and other memories of Billy for the *Texas and Southwestern Horseman*:

> You could get a dollar a head for wolves then so we did a lot of wolf running.... Wolves were bad. They'd kill our calves and the cowmen were glad when the wolf runners went out.
>
> The people all got together for this. They'd come from Hockley, from Waller, Katy, from Addicks, from Brookshire. From all around we'd come out to those big prairies.
>
> My horse's name was Billy. He was an outstanding horse. Billy was a gelding and must have weighed about nine hundred pounds. I don't think he was over 14:2 [hands].... He might have had some Thoroughbred breeding back there. But a good horse will pop out like good people. You'll sometimes find a good individual.
>
> Funny thing, the way I got Billy. He was about a three-year-old and I knew the fellow who owned him, name of Lomax. I wanted that horse first time I saw him. He had a real brisket on him, set out wide and good hips, too. Well, in those days I used to make a lot of bacon so I offered Lomax fifty dollars for that horse. He wouldn't sell. Then one day his son Claude came by and said, "Daddy said to come over and bring the fifty dollars for that pony and bring as much bacon as you can spare."
>
> I said, "I'm going to be pretty nice to you because I want that horse." So I gave Lomax fifty dollars and about twenty pounds of bacon.
>
> But to catch those wolves we'd set up in relays across the prairie. When we saw dust flying up, maybe two or three miles across that prairie, we knew they were after a wolf. Maybe they'd be after two or three. I've seen as many as six wolves in a bunch.
>
> Those wolves were fast and tough. They'd grow to maybe fifty-five pounds. And they'd stand up or jump up on their hind feet, to try and see you coming from away off.
>
> Sometimes we'd run those wolves to death out on that prairie. Sometimes you could shoot 'em. Because of Billy I managed to rope a few. The first time it happened I guess

we'd been running a wolf eight or ten miles. When we started, there were six of us on horseback after him. Everybody's horse played out but mine. We carried pistols so I started to shoot at the wolf when I got close enough. Every time I shot, the wolf jumped straight up. And I gained a little on him every time I shot and he jumped. I shot that pistol empty, stuck it on my hip and took my rope down. That wolf was about run down. He was just loping. The first time I made a loop at him he went right through it. Next time I hooked him, caught him around the belly and dragged him a little way.

Then I jumped off and pulled the wolf up to me. Thought he might still be alive. But he was just run to death.

We'd catch maybe thirty or forty wolves a year. And afterwards the cowmen would get us together and give a keg of beer and barbecue a calf on a Sunday for all the wolf runners. Of course there'd be a lot more show up to eat than just the boys on the wolf run.

This Billy horse must have been an accident because he was a powerful horse. I used to butcher some for the rice farmers and cotton people and they'd have me go out on the open prairie a mile or so from the house and rope a yearling, for meat. I'd put Billy on the trail that led back to the house, then I'd get off and walk around behind that yearling. I'd start to run the yearling while Billy kept the rope tight, going toward the house. That yearling might weigh six hundred or seven hundred pounds and maybe he wouldn't want to go—but Billy would strike a lope and take him back to the house.

Another time I was trying to pen two steers and had to take 'em over a railroad crossing and through some brush. I couldn't see where I was going through that brush and the steers turned. Billy turned to the right and jumped a ditch and I spurred a hole in the saddle as I came off. But Billy penned those steers. He put those steers in the pen without me. He didn't even know I wasn't on him.[14]

Then there was the time after I married when my oldest boy, Emory, ate all those green peaches and got sick. There wasn't any telephones then. Nothing but a telegraph down at the train depot. My brother-in-law, Thad Smith, jumped on old Billy and I said, "Be sure you get there."

He loped up to the depot but Old Man Carter, the depot agent, said it was against the rules to wire anywhere. So Thad loped on back to the house. Then he loped Billy to Katy—about ten miles away.[15] And then he brought him back. The last five or six miles he said he went at a good speed.

Next morning Thad said, "You might as well turn him out. I have an idea Billy's going to die."

I took Billy out to the pasture. About three days later I went out there and he was under a shade tree looking like he was asleep. I blew my horn and he threw up his head and away he went with those heels kicked up. You just couldn't hurt that horse. I kept him for the rest of his life. He must have been thirty years old when he died. Toughest horse I ever rode.[16]

As E. H. mentioned in his story of Billy, in his first years as a cattle raiser he butchered and sold meat to his neighbors, delivering it from a wagon at four or five cents a pound. When he butchered a steer for his family's table there was always more fresh meat than they could use, with no refrigeration and no methods to keep it other than salting and drying. He would put the extra cuts in a two-wheeled gig with a large box on the back, settle young Emory on the seat beside him, and go around to the neighbors. His customers included a black family among the rice farmers across the bayou. When E. H. drove up, the family's four or five youngsters would delight Emory with their sing-song welcoming chant of "Meat man, mama! *Meat man!* Meat man, mama!"[17]

As E. H.'s cattle venture grew, he began buying cattle from ranches all the way to the Brazos, driving them to market in Houston each week during the spring, summer, and fall. His selling grounds were in what would become a fine Houston residential section called River Oaks. It took at least a day to walk the cattle there from Addicks. "Up till 1913 I used to drive cattle into town every week, but the cars blew those klaxons so loud and scared the horses so bad, and the country got all fenced up so, we just couldn't herd 'em in any more like we used to," E. H. recollected.[18]

"We used to drive our cattle to Houston and herd them where Montrose now is. Then we would telephone the market men to come out and look them over. They would buy the cattle, then we would attend shows until midnight, ride back home twenty miles away and feel fine the next day." The beeves were so wild, men carried cow-whips to control the outlaws. It was considered bad practice, though, to use the whips on butcher cattle.[19]

Early in his cattle-trading career, E. H. learned to beware the tricks of unscrupulous cattle buyers. Those who thought to cheat the young rancher usually found their efforts turned against them in swift reprisal. Travis Marks recounted how his father squared accounts with one sharp operator:

> While being a good man in so many ways, E. H. did not subscribe to the admirable virtue of turning the other cheek. If he was wronged, cheated, or his character questioned, one could expect retaliation. In the early days of cattle trading and selling, E. H. made a deal with a buyer to deliver a bunch of steers to the buyer's pens where he had a cattle scale. The price agreed upon was four cents per pound or twenty-eight dollars per head, whichever the buyer decided to exercise when the steers were in the pen.
>
> E. H. drove the steers to Houston horseback and penned them before the set time of ten A.M. when the buyer was supposed to choose between buying them by the head or by the pound. The buyer was nowhere around at ten-thirty; at twelve o'clock still no buyer. E. H. knew the man was shrinking his cattle on purpose. The water trough was dry and there was no key or other means to turn the water on. E. H. fired his pistol into the ground, took the empty cartridge case and drove it into the recessed keyway and onto the square faucet control. Then, taking his barbed wire pliers which were always carried on the saddle in a leather holder, he turned the water on. His steers fell in on the water as though starved for it, which of course they were. The steers took on a good fill. When all had drunk their fill the water trough was dried out and cowpen dust applied to the bottom.
>
> About two-thirty the buyer drove up in his buggy complaining of being tied up and not able to get there in the morning. He walked over to the water trough and seeing

that they had—apparently—had no water said, "Let's weigh the steers," thinking he had shrunk the steers considerably.

The buyer got out a piece of gum and started chewing it. The scales were balanced and weighing began. The buyer would steady the scales with his fingers so they would not bob up and down so long. While doing this, from his vest pocket he retrieved a buckshot and used some chewing gum to stick the lead buckshot under the scale beam, which made the steers weigh less than they did. E. H. acted as though he did not notice the lead shot and gum placed on the scales to make the steers weigh light.

Only four steers could be weighed at a time. After one or two weighings E. H. said, "Let's balance the scales," which they did. Then, with some dexterity, he removed the lead shot and gum. This made the steers weigh heavier than they actually did.

When they settled up, the buyer paid about two hundred dollars more for the steers than he could have bought them for by the head. E. H. left the pens in a high lope, headed for the bank with the check. Throwing down his check at the cashier's window he asked for the cash. The bank teller asked if he did not want to deposit it. E. H. said, "Nope, would like the cash."

A few minutes later the buyer appeared at the bank and headed for one of the bank officers to stop payment on the check, but it was too late. E. H. was leaning on one of the bank tables as though figuring his profit; up stomped the cow buyer saying, "You think you are a pretty smart fox." E. H.'s question to him was, "Do you want your buckshot back?" The buyer's parting words were "Go to Hell." No doubt the buyer had worked his cheating tricks on other men but one had to get up early in the morning to get ahead of E. H.[20]

By 1913 or 1914, E. H. and Maud were doing well enough to replace their tiny shotgun house with something nicer. They lived in the backyard in tents while workmen built a fine house finished with beautiful woods to accommodate the growing family. The couple's second child, a daughter, had arrived 18 August 1910 and was christened Atha Elizabeth. The name "Atha" was suggested by Maud's father, Fred Smith, an avid reader. He said it was the name of an early Hungarian queen. "Elizabeth" was for both grandmothers: Elizabeth (Schulz) Marks and Martha Elizabeth (Clark) Smith.

The new Marks home had a long hallway that stretched from the front to the back door and separated the three rooms of the north end from two large bedrooms on the south. Stairs ascended to an attic. The house faced east. A bay window that Atha soon adopted as her favorite perch graced the middle room on the north end, which was a family and dining room warmed by a large double fireplace opening into the front room.[21] To get from one to the other, "we kids used to crawl through there and get all dirty," Emory recalled. "Mother would just eat us up about that."

Atha liked to sit in the bay window of the new house and watch the gypsies who came into the yard for water from their camp north of the railroad tracks. They came each year, traveling in colorful wagons as elaborate as a circus and wearing bright, flowing garments. Atha was enchanted. Mrs. Marks found them less appealing: The vagabonds openly stole pomegranates from the trees that grew in the yard near the well and hand pump. When Maud protested, the proud matriarch of the caravan offered a stately, dignified bow and said, "We'll be back tonight to get your chickens." They were.[22]

Along with the gypsies, a number of memorable eccentrics tramped over the Addicks-Barker-Katy area of West Harris County, most of them well known to the Marks household. Old Man Smith was forever going into Addicks and getting drunk, and on his way home he would trip on E. H.'s fences and hang upside down until someone came to his rescue. "Dad and I'd go out there, I'd stay back on the other side of the railroad tracks, and Dad would untangle him and get him going again. But as long as I can remember, if it wasn't Dad getting him out, it was his boy," Emory said. "He'd get in that fence and get all tangled up."

Lucius B. hailed from Brookshire, twenty miles up the road, but his antics were legendary throughout that territory. "Old Lucius was from a very prominent family, they had lots of cattle, lots of land, but he'd wear an old hat down to his ears, and his shirt was out, and his boots ragged, and he carried a slicker with him the year round, whether he needed it or not," Emory observed.

The Marks family had several colorful characters within its own ranks. Uncle Billy Schulz kept a parrot in a cage that hung from the eaves in front of his store at Addicks. The railroad tracks that ran by his place were not fenced, so Uncle Billy would send his dog to chase the cows off the tracks whenever the train came through. "Sic 'em, sic 'em, sic 'em! Shep, get 'em!" Uncle Bill cried when he heard the train coming. The parrot learned to say "sic 'em, sic 'em," too, and nearly ran the dog to death, siccing him on nonexistent cows to clear the way for invisible trains. The dog was soon ignoring commands to "sic 'em!" from either the parrot or Uncle Billy. "The old parrot really ruined that dog," Emory said. "The dog wouldn't pay any attention to Uncle Billy, he'd just lay there and go to sleep."

Uncle August Marks ran a saloon and hotel in Katy. He had three big hogs in back of the saloon, and for twenty-five cents, bar patrons could buy a bottle of beer and watch an inebriated swine guzzle it. "Beer was selling for ten cents a bottle then—twenty-five cents was a big slug—but they'd open the back door of the saloon and an old hog would come up and take the bottle in his mouth," Emory remembered. "Those old hogs were just a-sittin' there hollering for that beer all the time."

On the way home from Houston one day, Uncle August, E. H., and Emory stopped at Schotts Bakery at 3000 Washington Avenue. Across the railroad tracks was a beer joint. August wanted to buy beer for his saloon, but the price was fifteen cents a case higher than in the city. "Doggone the luck!" August exploded. "Hot dog the luck!" He wanted E. H. to turn the car around and go back to town, but E. H. reached into his pocket and said, "August, here's your dern fifteen cents! We're not gonna drive back to town."[23]

The Marks family got its first car in about 1913, a T-Model Ford from McFarland's Auto Sales. It had no doors and cost E. H. only two hundred dollars, but it made him "a big shot" by the standards of West Harris County.[24] The first chance he had, Emory, still a preschooler, climbed in and started down the road to Uncle Billy Schulz's store. "The Addicks store wasn't but a quarter mile from us," he said. "I got in that car and took off. And did a pretty good job, too. But after that, of course, I didn't get to drive for a while."

As the owner of one of the first autos in the neighborhood, E. H. assumed responsibility for providing emergency transportation. After the 1915 Galveston hurricane lashed the city with 120-mile-an-hour winds, he ran a gauntlet of destruction to get to Galveston Island and rescue the kinfolks of a neighboring family, the Wendlings. "E. H. took his Ford and, since the bridge was destroyed, drove across the railroad trestle," Travis related. "He found the people and brought them back to Barker."[25]

Telephone service arrived in the rural area about the same time cars became generally available. Lines were strung on fence posts in lieu of regulation poles. Anytime there was trouble on the line the first place to look was the pasture to see if a cow had knocked down a post or rubbed the wires loose.

One night the phone at the Marks house began to buzz like a deranged hornet. It was Uncle Willie, E. H.'s brother, a bachelor until he eventually married at forty-two. He lived on sixty acres adjoining E. H.'s property. Uncle Willie was excited. He wanted E. H. over to his place right away. Intrigued, the whole family went. "There's a *strange* creature under that woodpile," Willie told them. "It is a *strange* creature and I'm scared to death of that thing." E. H., Emory, and two ranch hands threw wood off the pile until they flushed Uncle Willie's alien visitor. It was an armadillo. At that time the armadillo, now so common across Texas it has become a popular symbol of the state, had just begun its spread into the southern United States from Central and South America. "They were a curiosity. Everybody in the country wanted to see that armadillo, so they caught him and put him in a trap, a little henhouse," Emory recalled.

By the time Emory started school, it was clear he shared the family genius for behavior others found extraordinary. He attended first through seventh grades at the Addicks school that his Aunt Sophie's husband, Uncle Judd Simpson, had helped to build in 1910. On the first day of classes, Emory remembered, the teacher asked each child to rise and say a few words: "We were all so scared, everybody had to say something.

They wanted you to introduce yourself, to get you acquainted with the crowd. I got up, and why I did it I don't know, but I recited a poem that I'd heard my dad say. The name of the poem was 'This is Texas,' and it went like this:

> "You can start out in the morning
> To give your health a chance,
> And you might come home at midnight
> With buckshot in your pants."

"That's enough, that's enough—Emory, sit down!" The teacher cut short the boy's risqué recitation. "She thought I had a lot of stuff behind that, and I did have, but I didn't know whether to say it or not."

J. M. (Milo) Frost, member of the prominent Houston family, kept a few cattle near the Marks place. When he came out to take them to market, he sometimes hired eight-year-old Emory to help drive the cattle cross country, at the princely sum of two dollars a day. Their association in the cow business led to an easy camaraderie between the young cowboy and the distinguished gentleman, Emory remembered:

> We were sitting under a shade tree one day. He was real bald on top of his head, so I said, "Mr. Frost, you've got a mite more hair on the side of your head than on the top. What kind of haircut is that?" He said, "That's a horseshoe cut. I'd have hair up there, but I get it cut out. The barber puts a horseshoe on top of my head and shaves out all the hair inside of it. It's cooler that way."
>
> Well, I bought that for a while. Joe Sills used to live across the road from us, and one day old Joe came over and I said, "Joe, I'm going to give you a horseshoe haircut. I'll give you one and you give me one." I gave him his first, and when I saw that it was looking awful I backed out. He went home, and that evening his daddy came over with a shotgun. He thought E. H. had give Joe that haircut, and he was about to have a fit. Dad said to me, "Did you give that boy that haircut?" I had to own up. "Yessir, I did. That was a horseshoe cut."

With Emory in tow, E. H. explained the situation to the irate Mr. Sills, who went home in a slightly less murderous mood. Frost's joke on his young friend was quickly forgiven. In

Emory's eyes he was a most respected figure: "I always admired Mr. Frost. When my first son was born I named him Milo, after Milo Frost."

Emory and his school chums played at the edge of a wooded patch on Buffalo Bayou, on low mounds that held a treasure of bones, arrowheads, bits of pottery, and fascinating artifacts: "We'd dig around there and pull bones out, and I found a skull one time. We were playing ball with it, Asher Hammond and Silas Waggoner and Johnny Habermacher and myself. When we left, I just took the thing and smashed it on a big post before I got home. I didn't think anything about it."

More than thirty years later, in 1947, a team from the Smithsonian Institution conducted salvage excavations of the mounds during construction of the Addicks Reservoir flood control impoundment. The excavators recovered a wealth of relics from the region's prehistoric Indian cultures. They found a burial site along Mayde Creek, a tributary of Buffalo Bayou, and turned up more burials at a site farther north along Langham Creek.[26] The remains and artifacts were put on display at the Smithsonian—minus a few pieces that had failed the child-proof test.

Emory Myron Marks, age four. (*Photo courtesy Atha Marks Dimon.*)

Atha Elizabeth Marks, age four. (*Photo courtesy Atha Marks Dimon.*)

E. H. Marks on "Romeo," in front of new home built in 1917 at Barker. (*Photo courtesy Atha Marks Dimon.*)

4

Barker Rancher

"Many men were on the move through early Texas, but ranchers drew respect because the drifters knew a man who could hold his own in Texas was a man to reckon with."[1]

Prospective land buyers rode westward from Houston after 1893 over the newly laid Missouri-Kansas-Texas rails. Speculators brought farmers from as far away as Iowa to inspect the coastal prairie lands, hoping to spark a land boom. The killing summer heat and voracious insect pests sent many back to their midwestern farms. Of those who stayed, some settled in the little country town that bore the name of Ed Barker, a contractor for the MKT Railroad.

Barker, Texas, was built along the rails twenty miles from Houston and had a train depot, a twine mill, a brick factory, a warehouse, and a combination store-saloon-post office and two-story hotel. There was a Catholic church and a Presbyterian church. The post office was inconveniently across the road from the train tracks. The postmaster reportedly had to "take the mail bag and throw it" to trains passing through.[2]

In 1917 E. H. sold his 63 improved acres at Addicks for one hundred dollars an acre and purchased a section of virgin prairie, 640 acres, at Barker. The new Marks home at Barker—a two-story, hollow tile stucco—was not yet finished when Maud decided to move out of the Addicks house and let the buyers have it. It was Christmas Eve, and E. H. was away hunting deer. Maud supervised as the family furniture and capacious icebox were loaded onto a wagon, and then she piled the children into the Model T and drove the three miles westward from Addicks to Barker. Supper that night was cheese and crackers, fed to the children on the sleeping porch.

"I had sort of vague feelings about it, I remember," Atha admitted. "It was kind of strange to me, what was going on. Daddy wasn't there, and we were coming up here to a new house. The living room wasn't finished; I remember how I played around in there. But when Daddy came home from the deer hunt, we had moved."[3]

E. H. found the family in residence at Barker with Atha the only casualty of the relocation. The seven-year-old had stuck a nail in her big toe while playing in the unfinished living room. She was in a Christmas holly drill at school, partnered with Laurence Groeschke. "So they wrapped my big toe, and I did the holly drill," she said. "We'd walk up to the center and hold our branches up, and then walk back. And there I went with my big ribbon bow on my head and also a bow on my toe."

Maud had designed the new house at Barker and was especially proud of the clothes closets, a double sliding door, the china closet, and the bathroom. Judd Simpson, husband of E. H.'s sister Sophie, built the house.[4]

With E. H. riding range across hundreds of acres and Maud busy with a new home and a growing family, their early years at Barker were full. The house was alive with the hubbub of children. Emory and Atha had been joined by little brother Travis Smith Marks, born in Addicks 15 December 1915, two years before the ranch relocated to Barker. A few months after the move, on 2 April 1918, the fourth and youngest child arrived, a daughter christened Maudeen Martha for her mother's side of the family.

E. H. and Maud turned the LH7 Ranch at Barker into a showplace. They finished the house and surrounded it with shrubs and trees, mulberry, mimosa, roses, Spanish dagger, redbud, yaupon, sweet bay, and holly. They planted an orchard of peach, plum, and pear trees. The peaches, especially, thrived. "I had peach trees and plum trees here twenty-three years old," E. H. later related. "They were big peaches. Everybody said, 'We want to see the peaches. We'll tell you what they are.' They never could figure it out. They called it everything except a peach." It seemed no one could say for sure how the fruit grew so large, even the specialists at the Agricultural and Mechanical College of Texas who named the variety the LH7 Peach and took buds for grafting. E. H. gave the trees no special care; in fact, he often was guilty of letting cattle browse the tender twigs: "I never did take as much care of my orchard as I should. My wife always told A&M College, 'I don't know what he does. When he gets a bunch of cattle, he might let the cows eat the tops off.' The fellow from A&M said that might be the answer to it. 'It grows so much top in this cussed country they ought to be cut back. If the cow eats the tops off, maybe that's it.'"[5]

E. H. always suspected the secret was in the soil: "This land had never been plowed up. Not a foot of it had ever been turned over, and all the minerals were still left in it."[6] A contributing factor also may have been the many steers fed out in that pasture, enriching the soil with their manure.

As the family settled in at Barker, E. H. enlisted the aid of neighbors and relatives to raise the necessary ranch outbuildings. Maud's father, Fred Smith, designed a grand barn with three enormous feed storage rooms, milk cow and horse stalls, tack room, haylofts, and a mansard roof over a loft large enough for community dances. The barn was built by Ed Romack of Katy. In the 1920s, a two-story cowboys' bunkhouse went up just west of the main house, built by Albert Weiman. Ranch hands' quarters were in a large dormitory room upstairs. Downstairs there was an area for cooking and eating and a garage for Maud's stylish maroon 1928 Dodge Victory Six.

Other ranch buildings included a hoghouse with a built-in self-feeder; a smokehouse for curing sausage, hams, and bacon; an engine house for the Delco electric system; two chicken houses, one for laying hens and one for raising baby chicks; a tool shed equipped as blacksmith's shop; and several long feeding pens. A second large barn, mansard-roofed with cupola, was a storehouse for hay and cottonseed hulls. Rounding out the facilities was a complete set of cattle-working pens including loading chutes, branding chute, and dipping vat.[7]

E. H.'s brother-in-law Judd Simpson built the LH7's slaughterhouse. The ranch negotiated yearly contracts to furnish meat each week for large Houston grocers including Henke and Pillot and many smaller, family-owned meat markets such as Lyons on Washington Avenue. Thousands of cattle were butchered in the slaughterhouse under federal inspection for Houston consumption. "They were grass-fed beef and that meat was always very good," Atha noted. The largest kill in any year averaged one hundred animals per week: 5,203 head, mostly calves with some cows and steers. All but a fraction of the cattle slaughtered were home-raised, LH7-branded stock.[8]

E. H. had ties to the dairy business through Maud's people, the Smiths; her father dairied at Fairbanks. It may have been because of this connection that Marks bought a herd of Shorthorns about the time he moved the LH7 from Addicks to Barker. Perhaps he thought to enhance the milking ability of the native Texas Longhorn by crossing it with the Shorthorn, a dual-purpose dairy and beef breed. "I like the Shorthorns crossed with the Longhorns," he said. "We had them here in the nineties. A fellow shipped in a bunch of Shorthorn bulls from up north somewhere and my uncle kept them over at his house quite a while and the strain got started between the Longhorns and the Shorthorns."[9]

When E. H. tried to introduce Shorthorns to his LH7 herd, however, the experiment was a disaster. The cattle failed to prosper on the best of pasture feeding, and many ended mired in mud holes. "The longer we had them, the more they faded," Emory recalled. "If there was a mud hole out there anywhere, that's where we'd see them, up to their breastbone in mud." The land was too boggy, the heat too intense, and the fever ticks too ferocious for a breed that originated in cool northeastern England.[10]

An innovative cattleman, not afraid to take a risk if the potential for profit looked good, E. H. continued to explore possibilities for crossing the native Texas cattle with another breed to produce bigger, faster growing offspring. His next attempt at crossbreeding, using Brahman bulls, was far more successful. The LH7 was one of the first Gulf Coast ranches to experiment with the hump-backed, droop-eared Brahman, the sacred white cow of India. The breed originated in a tropical climate and proved ideally suited to conditions on the sweltering, sun-blistered coastal prairies. The Brahman was free from pinkeye, ticks, and cancer eye and could survive heat and drought that would kill European cattle. Even on the hottest days, Brahmans did not seek shade but went about their natural business, grazing in full sun. They were resistant to flies, mosquitoes, screwworms, and other insect pests. Good range cattle, they gained weight on almost any kind of fodder and dressed out a high percentage of high-quality meat.[11]

J. M. Frost, Sr., who ranched to the southwest of Houston in Fort Bend County, brought the first Brahman cattle to the area in 1885. Frost had been skeptical of the "damned slick-haired cattle" until he saw how they thrived on the coastal plains. Won over, the ranchman imported two bulls, Richard III and Khedive, which he pastured on land out from Houston in what would become West University Place.[12]

In 1906 Abel Pierce Borden, nephew of Shanghai Pierce, imported fifty-one head from India to the Pierce Estate in Wharton County. E. H. bought his first Brahman bulls in the early 1920s. Unusually gentle "Bojan," a mostly Brahman crossbred, came from the A. P. Borden herd; two other bulls used on the LH7 were fullbloods raised in Brazil from imported Indian stock. They were brought up from South America through Mexico in 1924. E. H. paid a Mexican on the border twenty-five dollars to swim them across the Rio Grande. He named them "Atlas" and "Dan Moody," the latter for a Texas politician he admired. The man Moody justified E. H.'s confidence by becoming governor of Texas in 1927.[13]

Crossing Brahman bulls with the longhorned Texas cattle that were the common stock of the LH7 produced good beef animals that stayed healthy, cows that calved every year, and cattle that needed about half as much feed "as some of those pampered cattle you see nowadays," E. H. observed.[14] The hybrid vigor imparted by crossbreeding gave a great boost to the Gulf Coast cattle industry. Brahman-blooded cattle spread over the ranges of South Texas and across the Gulf states to Florida. The LH7 became a major supplier of quality Brahman stock.

"Dad saw the value in Brahmans because in that country they could stand the heat, and the fever ticks didn't bother them," Emory recalled. "The cattle were fast producing. E. H. would say they were half grown when they were dropped. And they could take the heat out in the middle of the prairie"—where the only shade a cow was liable to find was in the shadow of another cow.

E. H. particularly appreciated the breed's innate toughness. "These Brahmas may be compared to other cattle in hardiness as a mule to a horse," he told the *Cattleman* magazine. "We are running something near 150 Brahma bulls, which I consider the finest type of cattle for the coastal plains. It is not unusual to sell calves 300 pounds and up at five months old."[15]

Convinced that *Bos indicus* could make a valuable contribution to the cattle economy of the nation, a group of cowmen organized the American Brahman Breeders Association (ABBA), which has maintained headquarters in Houston since its founding in 1924. E. H. became a director of the ABBA, the first organization of Brahman cattle breeders in the world.

In 1923 E. H. acquired a partner in his ranching operation, W. A. Paddock of Houston. Paddock, chairman of the Texas Prison Commission, had a good name and plenty of oil money, but he was not a cattleman. "My father understood cattle, period. He was a cowman," Maudeen attested. "Mr. Paddock was more of a financier and did not understand cattle. They disagreed." Paddock wanted to raise heifer calves to maturity for use in the breeding herd. E. H. tried patiently to explain that it took too much time to bring the heifers along; the principal business of the LH7 was to breed cows to bulls to produce a marketable crop of calves.[16]

Paddock's uncertain grasp of the commercial cattle business would have posed fewer problems had he been content as a silent partner, but he persistently intruded himself into E. H.'s area of expertise. Lamented Emory: "Mr. Paddock was a wonderful man and a very wealthy man, but the trouble of it was he didn't know anything about the cattle business. He didn't know a thing about the business, but he wanted to have a voice." Sometimes it was more like an anguished gasp. E. H. did business in unorthodox ways that unnerved his conservative partner.

Marks once struck a deal with steer buyers who were to take eight hundred head at $42.50 each. The steers were being penned for loading into rail cars at Barker. "About that time a fellow came running from the old general store, flagging us down, and said, 'E. H., you've got a telephone call.' Dad went to the telephone and it was some other guy who wanted to buy the same steers," Emory related. "Dad didn't tell this fellow that he'd already sold them. He went back to the buyers that had already paid $42.50 for them and Dad says, 'I'll tell you what I'll do. I'll give you forty-five dollars for them if you'll back out.' Well, that's two and a half dollars a head on eight hundred head, that's two thousand dollars. They said they'd do it. He told the other guy on the telephone that he'd take fifty bucks for them. So he made five dollars a head."

His partner was more impressed with the risk E. H. had taken than with his four thousand dollars profit, Emory recalled. "Mr. Paddock said, 'I never heard of anything like that before in my life. You must be crazy.' But that's the way Dad operated."

Like all the Marks offspring, Emory qualified as a horseman as soon as he grew big enough to throw a leg over the saddle. He was five years old when E. H. took him to Houston and bought the boy his first shop-made boots at Scardina's, a pair of red tops. Like it or not—and he didn't much like it—Emory spent his boyhood looking after cows. E. H. put him on a freight train to Kansas when he was fourteen to watch over a shipment of LH7 cattle that would fatten on thousands of acres of bluestem on the Great Plains. From there the steers would be shipped to Chicago. Emory had a railroad pass that let him ride in the caboose, but the trainmen banished him from the lookout at the top of the car, a major disappointment. The train stopped in

Fort Worth to water the cattle, then went on through Oklahoma City to somewhere in Kansas.

"The next day we got up there and you couldn't see a house. The only thing out there was about ten cowboys, and an unloading chute," Emory recalled. "That's all there was. We just unloaded them, turned them out on the prairie, and these fellows took them. Where they went with them I don't know."

To Kansas by rail was a memorable trip for the young country gentleman from West Harris County. "Those old trainmen were having a lot of fun out of me, I'll tell you. That was the roughest bunch of people I ever saw. These two guys were squabbling and arguing, they got in a fight, and I thought they were going to tear each other up." Emory managed to dodge when one grabbed a bucket of cold, dirty water and doused his opponent. "That's the kind of business I had to put up with all the way. They were mean people.

"We got into Waco one night, we're on the railroad tracks with these cattle, and everybody quit the train. There was a honky-tonk; they had a lot of gals in there, and this gal walked by. She had her hand on her hip. I was sitting up on a stool, getting a Coke, and she came by and 'accidentally' bumped me with her elbow. I turned around and raised my hat off, and I says, 'Excuse me! Excuse me, ma'am!'

"Those brakemen nearly had a fit. They just laughed and laughed and laughed!" Well-bred Emory failed to see the humor. A gentleman, after all, always tipped his hat to a lady.

The train trip to Kansas made Emory the envy of the younger Marks offspring. Maudeen, especially, yearned to ride the rails: "That always bothered me because I never could go. I wanted to ride in the caboose so bad!" Her parents finally agreed to a short trip. "They knew I was eating my heart out, so they let me ride eight miles from Barker to Katy in the caboose one time."[17]

All four children practically grew up on horseback. E. H. made few distinctions between the jobs his boys and his girls could do; he needed all their help. During the twenties into the early thirties, the LH7 Ranch was growing into one of the largest beef cattle operations on the Gulf Coast. The peak number of cattle carrying the LH7 brand at one time was 6,670 head, running on thirty-six thousand acres west of Houston between Highway 90 and Hockley. Most of that land was prairie, useless for anything else, so E. H. could lease it for grazing for as little as fifteen and twenty cents an acre. It was a ride of twenty-five miles from the ranch's front gate to the back fence of the farthest pasture.[18]

In every aspect of ranch work the Marks children pitched in and did the job at hand, learning the cow business in much the same way their father had: by experience. From the age of twelve, both girls and boys were helping with roundups and brandings. They worked in the midst of the action, often encircled by milling cattle: "I didn't handle the branding iron when I was a child, but I would help poke up the fire," remembered Atha. "I also would stand on top of the cutting chute and move the gate to send a calf to the left or the right, or let a cow go out."

A man of action who believed in learning by doing, E. H. gave his offspring few formal lessons in ranch skills: "We were never taught to ride a horse," Atha added. "We were supposed to get on and ride. I was told to ride Billy to the post office but Billy didn't want to go. Daddy said, 'But you've got to go.' He hit Billy on the rump and we went to the post office!"[19]

Riding for recreation was an alien concept. As Maudeen remarked in later life: "I was accustomed to riding horseback for a purpose, for transportation and utility. To ride for the sheer pleasure of it seemed inconceivable. To this day when I get on a horse I feel like I have to have a destination."[20]

As a teenager Maudeen would ride with the cowboys, leaving home early in the morning and returning late. When necessary, she bunked overnight at the cowcamp about eighteen miles north of the main ranch house. She could cut cattle and work herd with the best of them, and she could shoot more than well enough to protect herself against snakes and other vermin.[21]

Some mornings the Marks siblings would rise at three o'clock to mount up and drive a shipment of steers to the railroad loading pens. The shipping pens were about half a mile north of the LH7 ranch house, at the end of Barker-Clodine Road just over the railroad tracks. The railroad operated at its convenience, not the ranchers', Atha remembered: "When we would ship a trainload of cattle, we would be expecting the freight train to come but we wouldn't know exactly what time. My father wouldn't want the animals to stand in the pens for hours on end, so he would leave them in the pasture in front of the ranch house. When we heard the train blow its whistle, we ran out and got on our horses and took the cattle up to the pens. I've done that sometimes in the middle of the night."

Occasionally, E. H. forgot that scattered among the grizzled old hands on the LH7 he had some youthful cowpunchers whose feelings were as tender as their years. In the excitement of a roundup he once snapped an order at Atha in a tone of voice that brought the girl near tears: "One time we were out in the front, holding cattle. There was a calf getting away, and Daddy yelled, 'Ride up! Ride up!' I *was* riding up, but not as fast as he thought I should. Later, at the lunch table, they said, 'Where's Atha?' They couldn't find me. I was sitting up on the stairwell, around the corner, hidden. Daddy came up there—he was pretty sensitive himself—and he asked, 'What's the matter?' I told him, 'You yelled at me.' He said, 'Oh, honey, I was just yelling out there, yelling at cows. I didn't mean to hurt your feelings.'"

Maud recognized that her daughters generally found cattle work more appealing than housework and gave them wide latitude to follow their interests. To help her in the house, Maud usually had a local girl or the wife of one of the cowboys to come in for half a day. Her helpers at one time or another included Eleanor Adkins, Louise Draemer, and Ruby Roberts. Ruby was married to champion cowboy Rube Roberts and was the foster daughter of Foghorn Clancy, longtime rodeo announcer.[22]

Freed from the narrow confines of convention, the Marks children had an unusually unstructured raising for children of the time. Said Atha: "I cannot remember any time when there was a big to-do about, 'You get out there and you get your work done.' We were just part of it. We fell in with everybody else and we did our work. Well, Emory was reluctant sometimes. But we didn't want to miss out. All of us kids, Maudeen, Travis, and I, had the reputation of eating fast. I think it was because we were afraid we would miss something."[23]

There was always some new adventure to get into on or near the ranch. As a teenager Emory went on wild horse hunts as E. H. had done at the turn of the century. The wild herds roamed the empty land north of Houston where Interstate Highway 45 would one day meet North Shepherd Drive near Little York Road. Intent on rounding up the broomtails, Emory and another LH7 wrangler, a black man named Mose Burton, would ride from Barker to Fairbanks and stay overnight at the Thad Smith place. The next day they followed the herd until the horses wearied of the chase.

"Joined by my Uncle Thad," Emory related, "we would begin to gather the horses that grazed on the prairies, always in a lope at first to wear them out. Fresh in the run they held their tails high. After a morning run we could always tell when we could corral them. Tails down and in a trot, they headed for an island of woods, trying to get away. After cutting out fifty or sixty head from a herd of about two hundred we would start home with them, tiring them out again. They would follow one rider, with one rider in the back to pick up strays. Of the fifty or sixty we might get eight or ten pretty good horses. Some could never be tamed. They brought five dollars a head." Emory also drove cattle to Piney Point, which would become an exclusive residential section within Houston.[24]

In the 1920s, E. H. was buying thousands of head of cattle in the East Texas piney woods from Huntsville to Center and shipping them to the Barker ranch, often five hundred head at a time. The region's pines and post oaks sheltered some of the last remaining old-time Texas cattle, the native stock on which the LH7 was built. "All our cattle at first were East Texas-type cattle, which were reds and brindles and blacks and multicolored cows," explained Travis, who would become a partner in his father's ranching business in the late 1930s.[25] Travis was too young to accompany E. H. and brother Emory on early roundups through the piney woods, though Emory gladly would have traded places with the youngster. Herding longhorned cattle through dense underbrush and low-hanging branches was exhausting and dangerous work. But for the rancher it had advantages:

"Bringing cattle from East Texas to South Texas was like taking a country boy who was used to grits and turnip greens and bringing him to town where they had orange juice for breakfast and Caesar's salad and steak for dinner," Emory observed. "The cows did better in a better environment.

"We used to buy cattle out in the switchbreaks and in the cane, and you couldn't gather but about ten or fifteen head a day. You could hear the cow running but you couldn't see her. They'd have to have dogs to head them off. It wasn't like going out on the prairie and getting three or four hundred a day. But we'd finally get a few hundred penned and then we'd drive them to the railroad."[26]

Driving a herd of half-wild scalawag steers near a human settlement was tricky business. During a Walker County roundup, one bunch of outlaws led sixteen-year-old Emory on a breakneck chase through the county seat. "On one of our trips north of Huntsville we were driving about three hundred head down a road north of the Huntsville post office," he related.

> The road went back of town to the river [the West San Jacinto]. You'd trail it out to the edge of town and go to the railroad and load them up and ship them. We were going down this hill and a couple of dogs came out. They started a-barkin' and those two brought six more and by the time it was over there must have been twenty dogs out there.
>
> They scattered the steers and a bunch went across the river. The river was low, it wasn't swimming. Dad says, "Get those from across the river." So I ran my horse across and went about two or three blocks, down where the old post office and the plaza used to be, and I saw these two steers go around a house north of the plaza. I was in a hurry, I had my horse at full steam—a real cow horse is intent on getting to the cow. I went around the house, and there was a clothesline with a bunch of clothes on it. It was barbed wire. I ducked just in time to save my head and neck, and got a gash on the shoulder. If I hadn't ducked, I'd have got it in the neck.[27]

The steers saw the rest of the cattle on the other side of the river and trotted over to rejoin the herd, leaving a shaken Emory trailing behind.

Hollywood brought a new kind of excitement to West Harris County when a 1924 silent picture, Emerson Hough's *North of 36*, was filmed on the Blakely ranch, which adjoined LH7 land on the southwest. The western photoplay starred Lois Wilson, Noah Beery, and Jack Holt. Ranch owner Bassett Blakely provided cattle for the herd shots—among them, several head of Marks-bred stock. In the first scene of cattle moving up the trail, an old Texas Longhorn cow from the LH7 stepped out to lead the herd as the camera cranked. Blakely told E. H. the cow did so well, the movie's director insisted it be in every herd scene.[28]

On the pretext of riding over to check on Marks cattle and to pick up strays, Emory and Mose Burton hit the trail to the Blakely ranch every chance they got, to watch the filming. "Mose and I were supposed to be riding the pasture all the time," Emory explained. "You always rode the pasture, to see if there's any sick cattle, if one was in the fence, if there's any trouble anywhere. We always had an excuse to go over to Blakely's, hunting for cows, while they were making the picture over there."

Young Emory's faith in Hollywood cowboys suffered a severe blow when actor Jack Holt, who portrayed fictitious Texas Ranger Dan McMasters, killed a horse while making the movie. "It was one of the best horses," Emory lamented. "He ran the horse all day long, and the horse just died from exhaustion." The incident occurred during a break in the filming. Holt took off alone across a fifteen-thousand-acre pasture and ran the animal to death, an act no real cowboy could conceive of.

Noah Beery, at least, lived up to Emory's expectations. "He was a very handsome man, and sophisticated looking," Emory observed. "He was a very commanding figure. We couldn't get too close to them, of course, we had to stay back, but I remember that nobody could do what he did. The feeling and the expression on his face was what told you he was a real actor. We went over there a lot. We had an excuse to ride the pasture everyday."

Emory and Mose spent so much time riding to Blakely's, they were gone the day Beery and Holt called at the LH7. Atha glimpsed the celebrities from the ranch house. "I recall looking out of the dining room window to see movie actors Jack Holt and

Noah Beery as they got out of a car and Daddy walking over to greet them as ranch guests," she later wrote. "They did not come into our home but visited with Daddy and some of the ranch hands. Of course, I wanted to go out to meet them, but Mother said no."[29]

Womanhandled, a 1925 film starring Richard Dix and Esther Ralston, also was shot on the Blakely ranch. ("I don't remember too much about that one," Emory confessed, "because about that time E. H. found out we were riding one part of the pasture too much so we had to ride the other way.") Cast and crew stayed at the Blakelys' large ranch house near Richmond, southwest of Houston. When the filming wrapped, Bassett Blakely staged a rodeo on Richmond's main street in the company's honor. E. H. was there, riding a little horse named Frenchie. A big Longhorn steer named Bowallopers was a featured attraction. He threw all comers.

The real stars of the show were the movie actresses who came as Blakely's special guests. One was a buxom, dark-haired enchantress from New Orleans. The rural West Harris Countians had never seen anything like her. "I will never forget, Mother saw this actress and she was *very* critical of her not having on enough underclothing. The men were bug-eyed!" Emory remembered.

Twice a year, spring and fall, E. H. and his ranch hands would ride to the Blakely ranch, help round up the herd, and cut out any LH7 stock that had strayed onto the neighboring spread. A week or so later, Blakely's men would come to the LH7, ride in another roundup, and take home any Blakely cattle mixed in with the Marks herd. After these neighborly cattle-sortings, it would not be long before each ranch again lost a few strays onto the other spread. "The cows were always crawling through the fence," Emory complained.

In shipments of cattle from either ranch, therefore, it was always possible some of the neighbor's stock might be mixed in. One day Blakely notified E. H. that he suspected a few head carrying the LH7 brand were in with a trainload of Blakely cattle being loaded southwest of Houston.

"Between Stafford and Missouri City they used to have a nightclub called Loma Linda. It was a gambling joint," Emory related. "One time Bassett Blakely was shipping some cattle down there, and he told us to come down because he thought he had three cows in there that belonged to us. So Dad and I went down there. The nightclub was right across the street from the loading pens and the depot. They were loading the cattle, and Blakely was telling the fellow that was taking care of it where the cattle were going and who had bought them.

"They had about six cars loaded, and Blakely said, 'I believe I'm going over and see the boys at the club.' Dad didn't go; he was looking the cattle over, to see if our cows were in the bunch. About an hour passed. Finally Blakely came out with another fellow, and he says, 'Well, you can take them off my billing. This man just won 'em.'"

Blakely had gambled away ten cars of cattle—about four hundred head. The ranchman seemed unperturbed by the loss. "Where do you want them to go?" he asked the new owner, then helped the freight agent make out new paperwork. "Just tear up that old sheet. These cattle belong to this man."

Ranchers like Marks and Blakely who shipped cattle by the hundreds kept the railroads humming. Orders for cattle cars had to be made in advance; it might be two or three days before the busy railroads could send cars to the loading pens to take on a shipment. Cattle cars came in two sizes, thirty-six and forty-two feet. "You would always order the biggest. You'd have to specify and just be set on it," Emory said. "Tell them, 'Boy, I want them forty-two-footers.'" The larger size could accommodate about one hundred calves or thirty-five cows. With Longhorn steers, the limit was about twenty-five head to a car because the horns took up so much room.

The railroad was a lifeline, taking cattle to market and bringing feed and supplies directly to the ranch. E. H. brought in carloads of cottonseed hulls and meal to fatten steers. A shipment spurred ranch hands to quick action, as the railroad gave them only three days to unload a boxcar. Feed was hauled either to cattle in the pasture or to the barn for storage. "One room of the barn was filled with corn, and another great big double room was filled with cottonseed hulls," Maudeen recalled. "They'd bring in the railroad cars and we'd go down in the big wagons and unload those hulls, and then drive the wagons and mules out to these big troughs. They'd let me drive sometimes; the mules knew where they were going." Shoveled into troughs eight or ten feet long, with cottonseed meal sprinkled on top, the otherwise useless hulls made a cheap, nutritious feed.[30]

A stack of rice straw also made fairly good cattle feed, except when it collapsed on the cows and smothered them, Emory noted: "You had to watch that stack, because the cows would chew into it and as soon as they got it pretty well eaten around the base, if you weren't careful that dern stuff would come down and kill 'em. I've seen it happen."

E. H. had about two hundred acres in rice, watered from an artesian well near Buffalo Bayou. The rice pond was a cool retreat for the children in summer. In hot weather they had their city cousins out from Houston to go swimming and feast on homegrown watermelon. Afterward there might be a cowboy sing-along at the main house, Atha recalled: "At night, we would sit around on the ground outside, there was a certain place just south of the house. There was nearly always at least one cowboy who could sing. We'd sit around out there and tell stories and sing songs."

At harvest time, threshing the rice left a mountain of straw for the children to play atop. "It was all flat around there, so that was the only thing we had to call a mountain," Maudeen reflected. "We would get up there and slide down. But rice straw is splintery. We'd come home with our little rear ends just full of splinters, so it didn't take long before we quit that."[31]

E. H. was a cattleman who believed in agricultural diversification. He raised a little rice and a little corn and rented land to farmers, furnishing the seed and in return taking a share of the tenant's cotton or rice crop. He had an interest in all things agricultural. Though never a dairyman, he would join with A. H. Kiefer, a Tomball banker; George Wilkins of Houston; and B. E. Stallones to organize the South Texas Producers Association in 1931. E. H. served as the dairy cooperative's president for twenty-five years; Stallones was general manager. The South Texas marketing venture would become one of the largest dairy farmer associations in the United States.[32]

For a while, E. H. also dabbled in the poultry business, raising turkeys for the Thanksgiving and Christmas trade. The enterprise proved successful for E. H. but highly disagreeable to Emory, who got stuck with turkey tending: "Dad would buy all these half-grown poults from people all around the country. We'd have six or eight hundred, maybe a thousand turkeys. He'd put me out there with a sack lunch, herding turkeys for about ten miles through the prairie. There weren't any fences up there at that time; all the way from Barker to Katy it was open. They'd put me out there with a stick and a lunch, and I'd get back of these turkeys."

With a mowing machine, E. H. would cut a swath several feet wide through the tall grass, stirring up grasshoppers to feed the turkeys and providing a lane where Emory could herd his birds: "They'd go right down this mowed place, just tumbling over themselves. Them son-of-a-guns was going twenty-five miles an hour, and I was trotting all the time to keep up with them.

"Then when the season was over and they were ready for Thanksgiving and Christmas, we'd load them up in a trailer. E. H. would set up on Houston City Hall Square, and later at the Farmer's Cooperative Market on Buffalo Bayou, and we'd sell turkeys. And of everybody who came up, nobody ever wanted the turkey right next to the gate. It had to be that one 'over there,' about six or eight back. E. H. would put me in there, I'd crawl around like a monkey and grab that turkey, and he'd slip away from me sometimes."

With a patient chuckle, Emory mused: "That's the kind of life we put up with. Dad would buy a rooster for ten cents if he could sell him for a quarter. Just anything to make a nickel."

A Marks family vacation to Pikes Peak, Colorado, in 1928. E. H. and Maud are in the back seat with Maudeen; Travis sits in the middle; Emory and Atha are up front with the driver. (*Photo courtesy E. M. Marks.*)

On a family vacation to Carlsbad Caverns, New Mexico, in 1928 or 1929, the Markses meet Amelia Earhart. Posing for the photo, left to right, are Jim White, discoverer of the caverns; Earhart, first woman to cross the Atlantic by air; Emory Marks; E. H. Marks; and Major Boles, with the National Park Service. (*Photo courtesy E. M. Marks.*)

BRAUHAUSER AND HENRY FORD

> "My father and I were on our way to Straack's mill near Tomball for some lumber, and we stopped at a farm home to ask the way. A boy at the gate called his father to give us directions to the mill. Said the father: 'You go down dese road and you turn the fence around de corner. You go right on till you come to a white house painted red. Then you come to a noder place and this fellow got two front doors in de back. But dot ain't Straack's mill. The next place is a fellow who got some hogs in a sheep's stable and turn the fence around there and go right on. Then you come to a place where a big dog come out and bite you on my leg, here, see? That is Straack's mill.'"[1]

The sturdy German folk of West Harris County were tough, self-reliant, and disinclined to change. They had no need of the world that lay beyond their quiet rural communities; their life was hard work six days a week with dancing in the local halls on Sunday. Houston could keep its bustle and bright lights, and its discourse. In settlements where the German tongue still held sway, English had a fractured, topsy-turvy quality that grated on the ears of younger and more cosmopolitan generations, who found their elders stubborn and clannish.

"They were a bunch of hardheads," Emory protested. "And they would get all their language mixed up. If one of them was going down to the store to get a loaf of bread or something, it was, 'Fritz is gonna go to dat store already yet once, again.' We went over to Fritz Kobs' one time and Dad says, 'You know, old Henry is pretty sick, I believe.' And Fritz says, 'Yes, you mean old Henry with his mustache across the creek?'"[2]

Though it may have made them difficult to deal with, obstinacy was a virtue for pioneers such as they. Hardheadedness saw these steadfast German farmers through the bad times. "They were good, hard-working people, though they clung to their ways and kept their language," Maudeen said. "They were really very admirable persons, and such industrious people. Whatever they did, they did well. Their places were neat and clean. They made everything count. Good people. But they were just old-fashioned. It was hard to communicate with them, and they didn't have a great sense of humor. They weren't much fun except when they went to the dances. The rest of the time they were so stern and serious. We had a little lighter atmosphere in our home."[3]

E. H. was different from the gruff and dour countryfolk of the bayou country. His world even as a boy had stretched far beyond old limits. While he honored the German community that held his past, he lived in the Texas of his time. "He went across the bayou," as Maudeen put it. "He went across the creek and got acquainted with the rest of the world."[4] Though he had grown up speaking German, E. H. from age ten was at home with English. He had an admiration for words well spoken, springing from his love of rollickin' cowboy songs and his respect for straight talk. Garbled communications were not allowed in the Marks home. His children were taught to treat language with as much respect as any native Texan shows for queen's English.

In the secluded German communities of West Harris County, most socializing was done at four dancehalls and gun clubs: Bear Creek, Spring Branch, Cypress, and White Oak. Each met on a different Sunday of the month, with families gathering at their local hall on the designated day for target shooting, dancing, and dining. A time for sumptuous feasts and kegs of beer, the shooting parties or *Schuetzenfests* also meant serious competition. The tests of marksmanship acquired an air of stylized ritual, each shootist eyeing the target with great deliberation, taking slow and careful aim, making infinite adjustments to the feet, head, hands, hat, and rifle before finally settling into a sharpshooter's rock-steady pose. "It'd take them five minutes to get the gun set," Emory said. "They wanted everybody to look at them shoot. And if they made a good shot it'd take them ten minutes to get away from there" so someone else could have the spotlight.

The contest judge stood near the mark, protected from stray bullets by a sheet of boiler plate. As each rifleman took his shot, the judge held up a stick with the appropriate score from one to five. The scorer sat in a shed near the firing line, recording each marksman's performance. Shootings were fiercely contested, Emory noted: "The Dutchmen from each community, the old men, all bragged on having the best marksmanship. They were very proud of it." Only men could belong to the gun clubs, but some women joined in the target practice, including Maud Marks, who was an excellent shot.[5]

Every third Sunday the Marks family went to the local Bear Creek club. The large round dancehall was located just north of Addicks, near the point where Highway 6 would one day cross a modern flood control levee. Atha remembered Bear Creek as the finest of the four German community halls: "We called the one at Cypress 'Tin Hall' because it was roofed with tin. I think the one at Bear Creek was the nicest—it was not barny at all. It had a beautiful floor. I've never danced on a floor that was any better. There was a large pole in the center, with braces going out from it, and the orchestra sat up there on a platform on top of that pole. They would go up a stairway, and after all the orchestra was up there they would raise the stairs like you would raise a disappearing stairway that goes in an attic."

On the appointed Sunday, amusements began at the club early in the day with the women's target shooting followed by the men's competition. There was a sort of coffee shop where families brought sandwiches and homemade pies and cakes to sell. Ice cream cones went for a nickel at the cold drink stand. "We didn't call it ice cream, though," Atha noted. "We said we wanted a Sayso," the trade name of an ice cream cone. Outside under the trees, an oompah band played through the day.[6]

The men's target practice usually took most of the day. The women bowled and visited in the coffee house until the men finished their shooting in mid-afternoon. Then came the event most anticipated by the community's young women—the dance. Atha remembered what pains each girl took with her appearance on these occasions:

"They would dance in the afternoon and then they would dance at night. Very often the young ladies would take a dress to wear in the afternoon and then they would change. The facilities weren't very good for changing, there was no running water, just a mirror and a curtained-off area and a place where you could hang your wraps. But the teenagers and older girls would change and put on a long dress for the evening dance. After they married and had little children running around, most of the mothers didn't wear long dresses, but it was a dress occasion. And you wouldn't dare wear the same dress next month that you wore this month. 'Mother, I can't wear that! I wore that the month before last!'"

To most members of the community, the get-togethers were well-deserved recreation after a hard workweek. Some, however, thought it sinful to go dancing and target shooting on a Sunday. "There was one family, also of German extraction, who thought it was pretty bad," Atha said. "The way their girls were brought up, that old Bear Creek hall where they had dances on Sunday was wicked. But we didn't think it was wicked. We thought it was very wholesome recreation."

At Bear Creek the dance floor was screened off with chicken wire. To one side was a curtained cloakroom. Wooden benches were built onto the walls where the women could sit back. The men stood in small conversational groups, occasionally coming over to the women's seating area to ask their wives to dance.

Babies were laid on the floor of the cloakroom on pallets made of quilts. While the children slept, their mothers danced or visited, once in a while going to the cloakroom to push aside the curtain and check on the infants. When the dance was over, mothers claimed their sleeping babies and everyone set off for home. Once when Emory was an infant, a confusion of quilts on the cloakroom floor sent him off with the wrong family.

"I got lost for three days one time. Somebody picked up the wrong kid and put me in their wagon," he related. "I reckon the quilts looked alike, and they just came in and grabbed me and took off. Dad went all over the country horseback, hunting for me. I wound up at the Gastmans'—I was just a baby, I couldn't talk and nobody knew. E. H. rode all over the country before he finally found me. Mother and I jokingly referred to the incident several times. I always told her maybe they thought they were getting the best deal by taking me—better than what they had. Or maybe it was the blanket they wanted."[7]

Once a year each club hosted a Big Feast and invited the neighbors. Before Henry Ford's adoption of the moving assembly line made the Model T more readily affordable, many rural families still traveled by wagon. For people in the fringes of the county, it might be a half-day's wagon ride to visit a distant gun club. Speeches and feasting lasted all afternoon, putting some travelers on the road home in the middle of the night. Isolated farm families, hungry for company and fond of ceremony, gladly endured the long ride to join their neighbors at the summer festivities.

On feast day each club marshaled its fifty or sixty men, and marching four abreast military fashion, they paraded down the road with flags and banners flying to meet at the hall of the host club just before noon. The visitors snapped to a halt at the entrance to the hosts' hall. A trumpet blew. The four club leaders, each carrying a ceremonial sword, met in the center of the gate. The host raised his sword and gave a welcoming speech, always in German. Then the trumpet blew again, signaling the men to file into the hall and take their places at several long tables.

One year during the First World War, E. H. carried the sword as grand master of the Big Feast at Bear Creek. There had been some unpleasantness, some anti-German remarks directed at the West Harris Countians. The children, especially, were hurt by the slurs of their schoolmates, the taunting accusations of "your granddaddy is a German."

The antiforeigner fervor spawned by wartime passions wounded the German community and inspired E. H.'s feast-day address. "Daddy made this speech, that they were so proud of their German ancestors, that they had seen fit to leave that country in the 1800s and come over here," Atha recalled. "I thought, 'That's a good way to look at it, to be proud that they came here.'"

With E. H.'s speech setting the tone for a celebration, the Big Feast began in earnest. Stewed meat, sauerkraut, and boiled potatoes were cooked outside the hall in huge washpots and big iron kettles. The stewed meat was excellent, Atha remembered, with fresh outdoor flavor: "At Bear Creek they would go out in the woods and get bay leaves right off the trees. They'd get a lot of their seasoning fresh from the woods and put it in their stew. It was really good. I don't know why we can't make stew that good now."

Another indispensable feast-day dish was stewed prunes, served by the kettle. The ubiquitous prunes brought snickers from Atha's elder brother: "Emory always got a kick out of it. They'd have these white, oval-shaped bowls and dishes, and there would always be stew, slaw, and prunes, the same food placed on every table and repeated about three times. Then there would be other things that people would bring, but the prunes and the stew were cooked right there in open kettles."

"Sauerkraut and prunes," Emory gibed with characteristic irreverence, "that was the backbone of the whole works. Atha and I used to call it the prune and sauerkraut mix. The men would sit down at the tables and the women would get busy and serve them. The men and the women were separated—the women didn't have any business in there. They'd stick their heads in and see if the men needed something, and that was as far as the women came."

"At the Bear Creek club," Atha added, "the wives could join the men and go in and sit down to eat. But at the White Oak club the women could not go in and sit with their husbands. Men were fed first. My mother's brother, Uncle Reed Smith, had married a lady from down in the White Oak area, and he belonged to the club down there. He would not go in to eat at the first tables because his wife could not go in. They used to kind of poke fun at him. 'Look at Reed, he's standing out there with the women. Why don't you come on in, Reed?' And Uncle Reed would say, 'When Freda can come in, I'll come in.'"

Beer flowed freely at feasts in the big halls. These German Texans saw drinking as recreation, not sin. Boys as young as six and seven years crisscrossed the room pouring the brew, frequently hotfooting it back to the barrels to have their serving pitchers refilled. Emory had the misfortune to act as serving boy early in the Prohibition era. His stolid kinsmen plainly thought he peddled a poor imitation of their favorite brew:

> These old Dutchmen would sit there with their beer glasses, waiting for that beer. That was the first thing, to get the beer. Well, when Prohibition came in, near beer came in. They wanted the real stuff, they didn't want that near beer. They'd give us a pitcher out of these big barrels and we'd go along and pour. The first one I got to was Old Man Hillendahl, he had a big cabbage patch and whiskers down to here. When I went to pour the beer, he says, "Vat? No foam?" and turned his glass upside down. I got to the next one and started to pour, and that guy says, "Vat? No foam?" Bang! Down went the glass. They wouldn't just all say at one time, "I don't want any of that beer." They waited until I got there, just sat there still—it looked like a mountain sitting there—and they'd wait until just before I went to pour it in their glass. "Vat? No foam?" Bang! Down would go the glass.

The men traditionally raised their beer glasses in a toast. A hearty, deep-throated cry resounded through the hall when the glasses were filled with beer; it came to the ears as "Feat-fot-ho! Knock 'em all!" Atha observed that Prohibition dampened enthusiasm noticeably: "The first year they had water in their glasses instead of beer, it was a very weak 'feat-fot-ho, knock 'em all,' because not all of the men joined in the toast. Whatever it was they were saying, you couldn't toast it with water." Atha was seventy-seven when she finally learned from a German-Texan acquaintance that the toast was *Vivat hoch* ("Let's live high") *Noch einmal* ("Once more!").[8]

As the rural population grew, candidates for county office began coming out from Houston to the community meeting places to shake hands and stir up support. Emory observed that the old-timers were glad to see them: "Those old beer drinkers would hang around the beer joints, and every politician there was expected to buy them a beer. They had to, if they wanted their vote."

Emory became a public relations opportunity for one local politico through an accident at the bowling alley:

> T. J. Harris ran for county judge for years. One time I was setting up tenpins. They would get us kids in a pit down there and we'd stand off to one side. The ball would go down the alley and knock down the pins and roll into the sawdust at the bottom of the pit. We'd set up the pins and return the ball. I reached down and got this ball and put it on the alley, and when I did I ran a big splinter way down in my thumb.
>
> T. J. Harris looked around at everybody, then he got his knife out, cut the fingernail, and pulled that thing out. Everybody was standing around looking; he looked at me and I knew he was about to make a speech. He wanted everybody to know he was running for judge. He put his hand on my shoulder and said, "Young man, you're one of the bravest persons I ever saw." He looked all around to see if everybody was listening and watching, then he reached in his pocket and said, "Here," and gave me a dollar for not crying. After that, all those old beer drinkers around there had to drink to me, too, for not crying, and he had to set 'em up.

A favorite recreation spot of the Marks family, less raucous than the local hangouts, was Sylvan Beach on Galveston Bay at La Porte. Sylvan Beach offered dancing, fishing, rodeoing, a lovely view, and fresh breezes off the bay. Atha described it as a good place for families: "There were two-story cabins, they had cooking quarters downstairs and an upstairs for sleeping. We would go and rent a cabin, and we might stay a weekend or we might stay a week. Whole families came.

"When we got a little older," she added, "we'd have dates and go down there just for the evening. That was quite a drive, because it's about twenty-five miles on the other side of Houston. It was a nice drive. And, oh, the cool breeze. They had a long pier that went out over the water, and hickory rocking chairs all around to sit in. It was all open, you could see through it. On one side you could see the water and on the other side the grass. Beautiful, just beautiful."

The Markses were good friends with the Millers, who lived up the road at Katy and had children the same age as Emory and Atha. The two families frequently vacationed together at Sylvan Beach. Transportation was no problem—the Millers had been in the car business in Katy since 1916, when they started selling Maxwells. Ollie Miller and his son Arthur had the Ford dealership in Katy from 1921 to 1933.[9]

Maudeen remembered family trips to Sylvan Beach highlighted by fresh seafood and big band music: "When I was pretty small, the Miller family and the Marks family would go down to Sylvan Beach and we'd catch fish and eat crabs and go to the dance. They always had a huge orchestra, someone like Rudy Vallee or whoever was big, and they had this huge open pavilion. And they had a rodeo down there. I remember that Emory and Arthur Miller were riding around in this car from the Millers' car business, and they came back without Emory's new cowboy hat. I was none too sure what had happened."[10]

Pressed for details, Emory confessed all. "You want me to tell the truth about that? It wasn't Arthur, it was J. F. McAdams from Huntsville. He got to be sheriff down there finally. He and I and Tommy Hicks were riding these two gals around on the hood of the car and Atha was giving me fits. She thought that was terrible. We'd promenade them all around. One of them got to be a movie actress—her name was Dorothy Granger. The other one was the 'boopoop-a-doop' girl—her real name was Bebe Kane.

"That night at the dance, it was about ten-thirty or eleven o'clock and these girls wanted our hats. J. F. says, 'Here, take mine!' He gave it to Bebe. I was dancing with Dorothy Granger so I gave her my hat, a great big white one. Next thing we know, these gals come up missing and we couldn't find them. Come to find out, they were leaving town the next day and going to California. Our hats were just gone—that's all there was to it."

To be a hatless cowboy with a rodeo on the morrow was a serious offense, as both boys well knew. Emory continued: "J. F.

and I got in the car and I said, 'Man, we're going to catch fits if we don't have a hat for tomorrow.' So that night about midnight we took off to Houston. We went to Shudde's Hat Company down on Preston at Travis Street and we sat there from about four o'clock till they opened up that morning. We got us a hat and we took off for Sylvan Beach again. That was the only way." The pair would just as soon have faced wild Brahman bulls as to have stood before their irate cattlemen fathers without the regulation headgear.

E. H. did not believe in hanging around the house when the chores were done and there was someplace to go. If it wasn't down to Sylvan Beach for the weekend, Atha remembered, then rain and roads permitting it was up to Pattison for a family visit with the Muskes. "On Sunday sometimes Daddy would say, 'Let's go up and see Uncle Rufe and Tanta Lula.' We would get to Katy, and he'd get out of the car and look down the road. Sometimes he'd say, 'I don't think we'd better go.' We'd have to turn around and come back home, because if it was muddy and wet the road would be impassable. But we'd have to drive to Katy to find out." Over the years E. H. negotiated the twenty-five miles from Barker to Pattison on horseback, by wagon, and in a Model T.

During World War I, E. H. was called to sell Liberty Bonds. The day before his call he took delivery at Katy on a new Model T touring car. Travis related that despite wet weather his father immediately set out in the car to sell bonds, ignoring the spatters and smears that soon covered the new Ford:

> As it was raining and the roads were all dirt and muddy, he put on the curtains to start his rounds selling war bonds. He was told it was imperative that he sell the bonds and bring the proceeds to the Harris County Courthouse. The only thing was that he did not wait for the license to be sent out from the courthouse, as he thought selling those bonds was the most important thing.
>
> After making his rounds selling war bonds, he headed to Houston with his proceeds and receipts. Parking his mud-covered Model T next to the courthouse, he entered and made his report, which was a good one. Completing his business in the courthouse he returned to where he had

parked his Model T, but it was gone. He took off his hat, scratched his head and tried to figure what had happened to his new car.

About that time two policemen walked up and asked him what he was looking for. He told them his car. They said, "You are under arrest, let's go to the courthouse." When he asked what he was arrested for, they told him for driving a car without a license and probably stolen. The policemen asked him if he knew anyone in Houston. He said he did; they told him to go in the other room and call. He called T. Binford, sheriff of Harris County and a good friend. He said, "T., this is E. H. and I need you." Binford asked, "Where are you?" E. H. said, "Almost in jail." "For what?" the sheriff asked. "For driving a car without a license," E. H. answered. "Well, you know you can't do that, E. H."

E. H. told him the whole story. He thought that selling $180,000 worth of war bonds was more important at the time than sitting around waiting for his license to be sent out from Houston. Of course, it's an old trick for policemen to listen in and garner all the information they can. When E. H. finished his story the door flew open and several policemen came in and patted him on the back. They gave him a cup of coffee and told him to go on back to the ranch and put the license on his Ford when he got it.[11]

One year a drifter named Dollar called at the LH7 ranch house. He had lately been to the high country and told wondrous tales of towering mountains where ice-cold streams brimmed with trout and magnificent forests of ponderosa pine and blue spruce sheltered deer, elk, and bear. "He talked about being up in that part of the country and, boy, the next year we started taking trips," Emory said. "We went there every time. Dad would have the cowboys take care of the cattle and the place, and we'd be gone sometimes a month."

Once E. H. hit the road, it was hard to bring him home until he was ready to come, Atha remembered: "One time we were in Colorado Springs, staying at the home of a friend. Mr. Paddock phoned up there and said, 'You'd better come home. The cattle don't have any water—it's very dry here. You'd better come.' And Daddy said, 'I'm on my vacation with my family. You tell the men there to get 'em some water.' I mean, Daddy believed in family vacations."

With their Model T groaning under the weight of kids and camping gear, Emil and Maud putt-putt-putted across Texas; in a succession of Fords, a Dodge Victory Six, and an early 1930s Dodge straight Eight, the Markses traveled from the Gulf of Mexico through the western states to California, and northward as far as Wyoming and Montana. The cattlelands of the north were as a foreign country to the Marks youngsters. Where the climate cooled, ranchers could raise Herefords and Angus, but these English breeds were unknown on the near-tropical Gulf prairies. The Marks children knew only Brahmans and Texas Longhorns. E. H. used the family car trips to broaden their horizons. During one trip west, as they crossed the High Plains of Texas, E. H. suddenly stopped the car and had everyone get out. Pointing across a pasture he announced to his startled offspring, "Now *that* is a Hereford." It was the first they had seen.[12]

Judicious travelers, the Markses carried in their well-provisioned automobile whatever supplies they might need in the thinly populated West. "We traveled when there weren't motels and restaurants," Atha said. "I remember stopping at the side of the road, and Daddy would hang a tarpaulin—a wagon sheet—from the car sloping down to the ground. We'd sleep under that, and we'd cook on a campfire." In the morning, tents, bedrolls and cooking pots were packed away on the running boards of the car. It was a stretch to step over all the gear when it came time to load up and go.

As every well-outfitted wagon ought to have a chuckbox, E. H. attached one to the back of his Ford and stocked it with bacon and beans—essential trail grub. He made sure there was a wagon sheet in the car before the family went anywhere. "Mother wouldn't let us leave home without a coat; E. H. wouldn't let us leave without a wagon sheet," Maudeen remarked. "When we'd go on trips, we always had the wagon sheet with us. We'd tie that tarp on the limb of a tree and we'd have a tent that would knock wind and knock rain. And if you went to the beach you had it to put underneath you to keep the sand off. So we didn't leave home without a wagon sheet."[13]

Thus prepared, the family took off for Yellowstone National Park one summer in an early-model auto equipped with a self-starter. "Well, it wasn't a 'self' starter," Emory amended. "You'd wear yourself out pulling that dern chain. *Rrr-iii-ppp! Rrr-iii-ppp!* You'd have to crank for ten minutes before you'd get it to catch." The starter was under the dashboard on the right-hand side; from the driver's seat the operator had to lean far to the right to grab the handle of the chain and give it a yank. Passengers could not get in until the car was started. "The crank in the front would have been easier than that, but this was something new. This was a 'self-starter.'"

Despite the balky car, E. H. and family did finally reach Yellowstone, only to have the car's chuckbox ransacked by a heavy-handed thief. "The first thing that happened, the first night we were up there, a bear smelled the bacon in the chuckbox E. H. had put on the back of this old Ford, and tore that thing to pieces. Sort of wrecked the back end of that old car, too," Emory recollected. "E. H. pulled off what was left of the chuckbox and we started home."

Their route led over Raton Pass, elevation 7,834 feet, in northeastern New Mexico at the Colorado state line. The mountain pass was almost too much for the family car, Emory remembered: "Before they put that new highway in there, that was a son-of-a-gun. It'd take you half a day to get across that pass. The road was dirt and rock, and it was steep.

"We were coming down, and Dad says, 'You know, we can save some gas if I turn the motor off.' Down we went. There's some pretty good slopes in there, and we were getting pretty fast after awhile. We got to the bottom and he turned the key on, and that was the dernedest noise you ever heard. The muffler and tailpipe and everything blew off. It had built up gas back in there, and just blew it off." They were stranded in Raton a day and a half for repairs.

For many years, Santa Fe with its ancient churches and adobe palaces was the Marks family's favorite vacation town. Maud would sit in the sunlit plaza and watch the colorfully dressed passersby, Emory related, while E. H. stole off to Burro Alley:

> They had gambling joints and women and everything, all up and down that section of town they called Burro Alley. Dad, he liked to gamble, and I remember one time he

went to one of these joints. They wouldn't let me go in because I wasn't old enough. I had to sit on the front steps.

So I sat there, and in about thirty minutes I saw a fellow go in with a red wheelbarrow. He wheeled it on in, and I thought that was awful funny. About ten minutes later E. H. came out, and he had 952 silver dollars in that wheelbarrow. He'd won 'em playing poker and blackjack, and rolling the dice—he did a little bit of everything. And he said to me, "You know, if I had forty-eight more silver dollars, I'd have a thousand dollars."

He wheeled that wheelbarrow out in the middle of the street, and then he said, "Now don't you ever say anything to Mother. I'm gonna go back in there and get forty-eight more dollars so I'll have an even thousand dollars." He wheeled the wheelbarrow in there, and about fifteen minutes later he came out with an empty wheelbarrow and he was shaking his head.

There was a little Indian boy coming down the street, and he says, "Pancho, you want a wheelbarrow?" The kid looked at him like he couldn't figure it out—"Why would he give me a wheelbarrow?"—figured he must have stole it or something. But that kid grabbed the wheelbarrow, E. H.'s brand-new, red wheelbarrow, and wheeled it down the street. As long as we could see him, for three blocks, he was still looking back at us.

Emory never did tell his mother about E. H.'s shiny new wheelbarrow with its short-lived silver lining.

The Markses also visited Carlsbad Caverns in southeastern New Mexico, which was established as a national monument in 1923. The sightseers posed for souvenir photographs with visiting celebrities, including Amelia Earhart, first woman to cross the Atlantic by air. As a memento of the occasion, Emory wrote on the back of his keepsake photograph that he was having a great time and found Amelia Earhart "very entertaining." When the family got home from the trip, he left the photo lying about the house. Maud found it and read his note. She was appalled by his familiar tone: "Entertaining! You're getting to be a big shot pretty fast, aren't you!" Emory was quick to explain that he had only had his picture taken with the aviatrix.

On a trip to the Painted Desert of Arizona in 1926, before the strictly enforced ban on removing objects from national parks and protected areas, E. H. cut out blocks of a hard surface in which dinosaur tracks were preserved. He hauled the blocks back to the ranch to become part of his extensive collection of rocks, fossils, antlers, and horns. Every vacation trip yielded more curiosities for his hoard, until the accumulation threatened to spill from the screened porch of the ranch house.[14]

Persuaded by Maud that he must do something with the pile of oddities on the porch, E. H. shipped in two carloads of logs from Montana and had an 1800s-style log shack built to house his collectibles. The interior reflected his eclectic tastes. In one corner hung a hornet's nest (abandoned), shaped like a Japanese lantern and measuring more than two feet long and fourteen inches in diameter at the center. In his bottle collection was an old-fashioned soda pop bottle of the type popped by striking a piece of U-shaped wire protruding from the neck. His curio collection included a rattlesnake-skin necktie and three objects supposed to be dinosaur eggs that were plowed up in the Santa Anna Mountains of west central Texas.[15]

The log cabin became an informal museum, filled with old guns, flags, musical instruments, pipes, copper pots, coffee mills, walking sticks, riding crops, spurs, and whatnot. Many of the antiques had been passed down through Maud's family and some dated to the Revolutionary and Civil wars.

Maud had relatives in Long Beach, California, so one year E. H. loaded up the family and drove to the West Coast. In a rare departure from family tradition, he sat behind the wheel of something other than a Ford. "Dad believed in Henry Ford all the way," Emory declared. "He said if it hadn't been for Henry Ford, the average man couldn't have had a car. He wouldn't buy anything but Fords, except once he bought a Dodge Victory Six. It had a covered spare on each side with oilcloth wheel covers that said, 'Houston—Gateway to the World' and 'Houston—Where Eleven Railroads Meet the Sea.'

"We got to California, we were sitting there on the street, and everybody who came by would laugh and laugh at the signs on the wheel covers. They thought Houston was just a little hick town. They'd laugh and it'd make Mother so mad she was just sitting there biting her lips. That was the Victory Six."

It took E. H. close to five decades to do it, but he finally had the last laugh on California. After he got to be an "old-timer," the colorful Texas cowman would be invited to speak to historical societies and businessmen's clubs all over the country. During a visit to New York City one year, he attended a Rotary Club luncheon and unexpectedly found himself called on to address the group. "We got people here from everywhere," E. H. recalled the Rotarian's introduction. "We got 'em here from California and Texas and Alabama and Louisiana. This old Texan is sitting right here and I'm going to call him up here."

Never at a loss for words, E. H. was happy to give them a story. He got on the mike and began a two-for-one tall tale:

> Well folks, I'm sure glad I got a jump on this fellow from California because we old Texans are gittin' to be pretty near as big liars as they are.
>
> I run a big ranch down in Texas, I've got eight or ten cowboys. There was a fellow there from California, he was taking pictures of the ranch and the roundups and the branding, and one day he came and told me and my cowboys, "You oughta been with me yesterday."
>
> We said, "What did you do?"
>
> "I caught a fish weighed a hundred and four pounds."
>
> An old boy winked at me and he said, "Where did you catch that fish?"
>
> He said, "Down on Goose Creek."
>
> The old boy winked at me again and he said, "Well, that's funny. I was down there fishin' yesterday. I fished there for thirty minutes and all I hooked was a lantern. And when I pulled it up that lantern was lit."
>
> That fellow from California said, "You can't make anybody believe that that lantern was lit!"
>
> The other old boy said, "If you'll knock a hundred pounds off that fish, I'll blow the lantern out."[16]

Maud Smith Marks, 1956.
(*Photo courtesy Atha Marks Dimon.*)

Maud May (Smith) Marks with children Emory and Atha, about 1912, at home near Addicks, Texas. (*Photo courtesy E. M. Marks.*)

6

Maud

"She reads more books I guess than half a dozen put together."[1]

Maud May Smith was a beautiful child, with hair the color of jet. She was born on the 10th of March, 1887, at Blue Earth, Minnesota, first of the four offspring of Fred Henry Smith and Martha Elizabeth Clark. As a tot of three or four years, Maud caught the eye of a Dakota Indian chieftain who tried to buy her from her father. Captivated by little Maud's resplendent black hair, the chief offered Smith one hundred dollars for the child. When the offer was declined, the Sioux doubled his bid. Smith refused to deal, and the chief rode out of town in high dudgeon.[2]

Smith owned the hotel and livery stable in Blue Earth. The hotel was a first-class operation. There were hand-crocheted tops for all the chamber pots to deaden the clatter of lids replaced during the night. When the new Ringling Brothers Circus came to town from nearby Baraboo, Wisconsin, in the

1880s and 1890s, the artistes had rooms in Smith's hotel while keepers and crewmen slept in the wagon yard with their animals. The circus made a strong impression on the innkeeper's daughter. Imitating acrobats who performed on the rosin-coated backs of well-schooled circus horses, Maud would plant her feet on the slick back of a surprised draft horse, take reins in hands, and stand erect as she urged the animal into a lope across the prairie.[3]

Maud's earliest American forebears settled in Connecticut during the colonial period. They hailed originally from Sussex County, England; Ayr in Scotland; and County Donegal, Ireland. All her people could read and write, an accomplishment in which the Smith and Clark families took great pride.[4]

The loss of her mother clouded Maud's Minnesota childhood. Martha Clark Smith was struck down in her twenties by an undiagnosed paralysis. Fred moved the family to a farm in northern Iowa, hoping the clean country air would foster a recovery. It was no good; Martha died in 1893 when her daughter Maud was six.

For his second wife, Smith chose Ada, the housekeeper at his hotel. The marriage produced two offspring and a family closet full of skeletons. Fred lived to regret his mistake, at least, which was more than could be said for some of the housekeeper's husbands: "This Ada turned out to be quite a harridan," Maudeen confided. "I don't know how many men she married, but there were at least six of them. It was suspected that she had done away with a couple of her husbands. And she was a child abuser. Her two daughters—my mother's half-sisters Athene and Marie—sat and cried as they told me they thought Ada was responsible for the death of a boy child."[5]

Ada indeed seemed capable of such an act. As Maud grew up, her luxuriant blue-black hair continued to attract admirers, including a very rich old gentleman who proposed marriage. "Ada told Mother that all she had to do was go ahead and marry him and pour lead in his ears when he was asleep," Maudeen said. "That would kill him and she could get his money."[6]

Doubtless horrified by her stepmother's suggestion, Maud might have hesitated to tell her father of Ada's gruesome plan. Fred, however, no longer had illusions about the kind of woman he had married. "Grandpa divorced her—and that was serious in those days," Maudeen said.[7] With the four children from his first marriage, Smith fled to Texas in 1899. He settled in the Fairbanks area northwest of Houston and became a dairy farmer.

Maud was twelve years old when her family moved to Texas. As a teenager, she became a schoolmarm, by default. When her teacher was incapacitated by a stroke, Maud took over a classroom in White Oak and tutored the other children. Many of her students were older than she.[8]

The young woman had a passion for learning that she never lost. She loved books and read at every opportunity, always keeping three or four volumes on the nightstand by her bed. Her tastes ran the gamut, from classical literature to the newest popular novel.

When she married Emil Marks, Maud undertook to broaden the cowboy's spotty education. E. H. was gratified by her attempts to smooth his rough spots. He was proud of her accomplishments and welcomed the civilizing effect she had on his life. No one was more aware than he of the gaps in his schooling. For a youth born into a German-speaking household, learning English by ear had its pitfalls, especially because the cowboys of E. H.'s growing-up years peppered their speech with slang.

"They shortened everything," he complained. "They didn't say *liable*—they said *li'le*. And *'im* for *him*. 'He goes downtown and takes the cow with 'im.' There were so many of those I had a hard time to try to master the English language. I was pretty far back. My wife used to get after me all the time. She's pretty well up on spelling and stuff like that. She was always correcting me in the early days and I was always glad to take advice because, by golly, the average old cowboy used his knife to eat peas with. One old fellow said one day, 'I can't keep these peas on my knife. I wonder if I could use a spoon.' We still don't know whether he was joking."[9]

With Maud's blessing, E. H. also became a voracious reader. He consumed Westerns, especially biographies of notable real-life Westerners like Jeff Davis Milton, famous Texas lawman. He also quoted Shakespeare from time to time. Among E. H.'s favorite passages were these well-known lines from *Othello*:

"Who steals my purse steals trash; . . . / But he that filches from me my good name / Robs me of that which not enriches him, / And makes me poor indeed."[10]

The literary pursuits of the LH7's owners spilled over into daily life on the ranch in curious ways. The names of horses, like Happy Hawkins, were taken from characters in popular novels of the day; dinner table conversations were sprinkled with quotes from great literature and classical philosophy.

At Barker the family had a black housekeeper named Gertrude. In Maud's employ, Gertrude discovered new worlds of knowledge. She was eager to learn and absorbed information like a blotter absorbs ink. Echoing Maud on the teachings of Socrates, Plato, and Aristotle, Gertrude often preceded her own remarks with a pedantic, "As the Greeks used to say . . ."[11]

Maud resolved early in her marriage to E. H. to improve the way of life for her family and other rural residents of West Harris County. When 4-H was founded in 1914 she became a 4-H leader and helped club members with dairy cattle projects. For years she supported the educational efforts of home demonstration agents sent into the countryside by the Agricultural and Mechanical College of Texas to bring modern methods to families isolated on farms and ranches.[12] Maud was president of the Barker Home Demonstration Club, which sponsored programs on food preparation, canning, family care, home improvements, and home economics. At first, the club met in the tiny Presbyterian church on Barker-Clodine Road. Later, the Katy Railroad abandoned its depot on the tracks near the LH7 ranch house. Maud seized the opportunity to turn the old passenger station into headquarters for the homemakers' club. Atha recalled her mother's efforts to gain use of the station:

"Mother wrote a letter to the president of the Katy Railroad, asking if the Home Demonstration Club could meet in the old depot. The answer came back, 'No, we cannot allow you to do that because of the legal liability. But we will sell it to you if you will move it off the railroad right-of-way.'" Maud offered two dollars for the building, and the railroad accepted. A group of local men moved it bodily from MKT property.

The station's floor was of four-inch-wide planks and had a small raised platform where the stove had sat, belching red-hot embers. To cover the burned places in the wood planking and raise the surrounding floor to the level of the stove platform, the homemakers installed new pine floorboards. A few other modifications finished the transformation from train depot to meeting hall, and the clubwomen were ready to host the rural specialists who came out from Houston and College Station. Atha attended programs that touched on everything from outhouses to energy-efficient cooking:

"One time a home demonstration agent from Harris County gave a demonstration on fireless cookers," she said. "You had this box, it looked sort of like an ice chest but it was a well-insulated cooker. You would heat stones on your woodstove, put your food in pots, set them down in the cooker, and then put the hot stones on top. After so many hours, your food was cooked. I was real small, but I remember that demonstration."

On another occasion the county agent came out to Barker to demonstrate the proper construction of a sanitary outdoor pit toilet. Atha missed the first part of the program, and consequently found the proceedings a mystery: "I walked up and didn't know what was going on. 'What is he showing them?' I thought. So I kept asking, 'What is Mr. Clinton doing?' Everybody was snickering, but no one was telling me what was going on. Finally someone said, 'He's showing us how to make a sanitary toilet!'"

"We never had one, however. We had the outhouse out at the back, with the Sears catalog in it. It was outside the yard." Later, with the installation of a septic system, the household progressed to indoor facilities.

Before rural electrification brought power to the Texas countryside in the 1930s, the Marks home had electric lights. The current was generated in an engine room that sat in the backyard on a concrete slab. The small building housed a gasoline motor and rows of primitive batteries, an assemblage known as a Delco plant. As the house lights drained the acid cells and began to dim, one of the boys would start the motor and recharge the batteries.

The small electrical plant powered only the lights. For ironing, Maud first used a flatiron heated on a woodstove. Later, she acquired a gasoline iron, exasperating to use because the tiny attached fuel tank demanded frequent refilling. Remembering the ornate trims and needlework popular for little girls' clothing when she was small, Atha winced at the thought of her mother meticulously pressing each ruffle and flounce: "When I think about my little mama having to iron the ruffles on my dress and the embroidery—just think of all that work."

The demands of running a large household in an age of few conveniences made rural homemaking a dawn-to-dusk job six days a week. As far as practicable, the Sabbath was set aside as a day of rest. One of E. H.'s early family edicts required "no fire in the kitchen on Sunday." Though noble in principle, as a practical matter the ruling may have brought little relief to those who kept the home fires burning. Atha acknowledged that strict observance of the Sabbath occasioned frantic activity the day before: "The women killed themselves on Saturday baking and scrubbing, but there was 'no fire in the kitchen on Sunday.'"

With the ingenuity of her Yankee forebears, Maud found ways to lessen the tedium of household chores and make more time for her children and her intellectual pursuits. One of the first modern labor-saving machines she owned was a Maytag washer. Maud put it to work churning butter as well as sudsing clothes.

"Pa," she said to Fred Smith one day, "if I had something that would sit down over the dasher, like a bucket, I could just churn the butter in there." Fred sketched a diagram of a bucket that would fit over the dasher and had a Houston tinnery build the prototype. It worked exactly as planned, Atha recounted: "Mother would put the bucket over the dasher that washed the clothes and put her cream in there and turn on the washer. It was out in the wash house. Then she'd go back in the main house and read a book or whatever she wanted to do." The slosh-slosh of cream in the Maytag butter churn was music to the ears of Atha, who no longer had to churn by hand.

(A gifted inventor, Fred Smith made life easier for many around the ranch with his creative problem-solving. Travis recalled that his grandfather invented an implement to remove bushings in a Model T Ford. Emory admired his grandpa's system for making walking canes: Fred went into the woods and selected small saplings, three to four feet high, which he wrapped from top to bottom with baling wire. He attached a flag to the top of each so he could easily locate the tree again in a couple of years. As the sapling grew, the wire caused ridges to form on the trunk. When Fred stripped the wire from the tree he had a naturally ridged walking cane, functional as well as beautiful.)[13]

Among Maud's treasured possessions were formal photographic portraits of her first three children, taken individually when each was very young. "We're all just really decked out," Atha remarked. "I said to Mother one time, 'How did you get the photos—did the photographer come out to the house?' And she said, 'Oh no. Your father took you to town in a horse-drawn buggy.' I asked how we ended up with our clothes looking so nice. 'I fixed your clothes and put them in a box,' she said, 'and then he took you in the buggy down on Washington Avenue to the photographer's to have your picture made.' So it must have been very important to Mother, to have photographs made of us." In Maudeen's case, snapshots substituted for a formal baby picture. The box camera had become available for general home use, giving proud parents a convenient alternative to the downtown photography studio.[14]

Much against her wishes, Maud was separated from one of her daughters for two years. For health reasons, Atha spent most of 1922 and 1923 on the rolling plains of Texas, reluctantly given up by her mother to board with a family of virtual strangers. It was a difficult time for a sensitive twelve-year-old girl. Cut off from her loving family, Atha began to think she was really no child of Emil and Maud's at all:

> I had the asthma, just very bad. Many times I'd think, "This will be the last breath that I take, but it'll be all right if it is." I was worn out from breathing so hard.
>
> Mother and Daddy took me to an old doctor out in the west end of Houston, his name was Doctor Beebe. He told them, "Well, she has a large lung capacity, she'll never have the TB, but she's got the asthma. The best thing to do with her is take her out in West Texas to a higher climate." So Mother and Daddy talked it out. "What shall we do? Shall we move?" That would certainly have been awful.

> Daddy belonged to a Masonic Lodge that a Mr. Carter belonged to, and Mr. Carter said, "I have a sister-in-law who lives out in Coleman County [near Abilene] with her husband and mother." The mother was way up in her eighties. "Would you like me to see if they would board her?"
>
> The Elmores took me in, and that was at the little town of Santa Anna. They lived on the side of a mountain. Mother and Daddy and Maudeen took me out there and they spent the night. The next morning they said they were going to go look at the glass mining. They had sand that they mined [for glass making] in the side of the mountain, and they were going to see that. Mrs. Elmore and I stood at the gate, and of course I thought they were coming back. They didn't come back. Mr. Elmore came and said my mother couldn't take it. She couldn't stand to say good-bye.
>
> I went to school up there two years and I stayed up there most summers. I only came home at Christmastime. You know, other children are cruel—sometimes they don't mean to be—but I remember some children would say, "Your parents don't want you. They just brought you up here and left you. If I were you, I'd save up some money and catch a train and go back home." They were feeling for me, but it certainly was not helping me.

One person made the experience bearable for Atha, and that was Mrs. Elmore's mother. She became the lonesome little girl's friend and ally:

> You see, we never had a grandmother. My mother's mother died when she was six, Daddy's mother died when he was quite small, so we never had a grandmother. I had one there, and she was one of those grandmothers who sat on the front porch and rocked and patted and sang. So that helped a lot.
>
> These folks that I stayed with didn't have a car. They didn't have a telephone. They just lived on the side of that mountain, and Mr. Elmore worked on the highway construction. I was sort of isolated. I walked about two miles to go to the Baptist Sunday School. So I missed some things at home. But it was certainly wise of my parents to take me up there, and I know it was quite a sacrifice.

Four-year-old Maudeen was far more impressed by the trip to Santa Anna Mountain than by her sister's absence: "I was just a barely talking butterball, but I can remember the trip in that Model T touring car and us being in the back seat. And these hills before they had all of them graded—we'd fly! I'd be trying to sleep and I'd roll off the seat and onto the floor. Finally, I had enough of it. Mother said I pulled myself up haughtily, punched Daddy on the shoulder and shouted, 'Can't you drive any better than that?'

"There was a question in Atha's mind for years whether she was actually born to the family," Maudeen admitted, "because they sent her off there all by herself, poor darling. She stayed out there a couple of years, but I was so small I hardly missed her." In the end it appeared the ordeal had been worth it. When long-suffering Atha came home, she no longer had the asthma.[15]

Quiet and rather shy, Maud Marks was as appealing in her serenity and gentle humor as E. H. in his flamboyance. Beneath her country gentlewoman's manners, she nurtured a spirit as lively and uncommon as E. H.'s own. The pair drew people like filings to a magnet. "The latch-string was always out" at the LH7 Ranch; Marks hospitality extended to strangers as well as friends. Whether drifter, welldigger, traveling salesman, newspaper reporter, or sightseer, a visitor could always expect an invitation to lunch.

Maud never knew how many places to set at the table—guests came and went in endless procession. Just as it was time to sit down to a meal, E. H. might walk through the gate with a party of strangers, the latter protesting that they could not possibly impose on Miz Marks at lunchtime. Maud would whisk another can of homegrown vittles out of the cupboard, pop another batch of made-from-scratch biscuits into the oven, and convincingly reassure the guests as they came in the door that it was no trouble at all. Her table always looked as if she knew they were coming.[16]

"[Mother] often glanced out the kitchen window to see our father bringing in two or three unexpected guests for lunch," Atha noted. "She responded with a bountiful table boosted by large bowls of home-canned foods and hot biscuits. I have always marveled at how fast Mother could whip out those biscuits! Ingredients were dumped unmeasured into her large wooden bowl. Presto! They were on the table by the time the men had washed up on the back porch. Daddy never failed to compliment Mother's biscuit-ability."[17]

Ranch-raised beef, of course, was the centerpiece of most meals at the Marks home. When E. H. was butchering to fill orders for Houston meat markets, Maud frequently would hand one of the children a bowl and send them out to the slaughterhouse to ask E. H. to send in something for lunch. Organ meats were a particular delicacy. "Quite often, he would cut off a hunk of the liver and the sweetbread and send that in, and Mother would fix it for our noonday meal," Atha recalled. "Sweetbread is a gland [the pancreas or the thymus] in a healthy, sucking calf—a very nice piece of meat. It is delicious. We just grew up on that.

"Now, Mother would never cook brains," Atha added. "There was never any need for Daddy to send brains in the house, because she wouldn't fix them. And she wouldn't cook frog legs. She said they jumped around too much and she was not going to have them in her kitchen. Those were the two things she wouldn't fix, brains and frog legs."

It was a wintertime ritual to butcher a hog and make sausage. Nothing went to waste at hog-killing time. "Daddy said they saved everything except the squeal, and that may be right," Atha said. When most of the meat was cut away, the pork bones were salted down in a five-gallon crock, covered with a weighted wooden lid, and left in the smokehouse to cure. From time to time, Maud would send a child to the smokehouse to get a bowl of bones. "We loved those pork bones," Atha remarked. "She'd wash the salt off and boil them, and we'd chew the meat off. To me, they were a treasure."

Travis recalled that the family always sat down together to eat, though the dinner hour varied according to circumstances: "The Friday evening meal was usually late as E. H. brought oysters from Houston. The Katy Highway (now Interstate 10) which E. H. came home on was not much traveled after dark so even though our house was one mile off Katy Road we knew for certain when we saw those dim Ford lights that it had to be and it usually was E. H. coming from Houston."[18]

Strangers who enjoyed the hospitality of the LH7 frequently insisted on paying for their meal with a song, a service, or a small gift. Sometimes it was the simple gift of gab. On Sunday afternoons or warm summer evenings, the family might gather on the porch for conversation. "The front porch was just for sittin', a Sunday sort of thing," Maudeen recollected. "The back porch was for comin' and goin', a slam-bang, push it open and let it swing shut thing.

"In earlier days, we had all kinds of folks stop by. Wandering cowboys, some of them with guitars, would sit and play and maybe take a meal with us. Sometimes an artist would come by and would paint while we sat and watched."[19]

If he arrived late in the day, even a traveling salesman could expect the courtesy of an evening meal and a night's lodging. Most of the roadmen went on their way the next morning, fortified by a cowboy-sized breakfast. Some, however, were so impressed with LH7 hospitality that they stayed until they risked their welcome.

"When we lived at Addicks we had a lot of drifters come through," Emory recalled. "Some of them would work, some of them were salesmen, but they saw a good thing when they were there and they'd stay. This one salesman heard Mother tell about the masquerade balls we used to have in those old-time dancehalls, and he gave her a Japanese kimono to wear to one of these balls." With long ivory pins adorning her soft black hair in the oriental style, Maud cut a striking figure in the exotic silk gown.

Another peddler who stopped by the Marks home in Addicks complained of a slight cold and asked E. H. for "a little toddy" to ease his discomfort. An old hand at doctoring children and livestock, E. H. was glad to fix him up, though not with the hot whiskey drink the peddler expected. Atha remembered that her father was a firm believer in the Watkins product line: "He always kept these big bottles of Watkins Cough Syrup, Watkins Vanilla, and Watkins Liniment. They all came in the same size bottle—big. Daddy went in and fixed the man a glass with some sweet milk, a little sugar, and about half a tablespoon of Watkins Liniment. You did everything with Watkins Liniment. You rubbed with it, you inhaled it, and you drank it, but only in very small quantities. So he gave the glass to the peddler, who drank it thinking it was a whiskey mixture. The man grabbed his throat and yelled, 'Poison! I've been poisoned!' He didn't know it was going to burn like that."

As Houston grew, so did its cultural offerings, and Maud took advantage of the city's proximity to introduce her family to dance, music, and the arts. "Mother saw to it that we were exposed to the celebrated artists of the day," Emory noted. "Galli-Curci, Pavlova, the Scottish singer and comedian Sir Harry Lauder, the pianist Arthur Rubinstein, the tenor John McCormack, and other celebrities." The children went willingly enough, absorbing their Stravinsky along with their Gershwin and learning to distinguish the Charleston from a *pas de deux*. Years later, Atha recalled the neat juxtaposition of simple rural pleasures with the uptown side of her life: "I appreciate having grown up on the ranch. I could sit on a bale of hay and listen to the Longhorns bawl or I could drive in to Houston to attend an opera and appreciate the cultural events we were privileged to enjoy."[20]

When a class act came to town, E. H. could be persuaded to shake off the dust and escort his wife to city lights for an evening of highbrow entertainment. They attended a performance by Amelita Galli-Curci, the unexcelled operatic soprano who retired in 1930, and they saw the great Russian ballerina Anna Pavlova dance her most famous role, *The Dying Swan*, before her death in 1931. E. H. responded with enthusiasm. He complimented Pavlova's artistry with, "That little girl looked just like a swan!"[21]

On one occasion when the family headed to town for a concert by a classical pianist, E. H. made it no secret he would rather play poker with the boys. Usually he was agreeable about attending such affairs, but this time he balked. Maud had to insist. "Mother just dragged E. H. down to about the sixth row," Emory related. "She went for that classical stuff, but E. H. just didn't like it. So we're sitting there, and this guy was just a-banging those piano keys; he'd bang here a little bit and then he'd hit it there." The pianist's fingers flew through a particularly intricate passage. As the musician neared the climax of his performance, E. H. turned to Maud and declared, "I bet he couldn't do it again!" For rows around, the audience roared.

In E. H.'s defense, it must be noted that his hearing was impaired from years of hunting, and accustomed as he was to bawling instructions to men and animals on the open prairie, he probably did not realize how far his voice carried in an enclosed space. Hunting was part of life in the country, and auditory damage from the sharp report of a rifle was common. "All our men that hunt have hearing problems," Maudeen commented. "It's just from the blasting. Daddy hunted because when he was a young man they needed the meat on the table."[22]

Despite his hearing impairment—and because he had married a lady of culture—E. H. was a regular symphony-goer. "We were sponsors of the Houston Symphony when it first started," Maudeen reported. "We had season seats. The conductor was a man of short stature. When the orchestra got into a spirited piece, you could hear his swallow-tailed coattails pop. I went to the symphony concerts on Tuesday nights and I went with Daddy to the wrestling matches on Friday nights and to the rodeos on Saturday and Sunday. That was our life. We were exposed to the best, regardless of what it was."[23]

The lighter selections performed by the Houston Symphony Orchestra usually lulled E. H. into blissful, snoring unconsciousness. His Dutch blood responded instantly, however, to the hearty, heavy tones of German composer Richard Wagner. Maudeen merrily recalled that a Wagner composition always brought her father wide awake.

Under E. H.'s influence, the four Marks children learned to rope and ride with the best of Texas cowboys. Maud saw to their cultural indoctrination. Both parents were determined that Emory, Atha, Travis, and Maudeen should receive the best formal education possible, no matter what it took. They were adamant that all four would go to college.

The Barker school closed soon after the Marks family had moved up on the prairie near that community, so the children had walked three miles to Addicks to attend grade school. The Addicks school, however, was not accredited, a drawback for students aspiring to college. When Emory was about fourteen, his father gave him the keys to a little black Ford so he could chauffeur himself and his siblings to classes in Houston, where the educational facilities outshone anything in the rural sections. It was a forty-mile round trip over atrocious gravel roads. If the children rolled up the windows, they suffocated; with the windows down, the dust was intolerable. They arose in the predawn, and by the time they arrived home each evening the day was all but gone. It was a hard way to get an education.

Emory and Atha went to Reagan High School off Heights Boulevard in Houston, Travis attended James Hogg Junior High, and Maudeen was a "Harvard girl," attending Harvard Elementary in the Heights. When she transferred from Addicks to the Houston school, Maudeen skipped from the third grade into the fifth. The only thing she missed was long division, which Maud patiently taught her on a blackboard each evening after school.[24]

Maudeen retained vivid memories of life as a grade-school commuter, spending hours each day cooped up in a Ford coupe with her three older siblings: "I remember there were all these fumes that were coming into the car, and Travis was always complaining about dying and telling us to let him get to the window."[25]

Emory confirmed that his brother seemed to be getting the worst of it: "Travis would get in the car and say, 'I'm dying. I can't breathe. I'm dying!' I'd put my hand on his head and push him down to the floor and tell him, 'Oh, be quiet and sit down.'"

As the youngest of the lot, Maudeen often got caught in the middle: "I sometimes would wind up on the floor. Emory had to pick me up off the floor where Travis was stepping on me to get to the window. And there was Atha trying to keep her clothes neat. It was terrible for the four of us in that little old Ford coupe. It had one seat. And trying to get to school and look decent when we got there—nothing was satisfactory to Emory or Travis or Atha or me."[26]

Emory's homeroom teacher called him "Old Ford Car" because his usual excuse for being late was that they had had a flat on the old Ford car. "But I did have a lot of trouble with that car," Emory maintained in self-defense. "That was a pretty good trip every day, on those old gravel roads. I don't know how we ever made it. Well, that's the reason I didn't graduate with honors. I had to be the mechanic."

Many mothers customarily deck out their children in all new clothes for the start of school in the fall. Maud rejected that practice. "Mother started us to school with the clothes we'd been wearing," Atha recalled. "Then when we needed some more we got them. We were some of the few children who didn't start to school with all new clothes. But I think my mother was certainly correct. And anyway, new clothes are always hot."

Shoes were exclusively of leather then, and a new pair had to be molded to the owner's feet for comfort and long wear. Maud had the children pour water into brand-new shoes and wear them until they were dry and properly set to the foot. During the shoe-setting ritual, the children impatiently worried their mother for permission to remove their soggy footwear. "Many a time we'd say, 'May I take it off now?'" Atha said. "And Mother would say, 'No, the shoe's not dry yet.'"

To Maud's satisfaction, the nation in these years was by and large "dry." During the 1920s and early 1930s, as the Marks children grew up, Prohibition was a part of their lives. Even if there had been no national law preventing the distribution of alcohol, there would have been a family ordinance against drinking. Maud was "almost radical," as acquaintances saw it, on the subject of abstinence. Drinking was strictly taboo in her household. To her consternation, however, enforcing the no-alcohol rule beyond the confines of her own home proved difficult. "Every time I used to go off to a party or something, Mother would say, 'Now stay away from the punchbowl!'" Emory recalled with a chagrined chuckle. He did not always heed her admonitions: "One time I went to Addicks and had a beer. On my way home Mother passed me going sixty miles an hour in the opposite direction. That evening when Mother returned home she asked me to come into the study. 'Ah-ha!' she said. 'You have been drinking. I smelled your breath when I passed you on my way to town.'"[27]

Maud's grandfather Myron Thaddeus Smith, born in St. Lawrence County, New York, in 1830, had at one time been Captain of the Great Lakes. He directed shipping and traffic through the five lakes and their connecting waterways. Alcoholism eventually cost him his position as well as the goodwill of his family.[28] Deeply troubled by her grandfather's drunkenness, Maud grew to abhor alcohol. E. H. could not offer so much as a near beer to his poker-playing buddies. "Mother fixed eggnog once a year, between Christmas and New Year's, and that was the one time that there was any alcohol in the house," Atha remembered.

So strong was Maud's aversion to drink that no circumstance could induce her to swallow the stuff herself. Atha recalled an episode, after she had married and was living nearby with her own young family, when her father telephoned with disturbing news:

> Daddy called me and said, "Your mother's very ill—I think maybe you ought to come over here." I went right over, and you could hardly tell where Mother stopped and the sheet started because she was so pale. Daddy called the doctor. He came back and told me—not in Mother's presence, of course—that Doctor Turner had said to get her to sip some wine, as a stimulant.
>
> "Knowing Miz Marks," Doctor Turner said, "she may not do that. If she will not sip some wine, then you boil some coffee as fast as you can." The only way Mother had to cook at that time was on a wood range, so we would have to start a fire and boil the water and make the coffee.
>
> So Daddy went to the medicinal pantry and got down some wine and took it in to her. He said, "Now Maud, Doctor Turner said that you should take a few sips of this." She said "No!" and tightened her lips.
>
> "But Mother, Doctor Turner *said* to take a few sips." "No!" She just wouldn't do it. So Daddy said, "You just as well go get the fire started." I got the fire started and got some hot water and made the coffee. She drank that, but no liquor was going to go down *her* throat.

LH7 rodeo arena, judges stand with bucking chutes below, before the stands were improved in 1936. (*Photo courtesy Atha Marks Dimon.*)

Weaver Gray was a trick rider who, with his wife-partner, entertained at several LH7 Ranch Rodeos. Photo taken in the 1920s. (*Photo courtesy E. M. Marks.*)

Cattle in pen gathered for branding, May 1929. Sitting on the fence: W. A. Paddock, E. H. Marks' business partner from 1923 until January 1936. The handwritten inscription reads: "Just acres of cattle at LH7 Ranch, Barker, Texas. E. H. Marks owner of ranch." (*Photo courtesy E. M. Marks.*)

7

Real Cowboys and Rodeos

"If he's a real cowpoke he'd rather be dead than ride out there without a good hat on his head."¹

The LH7's Sam Ward was a real cowboy. He wasn't a cowman, he wasn't a bullrider, and he didn't bust broncos. He worked cattle and he knew a lot of songs to sing around a campfire at night when Jim Herklotz played the fiddle, songs like "Red River Valley" and "The Old Chisholm Trail."

Bill Gorman was a real cowboy from way back. In thirteen years of riding for E. H. Marks, he never fixed a windmill or walked behind a plow. He chewed tobacco and rode horseback and worked cattle.²

The vaqueros of the LH7 were real cowboys: "They know which end of a cow gets up first," E. H. said. Mostly, they were slow talking, slow walking, and tobacco chewing. Three out of four chewed; the danger of prairie fire made smoking too risky. Most were rail thin—the demands of the job trimmed away the fat. "When you ride and rope and twist in that saddle every way, you lose a lot of that surplus," E. H. observed.[3]

Real cowboys tended to be passionate about horses. A buckaroo afoot resembled an aged and arthritic hound dog on a hot summer's afternoon; astride a good horse he was transformed. "The average old cowboy doesn't get in a hurry until he gets on a horse," E. H. remarked. "As my daddy always said in the eighties when they'd ask him if he was looking for a job, 'If I can do it a-horseback I'll take the job, but I don't want no walking.'"

LH7 cowboys had names like Charley Jones, Otto Thornton, Gerhardt Vandre, Charlie Grisbee, Moon Sullivan, Uncle Ben Hodges, Elmer Peek, Ed Warneke, Buck Stevens, Mose Burton, and Thelmore Jones. Commended by E. H. as "average old cowhands," these were men who knew that the secret of flanking a calf as it bounced and struggled on the end of a rope was to catch it by an ear and flank when the youngster was in midair, then drop it to the ground. Only a greenhorn would try to lift a calf to throw it.[4]

The ranch's top hands also knew how to throw a full-grown steer and how to keep it down with a minimum of effort. "You can hold the biggest steer in the world by putting his tail between his hind legs and your knee in his flank," E. H. explained. "I had old cowboys who could do it till the steer starved to death there on the ground. He could flounce and kick but every time he went to get up they'd pull that tail and gut him in the side and stick that knee in his flank, and down he'd go."

Experienced men had many tricks for controlling the half-wild range cattle. To get a Longhorn steer to lead, for instance, a cowboy could wear down the beast's resistance with a rope pulled tight around the base of the horns: "I don't know about these other cattle but I raised plenty of Longhorn steers," E. H. said, "and if you [tighten a rope on] one of them about thirty minutes it would get sore around the horns and he'd go to leading in less than an hour. You wouldn't have to chase him around much. When that would get sore [at the base of the horns] he'd give to the rope."

A good hand knew better than to try brute force on a range-toughened steer that outweighed him by a thousand pounds or more. The veteran cowboy tired his quarry into submission, like a fisherman playing out the line for a big fighting bass. "You can't lead [a steer] straight-away," E. H. emphasized. "You've got to jerk him sideways. You haven't got power enough to pull him forward but you can jerk him from side to side, and first thing you know he'll give. Whenever you get his head kind of sore, he'll come along."

Occasionally, a roper going for the horns would snag a steer by some other part of its anatomy, with disastrous results. "Every once in a while an old boy makes what we call a 'community loop.' Some people make too big a loop, you know," E. H. said. "They want to get everything that's going along. They generally catch them around the neck or maybe around the belly, and then [the steer's] got more power. He's going away from you; he'll go and jerk you along. You can't handle him like you can when you rope one around the horns."

Seasoned cowboys also knew a quick and effective way to teach a wild horse to lead. They would tie a log to a rope twelve to fourteen feet long and tie the rope to the horse's head. Turned loose in a grassy patch, the mustang soon wore itself out trying to shake off the unfamiliar weight dragging from its nose. It was a remarkably safe exercise for both trainers and horse.

"He'd run against that log and it would give and wouldn't throw him and bust him wide open," E. H. explained. "The boys would go on out there and run him around, and he'd run against that post that was tied to the end of the rope and he'd snatch it around, and first thing you know he'd give. He'd carry that log a little ways but finally he'd get to yielding and then he'd learn to lead."

A cowboy didn't have to be as smart as his horse, but it helped if he could keep a step ahead of the cow. He had to anticipate her moves and be ready to thwart her plans. "The average good cowhand will never wait till the cow gets away," E. H. said. "He heads her before she gets away. He knows the nature of a cow. He watches and he knows when she's going to try to make a break and he catches her. He doesn't wait till she starts running and then take after her and run her off so far that it takes two or three men to get her back."

A good hand need not be told that he could not drive a cow into a pen when she was looking at him anymore than he could drive the wrong end of a nail into a board. A cow would drive better if she thought she was getting away, reckoned top hand Mose Burton, whose opinion carried weight around the LH7. "Old Mose was one of the best cowmen that ever lived," Emory attested. "He could almost read a cow's mind."[5]

E. H. once told Maudeen that some of the best cowboys he ever had on the place were black men like Burton, because they worked cattle slowly and easily in the way that cattle should be worked. "Daddy always said that anytime you chounce a cow around, all you're doing is running off all the feed and care and time you've spent putting fat on that animal," Maudeen remembered. "So the cowboys always worked cattle real easy and slow and never ran them. They just walked them. But when Daddy would leave, sometimes they'd run those cattle. They wanted to hurry up and get through for the day."[6]

To E. H.'s mind, no cowhand worth his wages should have to be told when or how long to work. He tried never to hire a man who couldn't work without supervision. When other ranchers asked him what it took to run a successful cattle operation, E. H. advised them: "Get you a good cowhand and don't tell him anything. Let him alone. My man John Warnasch has been with me twenty-five years. I don't know what he's going to do next week and I don't care. I know he's going to do something. If he didn't . . . I wouldn't have him on the job."

A real cowboy watched out for the youngest calves at roundup to see that none was trampled under the milling hooves of the herd. He might gently stand a small, tired calf on its feet or carry it to roundup across the saddle in front of him.[7] Though legend holds cowboys to be a rough, carousing bunch, full of hijinks, there was none of that on the LH7 Ranch. The men were courteous and respectful in manner, knowing that wild behavior would not be tolerated. No animal was abused, be it cow, horse, or barnyard pet. Atha recounted how one cowboy's brutal act cost him his job:

"The men had been out branding and they had come in to eat. There were big shade trees in the backyard and the cowboys usually lounged around out there after they ate, until maybe two o'clock, and then they went back to work.

"On this day I went outside when they did, and when I got out there this man Leo was laughing. He had cut the ears off of a cat. I just went all to pieces. I said, 'Leo, you're fired!' He thought that was funny. He was telling the other cowboys about it as they came out of the house. 'Atha fired me!' He thought that was so funny for a little girl to do that. So when Daddy came out I told him, 'Leo cut the ears off of that cat and I fired him.' Leo just laughed—he still thought it was funny."

E. H. did not share his man's amusement. "You heard her," he said. "Get going." Incredulous, Leo shuffled to the nearby bunkhouse, got his clothes, and left the ranch. He wasn't laughing when he went.

No cowboy worthy of the name would maltreat a horse, and any man who did so was beneath contempt. To make the point, E. H. often repeated a conversation he had overheard between an old-time rancher and a newcomer. The greenhorn had been mercilessly overworking his small remuda of cowponies, and the animals showed the strain. He asked the old man, "What do you do for sore-backed horses?"

"Sore-backed hosses?" echoed the old-timer, astonished. "Don't you know what to do for sore-backed hosses? Buy more hosses! You ain't got enough!" To ride a sore-backed horse was to violate one of the cardinal rules of the West.[8]

On a wide-open grassland where shade, water, and human companionship might be well beyond the distant horizon, a horse could be a cowboy's best and only friend. Most men treated their mounts accordingly, E. H. noted: "We tried to be kind to a horse. If you hit a horse over the head around a cow camp you wouldn't get by with it. You'd be liable to lose your job. The other cowboys would tell you about it. And the horse would tell you about it. You could hit a horse over the head one time and the next time you raise your hand up, that horse would duck."

A horse's behavior could speak volumes about the temperament and character of its most recent rider. "A horse will give you a lot of sign of the last fellow that rode him," E. H. said. "I had a good horse one time—I called him Eagle—and I loaned him to a fellow. Later on when I threw up my hand and said hello to a fellow that was riding along, that horse jumped. I couldn't figure him out. He just kept jumping every time I'd raise my hand.

"Well, by golly, I loaned that horse to that fellow again. I told him to ride old Eagle and I was watching him. He had a rope and every time he wanted to start he'd haul off and hit that horse. That's what did it."

E. H. saw no justification for that kind of treatment: "When you raised your hand that horse was already gone. You didn't have to hit him. . . . You've got your persuaders on your heel—just let them know you've got those spurs. You don't have to spur the blood out of them."

E. H. did right by the men who worked for him and expected them to do right by him. He was seldom disappointed. Once he gave a young man a job against the advice of the boy's father-in-law. "Marks, that fellow is as big a liar as you've ever seen," protested the older man. "He can't tell the truth."

Despite this warning, E. H. put the boy to work riding range. One day the new hand reported the fence down in the corner of one pasture but said he had fixed it. E. H.'s brother Willie, who kept an eye on the upper ranch twenty miles north of the main house, rode in that evening and told E. H. he had passed by the fence in question and it was still down. True to form, the new hand had lied.

"Don't say anything," E. H. told Willie. "That boy rode that pasture and he said he fixed it all right. So wait until we get together and then ask me if he fixed the fence."

Later, the three met, and in the course of the conversation Willie casually inquired, "Did you fix that fence yet?" E. H. replied matter-of-factly, "This boy rode that pasture today and told me he fixed it, and when he tells you anything you can depend on it." The downed fence was up by morning. The young cowhand rode to the pasture late that night and made the repairs under cover of darkness, suddenly anxious not to be caught in a lie.

Hearing good reports of the boy's behavior on the LH7, the mystified father-in-law asked E. H. for his secret. "What did you do, Marks? Beat him over the head?" "No," the rancher replied, "I just bragged on him. You can't make a man any better by cussing him out. If a man tells a lie, just brag on him.

"I had a fellow working for me that wouldn't clean the box where you feed the horses," E. H. added. "I told the other boys, 'Do like old Joe. He cleans those boxes—that's one thing he's going to do. He won't feed a horse in a dirty feed box.' Well, if he never did anything from then on, he cleaned the boxes."[9]

Bill Gorman started work for E. H. in 1923 and by the 1930s was ranch foreman. Gorman knew well the rules of the range and the cowboy's code, but certain urban regulations, particularly traffic laws, eluded him. Emory remembered one adventure-filled weekend in the city with Bill: "One Saturday morning Bill said to Dad and me, 'Ya'll want to go to town?' We'd go to town and go to a cigar shop. All over town they had United Cigar stores, and everybody would go there and get cigars, smoking tobacco, and chewing tobacco.

"I was in the back of Bill's car, E. H. was in the front, and Bill was driving. We got up in front of the Rice Hotel, going down Main Street putt-putt-putt-putt in this old T-Model. They used to have a policeman on each corner of Main. Bill starts to make a U-turn at Main and Texas Avenue and a policeman yells, 'Hey, you can't do that!' Bill just keeps a-going. He yells back, 'I believe I can make it if I take my time, officer!'"

The perpetrator hurriedly parked his car in the alley by a shoeshine shop, and the three ranchmen fled inside, using the opportunity to get their boots shined while they hid from the law. As they waited in the shop, several policemen approached. "We've got to get out of here!" Gorman pleaded.

Knowing their cowboy hats would be spotted immediately, E. H. ordered Bill and Emory to take off their Stetsons and stash them behind the shoeshine shop. The three then ducked around the corner and stayed out of sight until the officers had walked on down the street. The relieved cowboys made it safely back to the ranch, where the only restriction on making a U-turn was the rider's ability to stick in the saddle while the horse executed the move.

Real cowboys were hard to miss in the city because they wore hard-heeled boots that clattered on the concrete and spurs with tiny bells that jingled as they walked. Their pants were khaki, not blue denim, and they wore chaps only when they rode in brush. A real cowhand always wore a hat, never a cap. Uncle Rufe Muske had a saying that said it all: "A man who wears a cap when it rains is sitting in the saddle in water and a man sitting in water ain't no good."[10]

On the job, real cowboys dressed for utility, not style. They put their money in a good horse and a well-made saddle, the best they could afford, because those were the things that counted. Fancy duds simply announced the wearer's greenhorn status. If worn around the cowcamp, they would start old-timers' tongues to wagging.

"We talked about a lot of things, and the biggest talk was when a man had on store-bought clothes and catalog spurs," E. H. said. "We didn't think a fellow was a pretty good cowhand if he had on Sears and Roebuck or Montgomery Ward spurs—we called them catalog spurs. And the old boy that had on a pair of rubber boots as hot as a coffee pot, we said he wasn't much cowhand."

Men who cowboyed for a living kept their gear in shape. The condition of a cowhand's outfit said as much about his character as the quality of a clerk's writing instruments told of his. "A bookkeeper that would get one of these two-for-a-nickel pencils to keep books with and didn't have a good pen isn't much of a bookkeeper," E. H. reasoned. "You can just tell. A cowboy wants a good outfit. He wants to look decent. He wants a horse that he can kick in the side and go ahead when it's necessary. We believed in riding a good horse. They always say you can tell the boss by the horse he rides. When you rode into a headquarters where there was a bunch of cowboys and you looked around, you could tell the boss right quick. He generally rode a good horse."

A cowboy's day on the LH7 began at five-thirty in the morning. After a quick wash and a breakfast of bacon, bread, hotcakes, syrup, and coal-black coffee, riders were in the saddle by 6:00 A.M. At midday E. H. called a halt. The cowboys ate and took an hour or two to rest from the sun, lounging in hammocks in the shade of trees and swapping tall tales. Then it was back to work until the job was done, with supper at six or eight o'clock.[11] The late evening often was given over to poker. Much to Atha's consternation, E. H. was so fond of the game he frequently got up all-night poker sessions in the log cabin he had reconstructed behind the ranch's main house.

"It used to really upset me," Atha admitted. "I couldn't understand how he could sit up all night and play poker. He played poker out in the log cabin, and he'd go other places and play. He loved it, just loved it. He had his cronies that he liked to have at the games. There was Mr. Tom Belew from Simonton and Mr. Chris Pillot, those two were always there. And sometimes they played all night. I'd get very upset about it. Of course, I could dance all night, but that was different!"

Travis Marks could remember nights when his father and Bill Gorman played for pinto beans until daylight. At dawn, Bill would feed horses, eat breakfast, then saddle up and ride all day.[12]

Oddly, as much pleasure as E. H. took in the game, he forbade his children to play. "He wouldn't let us play poker in the house," Atha recalled. "One time when I was in high school, I told Mother that we were going to play cards. She said, 'What kind?' When I said, 'Oh, poker, I guess,' Mama said, 'You'd better ask your daddy.'"

Atha was mystified by this stipulation, but obediently sought permission from her father. He surprised her with a firm "No." "We're just going to play with matches," she told him, thinking he objected to teenagers gambling for money. He would not be swayed. "I don't know why that was, unless he thought I might get the habit," Atha mused.

Cow camp headquarters for roundups on the upper LH7 was an old ranch house twenty miles north of Barker, off the Hempstead Highway on Barker-Cypress Road. The heart of the house was the spacious kitchen and the dining room with its long table and benches. This was the province of Henry Embry, camp cook, who served excellent roast beef and chuckwagon coffee strong enough to float a horseshoe. Houston newspaperwoman Wilhelmina Beane found that Embry "has the English of a college professor, and is well-read on current events and Texas history," attributes not often found on the range.[13]

Branding time always drew visitors from Houston, many with a yen to ride alongside real cowboys and to partake of Embry's memorable camp cooking. Long-time Harris County

The LH7 Ranch

Sheriff Thomas Abner Binford, Frank Arnold of the sheriff's office, and Houston cattle buyer Mason Habermacher were among the regulars to appear on the prairie as the roundup got under way. Even E. H.'s partner, W. A. Paddock, a bona fide city sophisticate, could sit a horse well enough to head off an escaping cow.

Not all who came to the LH7 in springtime came to work the brandings, however. Many wanted simply to watch and marvel. Houstonians were fascinated by the sprawling ranch with its Old West aura only twenty miles from downtown's modern multi-storied buildings. City dwellers were charmed to discover that, three decades into the twentieth century, cattle and cowboys could still be found on the doorstep of Texas's premier city.[14]

Brandings as a form of public entertainment on the LH7 dated back to 1917, the year E. H. had moved family and ranch from his small place at Addicks to the open prairie near Barker. After the relocation, with ten times the land and a prospering herd of range cattle, E. H. had found himself desperately short of help. World War I claimed the services of many able-bodied men. The scattered drifters who came through in those years looking for work usually wanted to pick beans or dig postholes, not punch cows.

Aware of E. H.'s labor problems because most of them were in the same straits, friends and neighboring ranchers first rode to his aid in the spring of 1918 to help gather Marks cattle and brand the new calf crop with the distinctive LH7. When the work was done, cowboys and visitors had stayed to enjoy a neighborhood picnic and have a little friendly competition on outlaw stock the ranchmen brought along for amusement.[15]

A festive occasion, branding day on the LH7 grew into a popular annual event that drew to the ranch an ever-greater number of friends and relatives, many of whom camped in a pecan grove on the banks of Wolf Creek. E. H. fed his guests barbecue beneath a towering sycamore where five Mexican horse thieves reputedly had been hanged in 1871, strung up by implacable frontier cattlemen for stealing a remuda. The five were said to be buried in unmarked graves on the creek bank near the rodeo picnic grounds.[16]

Each spring, city-bred visitors thrilled to the action as cowpunchers from local ranches worked cattle, then rode broncs and wrestled steers for sport. To add variety to the competitions, E. H. invented a branding contest, thought to be the only event of its kind ever staged. Three calves with their mothers were run into an arena. Men competing in teams of five cut the calves out of the herd, roped them from horseback, and burned the LH7 brand on the right hip of each. A team was disqualified if the brand was in the wrong place or if a calf was crippled so that it could not walk from the arena. The contest brought out some of the fastest branders on the range. (Winners of the 1940 event branded three calves in this manner in 1 minute 18.4 seconds.)[17]

The crowds grew larger each spring. During the 1920s the gatherings so overflowed the ranch's facilities that E. H. found it necessary to build grandstands and a rodeo arena and to begin charging admission. By 1930 the original neighborhood branding party had evolved into a major, two-day public rodeo that was attracting audiences in the thousands. The event was held at the ranch for thirty years on the first Saturday and Sunday in May. Feeding the crowds, which some years numbered eight to ten thousand, took considerably more preparation than spitting a calf for a neighborhood picnic. During the rodeo's heyday, head cook Eric Anderson, assisted by "Uncle" Aaron Jones, supervised the barbecueing of as much as sixty-three hundred pounds of beef, all from the LH7 herd.[18]

The scores of cattle used in the roping, branding, and bullriding events also were ranch raised. As a Houston newspaper reported at the approach of the twelfth annual rodeo and barbecue: "Mr. Marks says that they will try to brand about 1,000 head although he is not sure that they will be able to get them all done in the time allotted. These cattle are all home-raised and are all Brahma field cattle and represent the pick of cattle in Harris County. In fact, the LH7 Ranch is known all over the Southwest for the high quality of the beef it produces."[19]

E. H. took particular pride in the fierceness of his bucking bulls. Poison Ivy, Double Trouble, and Impossible were "notorious the country over" for lofting riders into blue sky. The ranchman had a standing bonus of ten dollars for the cowboy who could ride Poison Ivy across the arena.[20]

To add spice to the entertainment, E. H. booked novelty performers—trick ropers, clown bullfighters, fancy riding acts. Buck Hoover, the "cowboy of the clouds," tried a stunt at the 1932 rodeo that put him in the hospital. He proposed to bulldog a steer out of an airplane. Dangling on a rope ladder beneath the plane, he jumped for the steer but missed. Hoover was rushed to St. Joseph's Infirmary in a Houston funeral home ambulance but suffered only cuts, bruises, and a broken ankle. A reporter got this eyewitness account from E. H.: "He went up in the airplane and then climbed down the rope ladder. Some of the fellows ran the steer out so he could swing or leap on its back. Something went wrong. Hoover missed the steer and finally dropped into a sandy place and rolled several feet. I didn't talk to him. He left immediately in the ambulance for Houston."[21]

Professional rodeo cowboys included the LH7 on an itinerary that also listed Madison Square Garden, Oregon's Pendleton Roundup, and other national attractions. Eventually, only professional cowboys would compete in the LH7 event, at their own insistence, but in the beginning the rodeo was open to any wayfaring roper. Emory recalled that some of the earliest competitors were of questionable character. "These cowboys would come to the rodeos and a lot of them were good people, but there were a bunch of drifters, too," he asserted. "Them son-of-a-guns would steal anything and do anything. Mother would look out the back door and she'd see one of these guys coming in the gate. Most of them would have a great big belt buckle, and she'd say, 'The bigger the belt buckle, the smaller the brain.' That was one of her mottos."

The LH7 rodeo was well regarded by the competing cowboys because E. H. never shorted them on prize money. Some early-day rodeo promoters had a reputation for offering a song and dance instead of cash when winners came to collect their jackpots. As word spread of the ready payoffs and spectacular entertainments offered by the LH7 show, E. H. was elated. "The rodeo is going over big," he reported in May 1934. "I have been traveling about in different sections of Texas and everywhere I found the people interested and talking about the contests.

"We expect 200 cowboys from all parts of the United States to take part in the rodeo. If the weather is good, we expect to serve 4,000 pounds of barbecued beef. We now are very busy getting all details in shape and we are paying special attention to the culling out of poor performers among the animals."[22]

In addition to the annual spring event for the public, the LH7 Ranch staged made-to-order private rodeos. E. H. hosted the Humble Oil Club; Eastern Air Lines when World War I flying ace Eddie Rickenbacker was company president; parties of postal workers, Shriners, railroad men, advertising execs, and engineers; and even a delegation of French perfumers.[23] In a typical summer there might be contracts for five or six private shows; one season E. H. staged nine rodeos at the ranch. "Dad would feed them barbecue and then hold a scaled down show," Emory explained. "He'd have about six bucking horses, two bucking bulls, and maybe five ropers. They had enough, seeing that. If they had too much it'd take up the whole afternoon."

Of all the horsemen who came to the ranch, to rodeo or to work, Emory was one of the best. An expert rider, he could handle the most fractious beast. "He broke more horses, better, than any cowboy we ever had there," Maudeen said. "Emory just had a way with horses. He had a horse called Ben that only had one eye, and he could take the bridle off that horse and cut cattle with him."[24]

One of those who greatly admired Emory's horsemanship was Mose Burton, himself an exceptional broncbuster. Mose once saddled and rode nineteen wild horses in a day. But rather than talk of his own accomplishments, Burton liked to brag to ranch visitors about his friend Emory. On occasion, he would arrange demonstrations of young Marks's riding skill.

"We had a bunch of people coming out for a little barbecue, and Mose wanted me to show off on a bucking horse," Emory related. "He eared him down and we got out in front of the house, and here were all these people standing around. I got on that horse and that son-of-a-gun made two lunges—boom! boom!—and then stopped dead. I went off him. It was the first time I'd ever been bucked off like that. Mose was embarrassed. Here he had put me up to it and had been telling everybody what a good rider I was. He went off and hid in the garage."

As Emory began to discover life beyond the ranch, he became a reluctant cowboy and seldom rode in his father's rodeos. He found the sport painfully akin to work he did with growing distaste everyday on the ranch: "I had to do it out on the prairie too much, and I just got sick and tired of it." Even as a teenager, Emory was harboring suspicions that there were easier ways to make money than busting broncs and punching cows. Ironically, he had an undeniable talent for the cow business.

"He's excellent with animals," Atha said. "Judging cattle, he could look at them and tell you how much they weigh and how much they're going to butcher out. And he can look at a horse and say why you shouldn't buy him. 'Can't you see his eyes are set wrong? He's stubborn.' Or, 'Have you looked at his feet? He's not swinging his feet correctly. Don't buy him.' But he just didn't like the cattle business."

As that dislike grew stronger, Emory cast about for an alternative occupation. Sales work seemed infinitely more agreeable than cow work, so he started selling tickets at the rodeos and ran the soft drink stand. "Dad always let me have the concession stand, unless I was somewhere else," Emory said.

The Houston Coca-Cola Company posed a problem for the young wheeler-dealer. Negotiations failed to bring him a discount on the price per case, Emory recalled in disgust: "The Coke people would not budge one nickel. I don't care if you sold ten thousand cases or you sold two cases, Coke cost seventy-five cents a case." Before the show started, he sold drinks to the cowboys for five cents a bottle. When the rodeo kicked off, the price to the public was a dime. Patrons grumbled that it was highway robbery. Emory had eight or ten boys working for him, carrying buckets of iced-down soft drink through the stands. They could keep two cents for every bottle sold; Emory got eight.

When Prohibition was lifted in 1933, Grand Prize Beer of Houston approached E. H. with a proposition to sell its brew at the annual LH7 rodeos. The company offered the cowman a high percentage of the proceeds if he would agree. E. H. asked Maud and the children what they thought. The idea was coolly received, Atha remembered: "Everybody said, 'I don't think that's the place for it.' We didn't think it was a good idea. Daddy said, 'Well, that's what I told them. I just wanted to see what the family thought.'" Coca-Cola thus retained its monopoly on Emory's cold drink stand and was never persuaded to drop its exorbitant price of seventy-five cents a case.

Though the demise of Prohibition left LH7 rodeo refreshments still spiritless, it did bring back the traditional whiskey jug that helped watchers get through their vigil when holding a wake over a corpse. Travis was among those called from the community, according to custom, to take a turn sitting by a body before burial.

"I only did it once when I was about eighteen and the night sure was long," Travis recollected. "Usually the body was laid out in a bed and two people were asked to hold the wake. It was expected that the family of the dead person furnish (drinking) spirits to those performing the wake. I wasn't furnished any during my obligation. On one occasion in the community, two old boozers were asked to hold the wake. They never should have brought them the jug of whiskey to make the night on, because the next morning the two boozers were in the bed and the dead man was on the floor."[25]

With liquor banned and cola profits marginal, Emory did not become independently wealthy from his concession business. His stint behind the counter, however, convinced him his future lay in some line of work off the ranch. Subtle signs revealed his deepening discontent with cowboy life. To E. H., the most annoying manifestation of his oldest son's rebellion was Emory's choice of head and foot gear. Maudeen noted the aspects of her brother's attire that most offended:

"When they had the rodeos and Emory ran the cold drink concession stand, he would jump over the fence when it came his time to rope. They'd announce, 'So-and-so is in the chute, Emory Marks get ready.' Emory would jump the fence where his soda water stand was, with a baseball cap on his head and maybe a pair of tennis shoes on his feet. E. H. felt that a man who was going to be a cowboy *had* to have a hat and boots. It was a big deal, and he did fuss about it."[26]

Emory's ultimate act of rebellion came one summer when he was working on the upper ranch near Cypress and Hot Wells.

It was an eleven-mile ride from the main house at Barker. To Emory, each hour in the saddle was drudgery.

"We'd get in a trot on Monday morning," he complained. "We'd start out from home with a link of sausage from the smokehouse, we'd stop at the store and get a handful of cigars and a loaf of bread or some crackers, tie the bread on the strings of the saddle and take off up there, striking a lope every once in a while.

"I got tired of all this business, this riding. I was making thirty dollars a month and wasn't satisfied. We'd get up there in the prairie and drink hot water in the middle of the day. We were supposed to go home on weekends, but we didn't always get to because if there was a cow in somebody's cotton patch or eating up someone's corn, we had to stay up there.

"So I fooled around about two weeks and got so tired of that business, I told Dad one day that I'd like to go to town. 'Well, we'll see.' He put me off about a week. But I finally got away from there. I went to Houston in my old Ford car and got a baseball cap and a pair of tennis shoes."

In E. H.'s eyes, a man who rode horseback wearing tennis shoes and a baseball cap was an affront to all true western cowfolks. If a man couldn't turn a horse around and rein him smartly, E. H. called him a beanpicker. The beanpicker and the fellow wearing baseball cap and tennis shoes were the lowest creatures on E. H.'s scale.

About a week after Emory's surreptitious trip to Houston, he was back on the upper ranch eating breakfast in the predawn: "We had about ten men up there working. You'd get a cup of coffee and you could have breakfast, but by the time the sun came up you were supposed to have your horse saddled and tied up to the hitching rack. You'd go in and get your last cup of coffee and find out what you were supposed to do, and then ride off. E. H. would always be the last one to come out. The other men would be gone."

On this day, Emory was the last to break camp. He waited until E. H. mounted and rode away, then put on his baseball cap and tennis shoes and followed.

"E. H. was riding along turning his head, just scanning the countryside, and all of a sudden he snapped his head toward me and turned around. He looked at me, and he said, 'What the hell do you think you're doing?' I said, 'Dad, there must be a better way to make a living than this.' He said, 'By God, you're fired! Take your horse back and unsaddle him.'"

Free at last, Emory unsaddled the horse, got in his Ford, and went to Houston. He found a job painting cars and took a room at a cheap hotel in a decidedly seedy part of town. "There was every kind of person in there that you ever saw. They were plenty rough," he said. The car painting job was abominable: "That stuff would get in my throat and I got all choked up."

City life quickly lost its glamour for the rebel cowhand. "It was awful," Emory admitted. "I stood it about two weeks. Then I got my baseball cap and my tennis shoes, burned them up, and went back home." He still thought there ought to be a better way than ranching to make a living, but it was a while before anyone heard him say it again.

E. H. Marks and grandson Blevins Bundick in front of judges stand in the enlarged rodeo arena. (*Photo courtesy Atha Marks Dimon.*)

"Cow crowd" in front of cattle cars on Katy Railroad, Barker, May 1950. E. H. (center) and his cowpunchers wait for the train to arrive to load 1,500 head of cattle for shipment to a ranch in Montana. (*Photo courtesy Atha Marks Dimon.*)

8

DANGER ON THE RANGE

"Our winters average fairly mild with a severe spell at long intervals in this Gulf Coast area."[1]

Cattle on the plains of the Gulf Coast died in their tracks during the Big Freeze of December 1924, one of the most disastrous blizzards in Texas history. The freak ice storm turned the bald prairie west of Houston into a meat keeper for the thousands of animals that froze to death during the two-week siege.

Emory, then a teenager, remembered the freeze vividly sixty years later. "We were butchering. Dad looked out to the north and this big, blue norther was coming up. We had one driver, Milburn Adkins from Paige, Texas. That's all he did—fix windmills and drive. Dad said, 'Milburn, you better get the truck around here and load up.' We had a lot butchered, maybe fifteen or twenty yearlings, a couple of steers, three or four cows, a pretty big load. 'You'd better back up and get this loaded and get on your way.' The blue cloud was a-comin' on."[2]

Milburn started for Houston in the loaded truck to deliver the fresh meat. Before he got to Addicks, three miles down the road, the blizzard struck. Sleet came down in glacial sheets, encasing the countryside in ice. The meat truck skidded off the glazed roadway into a ditch and stayed there for two weeks, frozen to the ground, with the raw meat rock-hard within.

"Telephone poles hit the ground, right in the middle of the road," Emory recalled. "Cattle died, and horses, all over the place. The cattle, of course, weren't used to it. Any kind of wintertime was hard on them, but when that came, it was terrible."

Cattle caught in the teeth of the blizzard stood no chance on the exposed prairie, but the woods that grew along Buffalo Bayou offered protection and something to eat. LH7 cowboys cut moss from the trees, the only feed available on the ice-encrusted grasslands, and fed it to the animals sheltering in the woods. Some cattle drifted on their own to take cover in the wooded bayou; others helplessly walked the fencelines, aimless, benumbed by the cold. E. H. was determined to save as many as he could. Afoot on the treacherous ice, he and Emory tried to herd the dazed beasts to the trees and safety:

"E. H. and I went up to the Number Seven pasture, which was about two and a half miles from the house. We used about 150 acres in that pasture for a holding pen. Anything we wanted to ship to market the next week, we'd gather from the surrounding places and put in there. It was an easy place to drive cattle.

"We started out walking with about sixty head of cattle, and before we got to the gate, cattle were dropping. They froze and hit the ground. We got up to the gate, and three cows fell down dead right in the gate and the other cows couldn't get through. We had to take the fence down. We finally wound up with about twenty-five head that we got into the woods."

An abandoned house stood decaying on the Number Seven pasture, its walls and roof intact but windows and doors agape. Sixty-four cattle crowded into the empty shell, trampling and smothering each other to death in a desperate search for warmth and shelter. Emory was sure of the number, because he and E. H. counted the cold, stiff carcasses.

Ranchmen patrolled the pastures with mule-drawn wooden sleds to haul in the dead cattle. There was no way to make use of the tremendous quantities of meat the winter onslaught left lying worthless on the range, but the hides could be salvaged. "They could sell the skins—that was the one thing they could save," Maudeen explained. "They'd cover the hides with salt and wrap them, and they'd wind up with a neat, square package. The skins were taken to town to be graded and sold."[3]

E. H. paid the local boys a dollar a head to skin as many dead cattle as they could. Working as quickly as subfreezing temperatures would allow, the skinners brought in 425 hides. Then the thaw came and the carcasses started to rot. "We still had cattle on the ground that we didn't get to," Emory said. "The animals didn't decay because the cold took care of them, all during that two weeks. But, finally, it started warming up and it was too bad to skin them then."

One of the neighborhood boys E. H. employed as a skinner was in unseemly haste to strip the hides from fallen cattle. To him, down was as good as dead: "He'd find a cow and maybe she wouldn't be quite dead yet, but he'd want to go ahead and hit her in the head and get his dollar for skinning her," Maudeen said.

Added Emory: "She'd be struggling, and E. H. would have every hope that maybe the cow would get on her feet. But the boy would be ready to knock her in the head. E. H. really got on him about that."

Back at the LH7 ranch house, Atha and Travis braved the biting cold to rescue a flock of chickens and guineas on the verge of freezing to death in the yard. The birds were clinging to fence rails and tree limbs, immobile feathered clumps, many unconscious and with their plumes falling out. Gingerly, Travis and Atha gathered them up and bundled them inside. Tucked into a warm corner, away from the killing cold, some of the hardier birds revived.[4]

The two-story ranch house was hard to heat in an average winter. In December 1924, maintaining a livable inside temperature proved nearly impossible. The fireplace and two woodstoves roared without letup but managed to keep only the dining room and kitchen comparatively frost free. The family clustered there in the heart of the house, fortified against the cold by the coffee, chocolate, chili, and soup Maud kept on the stove.

With the telephone dead, its service lines and poles downed by thick ice, reports of the storm's severity came to the household only in snatches. Retreating from the benumbing labor of saving the living cattle and skinning the dead, men frequently came in from the pastures to sit a spell by the fire, bringing what news they had heard of the brutal conditions that prevailed as far south as salt grass country.

The most ordinary details of daily life took on new significance during the blizzard, as the children discovered each time they steeled themselves for a trip to the icicle-draped outhouse. At night their unheated bedrooms would have been nearly as frigid but for the comfort of a goose-down featherbed and a hot stove lid. Maud wrapped the woodstoves' heavy round lids in newspapers and scrap woolens and took the improvised foot warmers to the children's beds. "Sometimes we warmed bricks to slide down near the foot of the bed," Atha recalled. "Some people put hot water bottles in the bed, but we didn't do too much of that. Mostly we used the stove lids because they were already hot. A lot of stove lids warmed up the beds for us."

Mercifully, such severe winter weather as that of 1924 might strike the Gulf Coast only once in a lifetime. For the most part, ranchers found the coastal plains a good cattle land with plenty of native prairie grass and abundant water. But the low country had a less benevolent face that long-time residents knew and respected. The same climate that might blast the prairies with arctic cold in December then bless the land with ample grass in springtime could bring searing heat in July and devastating tropical storms in autumn. Sun and drought, hurricane and thunderstorm, bog and blizzard: all could injure, sometimes in spectacular fashion.

For flash and dazzle, few prairie hazards could rival lightning. Emory described the wild scene that erupted once when he was herding cattle during a thunderstorm: "Whenever there's a storm, you want to scatter your cattle because they draw lightning. One time we had about 150 cattle in a sort of catch pen in the front pasture, and lightning struck. It hit and killed two cows and down they went." The survivors spooked and raced pell-mell out of the pen. So much electricity was in the charged air that Emory could see sparks flashing on the horns of the stampeding cattle: "When those cows came out, there were sparks dancing all around the back of their horns, just sparkling and dancing. I've never seen it since, and we've had lots of cattle gathered together since then."

Cattle would stampede with far less provocation than a violent electrical storm. Any sudden movement, any small disturbance in the still of the night could put them on the run. Emory recalled an episode when a particularly restless herd had everyone suspecting the worst: rustlers.

"We had a couple of stampedes in our feedlots where we fed nine hundred to a thousand steers," he related. "We thought someone was trying to steal some and scared the steers, so we kept watch for about a week. According to one of the boys watching, the steers were peaceful, everything quiet, when out of nowhere came a big owl flapping his wings and flying low. He scared two steers, they scared ten, they scared fifty and the stampede was on. We gathered steers all the next day around the community."[5]

Among Nature's more subtle threats to cattle on the coast prairies were bogs and sinkholes. The Devil Springs, about a half mile from Buffalo Bayou, were known to have swallowed a number of deer and luckless bovines. The three murky springs lay at the bottom of a basin overgrown with willows, bubbling with activity as tiny aquatic creatures skittered and wriggled in their dark waters. E. H. observed that no snakes were ever seen there. An eeriness about the place convinced the more superstitious local folk that Satan was a frequent visitor.[6]

E. H. had a more scientific bent. He observed that the land around the springs rose and fell at intervals, presenting an especially treacherous trap for livestock and wildlife in the dry season when the surface water disappeared. The top of the ground might look firm and dry, but the surface hid a loblolly that claimed the unwary creature venturing too close. He was sure an excavation of the ancient oil seep would unearth prehistoric bones and Indian artifacts buried in the sticky black ground.

"I have ridden up to these springs and have seen tops of horns sticking a few inches above the ground, where some cow or steer was lost," E. H. told a newspaper writer. "I believe the springs have trapped animals of all kinds and descriptions for countless ages, and if excavated the bones of mastodons and other prehistoric animals could be found."[7]

E. H. related that one of his neighbors, John Schmidt of Addicks, had once undertaken to drain the springs so they would be less a menace to livestock: "He sank a shaft several feet deep in one of the springs, and he afterward told me he found bones which were not those of cows, horses or any domestic animals, and many Indian relics such as arrowheads and crockery. He described the bones as being of enormous size and running deep into the mire. He said he dug through a molasses-like ooze down to a white chalky soil."[8] (The springs were later lost inside the Barker Reservoir, built in 1945.)

To Gulf Coast cattle raisers, a menace greater than any other was tick fever, commonly called Texas fever because Texas cattle spread the malady. To combat the deadly fever, as early as 1906 the federal government had established a large-scale tick eradication program requiring dipping with an arsenic solution. By 1922 all counties were required to have dipping vats.[9]

The eradication program encountered violent opposition from stock raisers of all types. The program was expensive, difficult, and in the eyes of many, dangerous. Dairymen insisted the potent chemical dip needed to kill ticks would cause pregnant cows to abort. Cattlemen were appalled at the prospect of running their herds through a foul-smelling vat every two weeks, winter or summer, no matter what the weather. Trouble was inevitable. Many livestock owners flatly refused to comply with the law. Cattle were held back from the eradication program, and some dipping vats were dynamited.[10]

It was essential, however, that the fever tick be controlled if the cattle industry were to prosper on the coast. The native Longhorns of South Texas had lived with the tick so long, they were immune to the disease it carried. But when Texas cattle were moved out of state or when ranchers attempted to import other cattle breeds into Texas, the fever tick spread to the susceptible herds and caused grievous death losses.

E. H. was too good a cattleman not to accept the necessity of the tick eradication program. He had begun dipping his cattle even before the law made it compulsory. In 1913, on his sixty-three-acre place at Addicks, he had built the first dipping vat in Harris County. After the LH7 Ranch moved to Barker and grew to encompass some six thousand head of cattle grazing more than thirty thousand acres, four vats were required to dip them all.[11]

Cattle dipping was a fact of ranch life during Travis Marks's growing-up years. "We had to dip all our cattle every two weeks, summer or winter," he recalled. "You had to go out and round up your cattle in the wintertime, in the dead of the winter whether it was freezing rain or snowing or whatever; regardless of how cold it was you had to round these cattle up and dip 'em. It was extremely hard on them. We had to dip eighteen months to clean the cattle up. Normally it was a nine-month dipping period, but they found a tick on somebody's old milk cow and so we had to start over again. It was extremely hard on these cattle. But we did it, and in the thirties we eradicated the fever tick." By 1945, twelve of thirteen infested states had been declared tick-free.[12]

Ever eager to escape the drudgery of day-to-day cattle work, Emory Marks found employment as a dipping inspector. In that official capacity, he went all over the country west of Houston. The job lasted about a year and a half, until the politics of cattle dipping got so dirty he resigned in disgust.

Dip inspectors were responsible for seeing that the dipping solution in each vat was strong enough. By mixing iodine with a sample of the dip in a test tube, inspectors could tell by the intensity of the purple hue if the solution was adequately potent or too dilute. Inspectors were to ensure that every animal in every cattle herd was dipped every two weeks. "You had to keep perfect records on the cattle that people had, and if they sold any they were supposed to report it to you so you could deduct it," Emory explained. "When cattle came to the dipping vat, you had to count them. The owners were supposed to have them all or explain what happened to them."

Not every inspector was so conscientious about the job. Some who held the position before Emory went easy on their friends and family, looking the other way when stockmen dipped fewer animals than they owned. Dairymen might be allowed to put their cows in the drain pen and spray them lightly with tick-killer rather than submerge them in the dipping vat.

"It was crazy," Emory said. "They had previous dipping inspectors who were partial to some of those guys, but I wasn't. I knew that I had a job to do, that we were trying to clean the ticks up."

His earnest efforts on behalf of the eradication program made it all the more insulting when he was accused of failing to enforce the law on the LH7. "Gus Parker, head of the dipping program for Harris County, accused me one day of being partial to my dad's outfit," Emory related. "He said, 'You're not dipping all your dad's cattle.' I said, 'I am, too.' 'No,' he said, 'there's a pasture down there that you're not dipping.' I knew good and well we'd dipped them. He argued and argued with me, and finally I cussed him out and handed him my book and the dipping vat tester, the whole works, and I quit right there."

It was probably just as well; the vile potion of the dipping vat could be deadly to cattle and humans alike. At the Anderson Ranch, a part of the LH7's big prairie spread, inspector Dick Koy had the misfortune to fall in the vat. He lost his balance while standing on the "bullboard," a wide plank that was put across the vat to keep the bulls' and steers' heads down in the dip. Cattle jostled the board and Koy tumbled into the vat. It was teeming with animals, all of them thrashing about and intent on climbing out by any means possible.

"The cows were just kicking him good," Emory recalled. "We finally got him out, and Bill Gorman and I carried him to the car. Uncle Willie, Dad's brother, was there, and we got him in the car and Uncle Willie started driving. We got up on the highway and Uncle Willie was sitting there hunched over the steering wheel saying, 'Read it, Bill! Read it! Read it!'

"Bill said, 'What? Read what?' Uncle Willie says, 'The speedometer! How fast we going?' Bill looks and says, 'Hell, you're not going but twelve miles an hour! Get on outta here!'"

Never quite at home with that newfangled contraption, the automobile, Willie was afraid to take his eyes off the road long enough to look at the speedometer.

"Finally we got the fellow to Heights Hospital," Emory said. "He was all filled up with that dipping vat stuff, and that stuff was risky. It must have been about three or four years later that he died. But it killed him."

While natural forces made much trouble for Gulf Coast cattlemen, some threats were not of Nature's making. In the case of the LH7, the ranch was both near enough and far enough from big-city Houston to appeal to the mischief-maker, the rustler, and the bona fide criminal.

As the annual Marks Rodeo grew from neighborhood party to nationally acclaimed attraction, the gate receipts became so substantial that E. H. eventually brought in Brinks Security to handle the take. But in the beginning, when crowds were still relatively small, he relied on only a boy or two stationed at the front gate with a wad of admission tickets and a coffee can for a cashbox. That was an invitation to robbery and led to one of Emory's hair-raising experiences.

"Boots Simpson [Uncle Judd's son] and I were out there selling tickets at the front gate," he recounted. "I had a big, three-pound coffee can, and I'd sell a ticket and cram the money in there. A guy parked his car and walked up, and he tried to get to me. I knew what he was because the wind was blowing like the dickens, and his shirt flapped open and I saw the gun on his side. He wanted to hold me up. I kept a-backin' up, and Boots came over and rescued me."

E. H. was away from home that night, so Maud locked the doors and kept the day's ticket money with her in the big bedroom. Emory couldn't sleep. He went into the living room and sat by the fireplace listening to the radio, resting a pistol in his lap just in case.

"I'd been in there a little while, and I heard a scratch on the screen. A fellow says, 'Hey, you!' I was about half asleep, and I jumped up and the pistol flew out in the middle of the floor. I had to run out there and get that pistol. I was sort of scared," Emory admitted. Evidently the sight of the lanky cowboy brandishing

The LH7 Ranch

a gun was even more disturbing to the intruder. The burglar fled, and they had no more trouble that night.

Such incidents were far from rare. The prison farm at Sugar Land was only ten miles south of the ranch. Escaped convicts often made for Buffalo Bayou, hoping to throw bloodhounds off their scent. So many escapees hid out in the woods along the watercourse that Atha and Maudeen were forbidden to go down to the bayou or to cross it by themselves.

Once a fugitive was beyond the bayou and safe from trackers, he might strike out across the prairie to get to the next road. More commonly, he would wait in the woods on the LH7 near the railroad tracks until he could hop a train. "Our woods were a great deal for the prisoners because they were close to the railroad tracks at Barker," Emory said. "The trains used to run pretty regular. When they'd hear a train, they'd start slipping out of the woods and get closer to the tracks."

The prison farm notified E. H. when convicts were on the loose. If he caught any in his pastures, he rounded them up at gunpoint and ordered them onto the hood of his car, where the fugitives rode all the way back to prison. Twice Emory went with his father to return escaped convicts to Sugar Land. For the prisoners' recapture, E. H. would earn a reward of twenty-five dollars and a fill-up of gas and oil for his car.

One night in the early 1930s when E. H. was away from the ranch, a shadowy visitor came to the Marks home. The family sought safety upstairs, joining Louise Draemer, Maud's household help, in her quarters on the second floor. Maud suspected the skulking figure was an escaped convict from Sugar Land who wanted clothes to replace his telltale prison garb.

"Travis had just gotten a basketball sweater," Maudeen remembered. "When Mother said that it was probably a convict wanting some clothes, Emory or somebody just grabbed some stuff and started throwing it out the window. I knew that Travis was proud of that sweater, so I went over to the window, stuck my head out and said, 'If you don't have to, don't take that purple sweater!'"

Afterward, they were shaken to think the caller might not have been a Sugar Land convict but rather one of the Clyde Barrow and Bonnie Parker gang. The countryside was on the lookout for "mad-dog killers" Bonnie and Clyde, and anything out of the ordinary was suspect. One afternoon, Maudeen spotted a strange car on Barker-Clodine Road just beyond the ranch's front gate. Investigators found fingerprints on the abandoned car and identified them as belonging to robber Raymond Hamilton and the Davis sisters, gun molls from Houston. Hamilton, crony of Clyde Barrow, may have tried to break into the Marks home. Maudeen and Emory, at least, were convinced he had been there one night, though the family never knew for sure if the notorious Hamilton was one of the LH7's midnight callers.[13]

Among the most infamous of local outlaws were four boys from a single West Harris County family. They started small, stealing whiskey in the jug from moonshiners, but progressed allegedly to cattle rustling, armed robbery, bank holdups, arson, and murder. It was wisest not to provoke them, as the rural black community learned to its horror.

When trouble began between the blacks and the outlaw boys, Emory and top hand Mose Burton barely missed hearing the opening shot. One day while riding through one of the LH7's leased pastures, checking fences, doctoring screwworm cases, and looking out for newborn calves, Emory and Mose approached a house that local black families occupied from time to time.

"We noticed a horse grazing out there, with the bridle reins dragging," Emory related. "We got a little bit closer to the house, and we saw a man lying in the gate. Mose went up and looked at him and said the man was dead. He was shot right square in the middle of the head." The victim was one of the outlaw gang.

Mose urged Emory to ride on and tell no one what they had seen. "Mose didn't want to fool with it, because I think Mose knew what was going on," Emory said. It appeared to be a revenge killing. The outlaws had terrorized the young black women of the community until their menfolk could take no more. Knowing white law would always look the other way, the blacks knew it was left to them to punish the outrages. And so one of the offenders took a bullet in the forehead.

Some three weeks passed before the outlaw brothers and their accomplices retaliated, but when reprisal came it was merciless. The Blakely ranch to the southwest of the LH7, where Mose had been employed before coming to the Markses, now had a black foreman named Scott. Scott lived with his family and others in a two-story house near Clodine, a small town on the Southern Pacific Railroad south of Barker. Armed with a Winchester apiece, the ruffians surrounded Scott's house and set it afire. None of the residents survived. Some died, screaming, in the blaze. Any who tried to flee the burning house were gunned down.

The outlaws were never formally accused of the murders. When at last they were brought to justice, it was not for killing blacks but for stealing from whites. One went to prison for trying to sell five hundred head of cattle that were not his. The others got caught robbing a bank on Houston's near northwest side.[14]

The criminal element ranchers most often confronted was the rustler, who grew ever bolder when the automobile's advent made getaways fast and easy. Some cattle thieves specialized in calves. After nightfall, armed with a small-caliber rifle that made little noise, such as a .22, they would drive the remote country roads, shoot a calf in a roadside pasture, and haul it away in their car. Oftentimes, the damage was compounded as the mother cow knocked down the fence in search of her lost calf, and others of the herd followed her through the break.[15]

Forms of cow thievery with older origins included brand blotching and counter branding. "In those early days they would disfigure a brand," E. H. related. "If you branded U-H some fellow would make O-B out of it. You can tell a new brand from an old brand, but he'd carve it with a knife and put ashes on it and in twenty-four hours it would look like an old brand."[16] Rather than tote a two-foot-long branding iron with them—a dead giveaway of their criminal intentions—some rustlers carried small iron rings into which they could wedge sticks and fashion makeshift branding irons on the spot. After the rings cooled they were easily concealed, frustrating cattlemen's efforts to expose the thieves.

Another trick was to make sure stolen cattle became too skittish to allow close inspection by a suspicious former owner. E. H. outlined the procedure: "A man steals a steer, puts his brand on it and puts it in a pasture. When he rides out there tomorrow he gets his cow whip and gets after that steer, but he doesn't try to catch him. The next day he goes back again and runs him. Now if you wanted to go out there and see if that's your steer, you never could get close enough to see what brand was on it."

One cow thief using this method went to prison after E. H. found him out and notified inspectors of the Texas and Southwestern Cattle Raisers Association. A steer had been stolen from Matagorda County on the coast and brought to a pasture adjoining Marks land. The nervous animal bolted as E. H. rode up, but with the help of another cowboy he was able to rope and throw the steer. A close examination showed a new brand on the left shoulder with an older brand almost obliterated on the right side.

E. H. carried a Winchester behind the seat of his pickup to discourage trespassers, who got to be more and more of a problem as Houston grew larger and nearer. One year he prosecuted seventy-six. "When I drive out in the pasture I've got my gun, because you never know," he said.

One time, he found four armed strangers in his pasture and ordered them to leave. When they refused, E. H. retreated just far enough to get the drop on the insolent intruders: "I said 'All right' and got in my pickup and drove off near the gate. I got old Winchester out and shot the bark off a tree about thirty feet off to the side of them. Gosh dog, they didn't know what was fixin' to happen. I said, 'Throw them guns down and come over here. I don't want any foolishness. I'll kill you and let the buzzards eat you if you think you can run over me in my own pasture.'"

E. H. pressed charges and was disgusted when the judge fined the interlopers only $27.40 apiece. It had cost him $5.00 to hire a man to take them in to the sheriff. Afterwards, when they wanted to retrieve their guns, E. H. obligingly led them back to the grassy spot beneath the sycamore where he had invited them to drop their weapons.

If a suspected cow thief or other suspicious character was spotted in the county, it was not always easy to get hold of the sheriff. The early telephone system was markedly unreliable. Lines strung on fenceposts were often downed by cattle, and sometimes by inattentive cowboys. "When they worked cattle," Atha recalled, "sometimes the boys would ride along and tie pieces of paper on the telephone line to warn the others not to ride into it. They wouldn't see it."

When the Barker Rural Telephone Company first established service in the community, the switchboard was in the home of Mrs. Albert Matzke. Calls were put through at her convenience. "Sometimes we would have to crank a long ring to get the operator, and sometimes she wouldn't answer at all," Atha remembered. "Finally you'd say to yourself, 'I'll wait ten minutes and try again.' When she finally answered she might say, 'Well, honey, I was out milking the cow.' That was our operator—she'd just leave the switchboard and go milk the cow and come back in when she was through. We didn't think there was anything unusual about it."

While run-of-the-mill calls might be handled in this haphazard fashion, let there be a fire or some community-wide emergency and the rural telephone system proved its worth. By means of a "general ring," which went through at the same time on all phones connected to a given party line, the operator could quickly sound an alarm throughout the community.

"You talk about communication," Atha remarked, "if there was a fire someplace the operator would put on a general ring for all the different lines, like the four hundred line or the three hundred line, and people would run to the phone to get the news. If the operator said, 'The Waggoners's barn is on fire,' that would alert the neighbors to go over there. Another time she might say, 'Mr. Saums has died, and the funeral service will be at such-and-such a time.' It was a fast way to get the news."

Operating the neighborhood switchboard became a tradition for the Matzke family. Jessie Matzke Petrick, Gussie Matzke Neuman, and Helena Matzke Ehlert all served as Barker "telephone girls." There were great benefits to keeping the telephone system in local hands—operators on a first-name basis with their callers could create an unsurpassed grapevine for relaying information. One time Atha called home and the switchboard operator told her, "Honey, nobody answers at your house, but I just saw your daddy go in the store." The operator rang up the general store and put Atha through to E. H.[17]

Some years later, Atha tried to phone home during a trip to New York City. The city operator told her there had been a tornado in the Barker area and her home phone was out of order. "Who told you that?" Atha wanted to know. "The switchboard operator at Barker." "Let me talk to her," Atha said.

The New Yorker was dumbfounded. "You want to talk to the operator?" Before Atha could insist, a voice came on the line from the Barker end: "Atha, is it you?" "Katy? Are you there?" With the anonymous New York operator listening in, astonished that the pair knew each other by name, Atha learned from Katy Bodak, incumbent Barker telephone girl, that the storm had knocked out the line to her home but her folks were all right. "I can imagine what that New York operator must have thought," Atha commented. It was perhaps an irregular means of crisis communications, but as effective as later systems devised in the name of emergency preparedness.

Tex McDaniel with "Barker," the LH7 Longhorn steer he rode from Texas to the White House in 1932-33. (*Photo courtesy E. M. Marks.*)

Baldwin Parker (son of Quanah Parker, last great Comanche chief), with his wife, children and grandchild. Emory Marks met the Parkers at the 1936 Houston convention of the Old Pioneers Association and gave them a tour of Houston and environs. Photo taken in the yard of the Marks' home at Barker. (*Photo courtesy E. M. Marks.*)

1936 — some members of "Old Pioneers Association" meeting in Houston. Man in front row in white is Kit Carson III. (At this convention, Emory met and volunteered to show Houston to convention guests. He hosted Baldwin Parker.)

9

DELIRIUM AND DEPRESSION

"The brand has never been for sale and never will be. When Paddock bought my cattle in the partnership dissolution I retained the LH7 brand. It is in writing."[1]

The catastrophe of Black Tuesday, 29 October 1929, was a long time reaching the LH7 Ranch at Barker. While newspapers carried grim tidings of a national economy in collapse, with prices plummeting and unemployment soaring, the *Houston Chronicle* in the spring of 1930 also was telling its readers that "Picturesque Cowboys and Herds of Milling Cattle" could still be "Found Near City." Giving the LH7's value as three hundred thousand dollars, the newspaper found it noteworthy that a 33,000-acre ranch with scores of cowboys and a touch of the Old West was operating just a short drive from the new Gulf Building, an art deco skyscraper rising thirty-seven stories over downtown Houston. Observed the reporter: "The only thing that fades the pioneer-day illusion is the presence of several automobiles. Occasionally a cowboy jumps from a gallant steed, gets into an automobile, and dashes to some distant point."²

These were the LH7's glory days. Its spectacular rodeos and quality herds of Texas Longhorn and Brahman cattle made it nationally known. The ranch hosted a stream of notable visitors, among them Houston civic leaders who met there for regular all-night poker sessions. Eastern tourists arrived by carloads for a look at a real Texas spread. Urban newshounds went often to Barker to interview E. H., middle-aged by now and more colorful than ever. He gave them plenty to write about, collaborating with his cowboys to put on the show expected of the local cattle king.

In 1932 a twenty-eight-year-old broncobuster named Samuel Franklin "Tex" McDaniel hatched a scheme that would put his picture in the papers and the cowtown of Barker on the map. Fellow Texan John Nance "Cactus Jack" Garner was to be sworn in 4 March 1933 as vice president of the United States in the administration of Franklin D. Roosevelt. Claiming to have a personal invitation from Garner, McDaniel proposed to ride an LH7 Longhorn from Texas to New York City and then to the White House, intending to take an active part in the inaugural ceremonies. The 2,500-mile trip, at the steer's leisurely mile-an-hour pace, would take the better part of a year.

E. H. and family gave the plan wholehearted support. The chosen LH7 steer was an impressive solid red seven-year-old weighing twelve hundred pounds, with a hornspread of fifty-two inches following the curves. He was named Barker after his home pasture. Teenager Travis Marks, a knowledgeable cattleman even then and a full-time cowboy on the LH7 during school vacations, broke Barker to snaffle bit and saddle. "I don't want to make this too strong, but I rode that steer first, myself," Travis said, telling the tale half a century later.³

Before mounting, Travis took precautions against Barker's sharp horns. "I thought Barker might hook me out of the saddle," he explained, "so I got a long persimmon stick, drilled holes in the ends and tied it to the D-ring on the saddle and to his horns, leaving slack enough to guide." With a stick on each side of his head, the steer could not toss his horns far enough to hit his rider.⁴

Delirium and Depression

Travis first rode Barker in a pen; finding the steer well behaved, he unlatched the gate and rode to the Barker Store. The second time out, they went halfway to Addicks without mishap. Nonchalantly accepting his new role as saddle steer, Barker was quickly trained and handed over to McDaniel.

Tex and Barker were a striking sight when they made their public debut in March 1932. The steer was a prime specimen from E. H.'s hand-picked herd of authentic Texas Longhorns; its tall, satin-shirted rider was "good-looking enough to be a motion picture cowboy."[5] Photographers' flashbulbs flared when E. H. and the pair arrived on the streets of Houston to promote the forthcoming Marks Rodeo. Everyone seemed to want a piece of the action, including Houston Police Superintendent Percy F. Heard. A news account described the meeting:

> When E. H. Marks, owner of the LH7 Ranch at Barker, and his bronco-buster, S. F. "Tex" McDaniel, came to town Wednesday herding a big, rangy Longhorn steer, Chief Heard promptly summoned them to the police station and telephoned a photographer.
>
> Marks and Tex McDaniel were worried. They thought they had run afoul of the law and were to be called on the carpet. But they were in for a pleasant surprise.
>
> "Lemme ride that feller," Heard pleaded with the cowboys. "I'm a bronc-buster from way back yonder."
>
> Relieved, Tex McDaniel clapped his 12-gallon hat—mind you, Sheriff [T. A.] Binford's is only a 10-gallon one—on the police chief's head and Heard mounted the steer to the clicking of cameras. The whole detective force was on hand.[6]

Immediately after the rodeo, on Easter Sunday 1932, Tex and Barker left the LH7 bound for New York City and national fame. The flashy Texans were a spark of excitement that briefly lit the dark Depression days and diverted attention from the gloomy economic news. Tex was attired in typical cowboy custom with wide-brimmed Stetson, fancy silk kerchief, checked shirt, leather vest, chaps, and high-heeled boots, and guided his mount with a halter of rattlesnake skin. Papers in every city they visited carried the story of the cowboy and his Longhorn, usually on page one and always with mention of Tex's slow drawl and Barker's imposing horns.

Barker had his endearing traits, and some not so lovable. McDaniel insisted his mount was bilingual, cognizant of commands in either English or Spanish. The pair reportedly played hide-and-seek together. "Ah raised him right off the range," Tex informed one reporter. "After he knew Ah was the one that fed and looked after him that animal has been plumb affectionate to me. He's got moah hawss sense than any hawss."[7]

The two were such fast friends, the steer showed resentment toward any who came between them. Tex told one writer that Barker was jealous of women. As the pair traveled through the South, the steer allegedly tried to gore a woman friend of the broncobuster when she began to claim too much of McDaniel's attention. A tall Texas tale told for the benefit of gullible reporters? Possibly. The press clearly was in no mood to be critical of the cowboy, preferring instead to dwell on "that matinee idol appearance and personality when he smiles" which made McDaniel a popular favorite.[8]

Passing through the South during the summer months, Tex and Barker often had to travel at night to escape the sun. They lived on prize money won at rodeos, fairs, and exhibitions, and by selling souvenir postcards. By the time the cowboy and his steer covered the two-thousand-odd miles from the LH7 to Buffalo and Syracuse, New York, summer was long past. The journey that began as a pleasure trip had become "a mighty long, hard grind," Tex admitted.[9]

Still the Gulf Coast denizens pushed on, reaching New York City late in the year. According to Emory, Tex sold crab apples on the street outside the Waldorf-Astoria Hotel to make expenses. "The steer ate so many he got the colic," Emory said. "Almost lost him right there."[10] After leading a parade through New York City streets, the Texas travelers went back on the road, walking the Philadelphia pike.

Unfortunately, Tex's plans went awry. After nearly a year of travel, he did not reach Washington in time for the inaugural ceremonies. The 4th of March 1933—Inauguration Day—came and went, and still the two plodded on. Tex was determined to make Washington even though he would arrive too late to hear

Roosevelt's address with its now-famous admonition: "The only thing we have to fear is fear itself."

Like an incarnation of the Wild West, Tex and Barker arrived in Wilmington, Delaware, on the last of April and sought shelter for the night at the Pennyhill station of the state police, who swallowed their shock and obliged. The *Wilmington Morning News* reported that the Texas steer had worn out nine pairs of steel shoes since leaving home but had gained 200 pounds. By journey's end, Barker would destroy twenty sets of ox shoes, yet increase in weight from 1,200 to 1,440 pounds.[11]

Making eight to twelve miles a day, Tex and Barker ambled on and finally arrived in the nation's capital. They were met by neither President Roosevelt nor Vice President Garner, but were saved from embarrassment by Mrs. Garner, who gave Tex an escorted tour of the White House. Barker had to stay outside.[12]

It was an anticlimactic reception after Tex's grand plans and received little notice back at the LH7 Ranch, where the Marks family was experiencing its own sudden letdown after the heady years of the twenties and early thirties. Cattle prices were plummeting, and E. H. was beginning to worry. His pride prevented much talk of money troubles, but his wife and children knew hard cash was alarmingly scarce. For one thing, as Maudeen remarked, "you didn't eat at anybody's house." Families were hard-pressed to feed their own youngsters. No one's table held enough for extra mouths.[13]

Shortly before the bottom fell out of the cattle market, Emory recalled, good cattle were worth from fifty to seventy dollars. After the crash, the same stock might bring a fourth as much. Prices continued to sink, to three cents a pound and less. "We used to sell calves at fifteen, eighteen, or twenty cents a pound," Emory said. "Mason Habermacher came out during the worst of the Depression and offered Dad a cent and a half a pound for weanling calves. They weighed 300, maybe 350 pounds. So that was about $4.50 an animal. Dad shook his head. He said, 'I need the money, but I'm not going to do it.'"[14]

Even as he refused the offer, E. H. knew he had to have cash to keep the LH7 going. The ranch was a big operation with substantial fixed expenses. "You had to have the windmills, you had to pay the land lease, you had to have men looking after those cattle, you had to have good horses, you had to feed the horses, you had to do whatever it took to get the cattle through the winter," Maudeen enumerated. "So every cow we had was costing us."

Eager to convert cattle into cash, E. H. directed his men to round up the market-ready steers for any buyer who wanted to see them. So often did steer buyers come out for a look, and so seldom did any have the money to buy, E. H. joked to his cowboys, "We've rounded up these steers so many times all we have to do is go out there and hold our hats up and they'll round up by themselves."[15]

Exacerbating the situation, the LH7's brisk business filling orders for Houston meat markets ended in the 1930s when the city ruled that no meat could be brought in from the country. Cattle for Houston consumption had to be slaughtered inside the city limits, a regulation that deprived E. H. of a market he had served for more than a decade. "It was considered a political move to close the country slaughterhouses in favor of city operations," Maudeen noted.[16]

Like many cattlemen, then or now, E. H. owed the local banker. In view of his excellent reputation, lenders in normal times were content to let the man run his business as he saw fit. They knew their money was safe, but with the economy collapsing around their ears, bank officials grew as jumpy as the frog legs Maud barred from her kitchen. Emory described a dramatic confrontation between his father and a panicky bank president:

"Dad had borrowed some money, I think it was thirty thousand or thirty-two thousand dollars, from the Houston National Bank, on the corner of Main and Franklin. He had mortgaged cows for this money. He was selling steers all along, and he sold a bunch of steers. Melvin Rouff, the president, nearly had a fit. He said to E. H., 'You've sold those cattle and here you owe me and you've collected the money.'"

Rouff was wrong in suggesting any wrongdoing on E. H.'s part. The note was against the cows only. The steers were in the clear. Maudeen remembered her father's indignation at the banker's accusations: "E. H. felt his reputation for honest dealing had been questioned. He clenched his cigar in his mouth and told Rouff, 'You sit right here and I will run every damn cow on that note right through this bank.'"[17]

E. H. acted at once to settle accounts with the alarmed banker. Emory witnessed the scene in Rouff's office: "Dad said, 'I'll tell you what. I'm going to pay you off.' He got on the telephone and rang up a fellow named Bonner at the South Texas Commercial National Bank, right across the street. Bonner was a big shot. Dad says to me, 'You go over there and see Mr. Bonner.' I walked across the street and asked for him, and Bonner handed me a sack. I didn't know what was in the sack, I didn't have any idea. I just walked back to the other bank and gave it to E. H.: 'Here's your sack, Dad.' E. H. went into Rouff's office and threw the sack on the desk. 'Here's your blankety-blank money. Gimme my note.' He paid them off, and that's the way he operated."

Thoughtfully, Emory added, "I don't know what I'd have done if I'd known that thirty-two thousand dollars was in that bag."

Jittery bankers and penny-a-pound cattle were not E. H. and Maud's only worries in the 1930s. They also had three children to put through college. By virtue of a birthyear that coincided with Henry Ford's introduction of the Model T, Emory alone of the Marks offspring made it in and out of college before the onset of the Great Depression. After graduation from Houston's Reagan High, Emory attended North Texas Agricultural College (now the University of Texas at Arlington) for two years. The college offered a course of study in veterinary medicine. E. H. had the idea his son was going to school to become a veterinarian, but Emory had other plans.

"I went up there and joined the glee club and beat the drums in the band," he recounted. "That first year was fine. I was having a big time."

"We had never heard him sing a note in his life, but there he was in the glee club," Maudeen marveled.

"Oh yeah," Emory said. "We made trips. That medicine could wait. But Dad had already told everybody, 'My son's going to be a veterinarian.' And the first fall that I went back home all the neighbors started ringing in, wanting me to do something about their sick cow or horse. I'd just use common sense that I was raised with. A horse with colic, for instance, that's sort of a rough business, and most of those people didn't know what to do. I'd do something for it and they would think, 'Man, he's going to make it.'"

Emory brought home from college no degree in veterinary medicine but was held in high esteem ever after by local stockraisers who called on him for medical advice. The neighbors awarded him the honorary title of "Doc," as he was known to all but wrangler Mose Burton. Mose called him "Flutes" after his boyhood trick of punching holes in the hollow limb of an elderberry bush to make an off-key flute.

Atha was the next to head off to college. Graduating from Reagan High School in 1928, she enrolled in the College of Industrial Arts (now Texas Woman's University) at Denton. By the time she earned a degree in speech in 1932, the specter of hard times had come to haunt the apparently prosperous LH7. Not yet ready to face what might happen to his big prairie spread with its six thousand head of fine beef cattle, E. H. refused to admit to his children that money was much on his mind. But Maud knew, and counseled frugality to her older offspring. Atha got the message when her mother took her aside before a trip to town:

"There was a Lewis's Oyster Parlor in Houston that Daddy loved to take us to on special occasions. One time I was home and Mother and Daddy were taking me to catch the train, the Southern Pacific, back to CIA at Denton. Before we went to meet the train, Daddy wanted to take us out to eat at Lewis's Oyster Parlor. I remember Mother said to me, 'Your father doesn't want you to know it, but we really can't afford a big dinner. So don't order a whole lot.'

"Of course I nearly choked while I ate! But I ate, because I wanted Daddy to enjoy taking me out. Mother knew that things were pretty bad, but Daddy didn't want us to know it."[18]

Although cash was tight, food was always plentiful on the table and in the cupboard at the LH7 because much of what the Markses ate they raised. Maud and her helpers canned iron washkettles full of meat and vegetables. A visitor to the ranch in June 1932 reported seeing Maud's pantry filled with three hundred quart cans of beef, chicken, chili, steaks, stews, corn, and other home-raised staples. With an average household of ten, including family and full-time cowboys, Maud kept her weekly grocery bill at less than four dollars.[19]

"Mother put up chili meat and stew meat and roasts in tin cans, and sometimes there would be a neighbor who'd share the work," Atha remembered. "Mrs. Armaderry (Fairy) Jordan used to come over and they would share the responsibility. Canning took all day long because they slaughtered the meat themselves, and it had to be cut up, and then they cooked it in a great big washpot. And then they'd have to put it in the cans. It was a very tedious job.

"That was what was sort of amazing. We didn't have a lot of money to spend, but we always had a lot of food at home because we grew it."

By the time Travis and Maudeen were finishing high school in the early 1930s, the curriculum at Addicks had improved sufficiently that they could give up the long daily drive to Houston and return to the home school for graduation. Travis then pursued his education at the Agricultural and Mechanical College of Texas, majoring in animal husbandry, and Maudeen followed her elder sister to Denton, where the College of Industrial Arts had been renamed Texas State College for Women.

The lessons of Depression-era living greatly influenced Maudeen in her choice of college career. All supposed the young woman would follow tradition and study home economics, so skilled was she already in the art of household management. But too many pantry shelves to line with home-canned goods set Maudeen on a different course.

"I didn't want to go into home economics because I felt like I already knew everything I needed to know," she explained. "I'd canned hundreds and thousands of cans while I was a 4-H Club girl—we had to during the Depression to feed all those cowboys at the ranch. I was thirsting for new fields of knowledge. I wanted to be part of the larger world." Deciding against the study of music, which she had pursued from childhood, Maudeen chose to major in journalism. But finding those classes already filled, she switched to speech arts with a minor in education.[20]

Out of her Depression childhood Maudeen carried vivid memories of tragedies that struck the poorest families in the county when economic conditions were at their worst. She recalled accompanying her mother to an impoverished home where an undernourished child lay dying. When the end came, Maud quickly and quietly made the necessary arrangements for interment.

"She told me to get the boys to stop everything and cut some lumber and bring it over," Maudeen related, her voice subdued. "She said, 'Tell the men I need some lumber, hammer, nails, and so forth, to make a coffin. And she told me to go get the cloth we had at the house. I took it to her, and I watched her line the coffin. Then she said, 'You can go home now,' so I did not wait to see her lay the baby out. Because I was too young, she thought it was a little bit too much. But she laid the baby in the coffin and took care of everything, and they had the burial."[21]

With such grim episodes casting a pall over the times, the four Marks children uneasily noted the growing distress of their father. The LH7 was in trouble, and try as he might, E. H. could no longer keep that fact from his observant offspring. Maudeen caught the worry in her father's face and in snatches of conversation: "I heard Daddy tell Mother, 'Maud, we are going broke and there is nothing I can do about it.' I saw my father pace up and down on the north side of the house, which is kind of a hidden place. I saw him walk up and down and up and down, and I saw him age right before my eyes. Even as young as I was, I could see him age. Something had to happen."[22]

When it did, the event was news. "Passing of LH7 Ranch Looms as Paddock-Marks Partnership Is Dissolved" blazoned the headline of a newspaper story dated 17 January 1936. Two days earlier, E. H. Marks and W. A. Paddock, partners since 1923, had reached agreement on a partnership dissolution. In effect, the settlement gave everything to Paddock except the section of land immediately surrounding the ranch house and smaller parcels at Fairbanks, Devil Springs, and on the prairie north of Barker, totaling 1,008 acres E. H. owned outright. But for those properties and his personal herd of Longhorn cattle, E. H. relinquished all. Paddock assumed the assets and liabilities of the former partnership and began disposing of land and cattle. Long-time ranch foreman Bill Gorman was dismissed.[23]

News accounts gave as the reason for ending the partnership a desire on the part of both men to curtail their ranching operations until economic conditions should improve. However, it was E. H. who had the most urgent need to cut expenses. Paddock had amassed substantial sums from his oil interests and could fall back on his cash reserves until the cattle business picked up. E. H. had since boyhood put every nickel he made into his ranch, its cattle, and improvements. He had no cash, except what could be borrowed, to see him through a prolonged market downturn. The alternative to losing everything he had worked for over a span of thirty years was to bow out of the partnership with Paddock as painlessly as he could, though it meant the end of the LH7 as one of the largest ranches in the Houston area.

"He was able to keep the section of land he had bought right around the home place, and by getting rid of the cattle he got rid of a lot of overhead," Maudeen said. "They took almost all the cattle; he had just a few head left. Mother went through the whole thing and never cried. She was stoic. Our people were kind of stoic when it came to major problems like that. But they forgot the milk cow, and when they came back to take the milk cow, that's when she let it all go."[24]

Almost in defiance, E. H. made it clear to reporters covering the story that he had retained his LH7 brand when the partnership with Paddock ended. The brand was registered as his property, E. H. declared, and was not for sale. Putting on a show of confidence for the press, E. H. said he planned "to take things a bit easier from now on." It was his intention, he said, to raise smaller herds of finer cattle.[25]

Privately, he was preparing for disaster. Emory described the scene that took place on the LH7 soon after the breakup with Paddock: "Dad said to me, 'Get your horse saddled.' 'What are we going to do?' I wanted to know. 'We're going to go out and get twenty head of cattle and one bull. They can't take those away from me.' And he said, 'We're going to take a plow and go around this two hundred acres.' That was the homestead. 'They can't take my homestead away from me.'

"He was expecting to get wiped out," Emory admitted. "He plowed up a big furrow around the place. I don't know what good the furrow did, but that was the homestead and he said they couldn't touch that or the twenty head of cattle."

Fifty-four years old and left with little more than he had in 1917 when he made Barker the headquarters for his LH7 Ranch, E. H. proved himself master of the situation. If secretly he feared he might lose the LH7, outwardly he was bold as ever. His customary good humor again in evidence, barely two months after the breakup of his ranch, he harnessed a team of Longhorn steers and joined in celebrating the 1936 Texas Centennial. The steers stole the show during ground-breaking ceremonies for the San Jacinto Memorial shaft to be erected the following year on the San Jacinto Battleground east of Houston. E. H. drove the Longhorns as they pulled a hundred-year-old wooden plow guided by Andrew Jackson Houston, son of Sam Houston. The indomitable Texas cowman was once more the center of attention, and loved it. Reported the *Houston Chronicle*:

"The crowd pressed so close that the oxen, Bald and Spot, became excited and tossed their horns, causing a small panic in the line which was pushed close to them by spectators. Emil Marks..., the owner, handled the oxen. Motorcycle patrolmen had a hard time clearing back the crowd for the movie and newspaper cameramen. When enough space was cleared... Mr. Marks called on the oxen. They lunged and the ground was peeled away a few feet. There was a splintering sound. The plow had broken the ground but the ground also had broken the plow."[26]

The plow, from E. H.'s collection of antique farm and ranch implements, was placed in a showcase on the first floor when the San Jacinto Monument and Museum was completed, Emory noted. He recalled that during the ground-breaking exercises, President Roosevelt was seated in a car in back of the crowd.[27]

Also in 1936, the Old Pioneers Association made E. H. a member at a meeting in Houston attended by such characters as showman Pawnee Bill, New Mexico law-and-order man Elfego Baca, ex-train robber Al Jennings, "and many others—

reformed bank robbers and show people," as Emory summed them up. The celebrities included Baldwin Parker, son of Quanah Parker, the last great Comanche chief. The Parkers were Emory's special guests. He took them to the country, and they performed Indian dances in front of his restaurant at Addicks, Emory's latest off-the-ranch venture.[28]

The 1936 edition of the LH7 rodeo was held on schedule, the first Sunday in May and the Saturday preceding. No member of the audience could have guessed E. H. faced bankruptcy only months before. Reportedly, the rodeo was the most spectacular seen in that part of Texas: "The LH7 Rodeo at Barker . . . drew the largest number of cowmen and the greatest attendance of any rodeo ever held in South Texas. Some 200 rodeo stars and ranchmen headed by Emil H. Marks . . . paraded before a throng which far overran the two large grandstands. Attendance exceeded 7,000 and the sponsors ran out of barbecue and cold drinks."[29]

That E. H. not only saved the LH7 Ranch but had it back on the way to prosperity within months of his breakup with Paddock is evidence of the rancher's strong resolve. He met adversity with ingenuity, doing anything he could to make a dollar, as he had learned in his young adventuring days. Travis recalled that his father built a thriving trade selling Longhorn steers to pose with tourists for Texas Centennial souvenir photos. "People would buy these steers and break them, and for fifty cents a throw they'd take pictures of you grabbing hold of their horns, or sitting on them, or whatever you wanted to do," Travis said. "We sold a lot of steers that way."

The greatest resource E. H. could draw on in rebuilding the LH7 was his reputation for honesty. He was highly regarded as a fair trader who drove a hard bargain, then stuck by it. It was a policy that won the trust of business associates, as illustrated by a story E. H. often told:

> When I was buying cattle from various people around, there was a man by the name of George Groeschke. He had a little goatee and he drove a mule and buggy. He told me, "I've got twenty-two steers I want to sell. I want twenty dollars apiece for them. You look at them, Marks, and see if you can use them."

> I met him one day and I said, "Mr. Groeschke, I looked at the steers and I'll give you eighteen dollars a head for them." He said, "I won't take it." "Well," I said, "that's all right. That's all I can do."
>
> But a few days later he saw me and he said, "Marks, I'm going to sell you them steers. You're going to take twenty-two of them at eighteen dollars apiece." They were running on open range so I said I'd get them in a week or ten days.
>
> By golly, it wasn't over four or five days later he sent his son over. "Papa sent me to tell you that lightning killed two cows and two steers at the alligator pond." That was out here on the prairie. I said, "Well, George, I'm driving a bunch of cattle to Houston today so tell your daddy I'll be over there tomorrow and see him."
>
> So the next day I got enough money out of the bank in Houston and went over there. I'd studied about this thing all day, about the two steers that the lightning killed. When I got there he said, "What about those two steers?"
>
> I said, "Mr. Groeschke, if I had had the money in my pocket when I bought them steers I'd have paid you for them. And you wouldn't have given me any money back and I wouldn't expect you to. I bought them steers and I'm going to pay you for them."
>
> The old man looked down and he said, "By gosh, that's what I call a man." I paid him for the steers and I just got twenty head and didn't make much money, but I figured that that was right.

The story's end came later. E. H. did not specify under what circumstances he next met the old man, except to hint that times were hard:

> He was at the hitching rack one day and he called me off to one side. He said, "Marks, you need any money?" I said, "Mr. Groeschke, I haven't got much money to buy and sell cattle. If I had more money I could do more business."
>
> He said, "Well, if you need money come on over and see me." So I rode over a couple of days later and he said, "How much money you want?" I said, "Whatever you can let me have at eight percent interest. I could use two or three thousand dollars."
>
> That old man went down in the cellar under his house and came out with three thousand dollars. He counted it out to me.

"By golly, that was an experience for me," E. H. concluded his tale. "If it had been that morning I might have let him lose a steer. But I studied about it all day and decided I'd bought those steers and owed him for them. That kind of business made me more money—the old man told it everywhere, that I'd paid for those two steers that lightning killed. I made what I got because people trusted me."[30]

That trust enabled E. H. to borrow from his neighbors, after several bankers had refused him the loan, to purchase two hundred acres adjacent to the old Anderson Ranch north of his land at Barker. He dubbed his new property "The Duck Ranch." Maud knew nothing of the deal—"She'd have thought he was sticking his neck out too far," Atha figured. Shortly after E. H. acquired the Duck Ranch, an oil company leased it from him for enough to cover his debt, then brought in four oil wells. If the ranchman was tempted to wave his royalty checks beneath the noses of a few recalcitrant bankers, no one could have blamed him.[31]

Oil money helped see the LH7 through the lean Depression years. But long-term prosperity for the Marks family was built on land and cattle, as it had been since Grandmother Sophia obtained her homestead on Bear Creek and August Texas drove cattle north. Atha recalled the advice that guided her father when things looked blackest: "Daddy said that his father used to say, 'Emil, you hang on to that old cow's tail and she'll pull you out.' So that's just what he did during the bad times. He held on."

E. H. Marks hand feeding one of his favorite longhorns. (*Photo courtesy E. M. Marks.*)

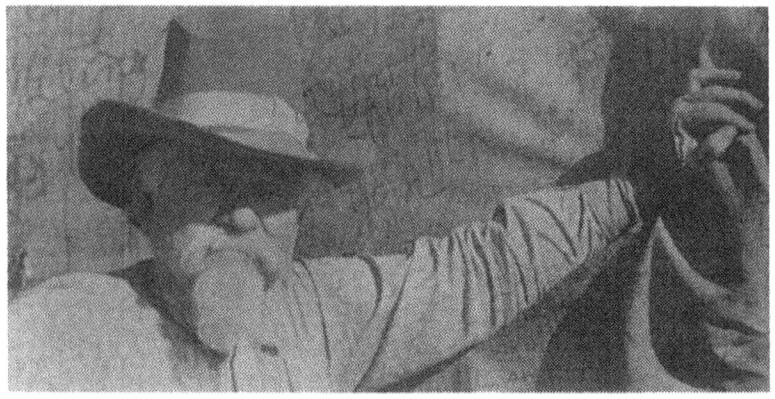

"Uncle" Jim Fairchild traveled to St. Augustine, Florida, in 1940 in a covered wagon pulled by LH7 Longhorns. Fairchild later returned to the Houston area and played Santa Claus. (*Photo courtesy E. M. Marks.*)

Ground-breaking ceremonies for the San Jacinto Memorial, March 1936. E. H. (right) handles the team of LH7 Longhorn steers as Andrew Jackson Houston, son of Sam Houston, guides the plow. (*Photo courtesy E. M. Marks.*)

10

LH7 Longhorns

"Some of these days the boys are going to wake up and find there are no other Longhorn cattle in the state. Then I will show them what I have been building up."[1]

An anachronism. A thing appropriate to an earlier age. That was the Texas Longhorn, to the minds of most of E. H.'s peers. Though superbly adapted to an area its forebears had occupied for four hundred years, since the days of Spanish exploration, the Longhorn by the twentieth century had fallen into general disfavor. When the great northern trail drives ended late in the 1880s, so too had much of the Texas cattle's apparent value. Barbed wire now chopped the once open range into private parcels; safe within these enclosures ranchmen could run "improved" breeds of cattle—Herefords, Angus, Durhams. Modern cowmen spurned the Longhorn, one-time monarch of the Western cattle empire, preferring the beefier, more placid British breeds.

English cattle, however, were ill-suited to the hot, muggy climate of East and Southeast Texas. There, the Longhorn made its last stand, defying the region's cattle raisers to find any breed that could match it for heat tolerance and pest resistance. Gulf Coast ranchers responded with the Brahman. Remarkably vigorous, hardy and adaptable, the Brahman took hold, pushing the Longhorn from its niche along the Texas Gulf Coast.

Excited by the new breed's promise, many Gulf Coast ranchers saw the Brahman as the future of the cow business and dismissed the Longhorn as a remnant of another era. E. H., however, tempered his enthusiasm for the imported Indian cattle with a keen appreciation of what the native Longhorn had meant to the Texas beef industry. At a time when rail transportation was nonexistent and steamship freight rates prohibitively high, the Longhorn had been able to pay its own way to market on grass and fresh air. "The first real money that this state received was the returns on Longhorn cattle," E. H. emphasized. "We had a product that transported itself to the market before we had any railroads."[2]

Years before preservationists warned that the Longhorn was endangered, E. H. realized that the changes in Western stockraising methods threatened to annihilate Texas's only indigenous breed of cattle. He had a knack for knowing what was going out of style, and he knew the Longhorn was fading fast: "They went out overnight, you know. Everybody got rid of them." But not E. H. To keep the breed alive, he had begun as early as 1923 to gather good examples of old-time Texas cattle from the comparatively pristine herds of the piney woods.

"He bought thousands of head of cattle up in East Texas which had a lot of Longhorn blood in them," Travis said. "It was primarily piney woods and post oak country, and he found out that those cattle coming out of there all had Longhorn blood."[3] Herds in that isolated region had not felt the pressures for change that influenced most Gulf Coast cattle operations. Their makeup remained much the same as it had since pioneer days: tall, long-horned, rangy cattle of Spanish origin intermixed to some degree with the domestic cattle introduced by early Anglo settlers.

Choosing carefully from the thousands of East Texas cattle he traded in, E. H. saved the best for his own herd. "Out of all these cattle he'd take the really good ones that he thought were the true old-type cattle, and he would put them aside in another pasture," Maudeen said. "We had as many as five hundred at one time. That was when we were running almost seven thousand head."[4]

Over the years, one hand-picked specimen at a time, E. H. built one of the finest and largest herds in the nation of authentic Texas Longhorn cattle. His intent, according to contemporary newspaper accounts, was to raise Brahmans for profit and "old-fashioned longhorned cattle for color and romance." The Longhorns indeed presented a colorful contrast to the more uniformly shaded gray Brahmans; E. H.'s Texas cattle were multicolored, speckled, spotted, blue, and red, and some had the coveted brindle pattern—gray or tawny with darker streaks. Many grew horns of majestic proportions, spanning up to six feet tip to tip. Cows and steers sported the prized "Texas twist," with horns spreading gracefully outward and spiraling back in a corkscrew.[5]

To say that E. H. raised Longhorns solely for their color and romance, however, did a disservice to both the rancher and the cattle. While the breed's striking appearance certainly appealed to his sense of showmanship, E. H. was a hard-nosed businessman who respected the qualities he had seen Longhorn cattle demonstrate over many years.

"They are hardy and can rough it and make out on forage that purebred cattle can't make a showing on," he observed. "They can resist tick fever better than Shorthorns and Herefords, and a rattlesnake bite doesn't even faze 'em. Time and again I've seen these ordinary old range cattle, descendants of the Longhorns, get bit by a rattlesnake or a moccasin and never let it slow them up. You never see one of these purebred animals with a pedigree a mile long do that. If one of them gets bit by a poisonous snake, it dies."[6]

Besides snakes, ticks, and fevers, Longhorns could cope with droughts, heat waves, and cold spells, E. H. said: "It's like a catfish can live in a mud hole that would choke other breeds; so the Longhorns could survive in Texas in the days of the open range."[7] Years before agricultural researchers began to endorse the Longhorn's remarkable qualities, E. H. was defending the breed based on the observations of a lifelong association with the cattle. He noted that Longhorn cows are highly fertile and that they are good mothers, able to care for themselves and their offspring under range conditions. Cows are known to lick cuts and scratches on their calves to remove screwworms. They will even baby-sit each other's calves, E. H. observed, with those on duty standing guard while the rest seek forage and water, so that the young are never left unprotected: "In those early days when they had to go to water a long ways on these prairies, I have seen time and again where there would be two cows and thirty or forty calves. Where are the other cows? They're gone to water. When those other cows come back these two will go to water."

Cows on the open range responded instantly to the sound of a calf in danger, whether their own or another's. "You go out there and rope one of those calves and let him bellow one time, and cows will come to his rescue from every direction," E. H. said. "There ain't no wolf going to get one of those old Longhorn's calves.

"A Longhorn cow will trail her calf like a dog will a rabbit—by scent," he added. "They are the only breed of cattle that will wean their calves. Cows hide away from their calves, in the thickets, in the draws, anywhere."[8]

Unlike some domesticated cattle, bred for greater size until calves are too large for natural unaided birth, Longhorn cows characteristically give birth easily, like their wild ancestors. At calving, they rarely need assistance. E. H. told Maudeen, who recorded many of her father's comments about the cattle, that he could not recall any trouble with a calf backwards, or hindquarters first.[9]

This was a breed shaped and refined over centuries by the demands of self-preservation. Generations of coping with the disease carriers that thrive in a warm and wet climate made the Longhorn unusually resistant to the ills and parasites that commonly afflict cattle. E. H. reported no veterinary bills on any of his Longhorns: "During a cattle inspection, government vets told me my Longhorns were the healthiest bunch of cattle they had come across. They're the only cattle that could survive the salt grass country before modern veterinary medicine.

These are the survivors. The weak ones died off two hundred years ago.

"Longhorns shift for themselves. Almost like a razorback hog, they hunt their own medicine if they need any. They'll browse on bushes and eat twigs, weeds, sagebrush, whatever they need; that's their medicine. They know when they need it."[10]

Ranging over a territory that included diverse habitats, from mosquito-infested salt grass marshes to dry sagebrush flats, Longhorn cattle in Texas possessed the ability to eke out a living on poor pasture, in brush country, and during droughts. "Longhorns thrive where other breeds would starve to death," E. H. observed. "They are not much trouble to raise because they are adapted to this region. They adjust to existing conditions. [During droughts] I have seen them straddle trees and walk them down to get moisture and food from the leaves." When the water failed halfway through the growing season, as sometimes happened, blighted rice crops also became feed for the economical Longhorn.[11]

If a rancher could afford to provide extra fodder, Longhorns would respond to feed as well as any breed, E. H. maintained, though he cautioned that "Fat is the most expensive thing you can lay on an animal." But one memorable old steer from the Marks herd seemed determined to eat only what he foraged for himself. "Old Spot was never in a feedlot. Wouldn't even eat hay," E. H. admitted. "He would stand on his hind feet and pick moss out of the trees. He lived on moss during the winter."[12]

Acknowledging that Longhorns generally take longer to reach their maximum body size and weight, E. H. observed that in the days of free grass and open range, that was not a drawback. By age five or six the cattle reached respectable market weights: "I bought lots of cows that dressed six hundred pounds and that meant better than twelve hundred pounds on foot, running on the grass on open range, and that's pretty good cattle in any man's country," he said.

Though slow to mature in bone structure and stature, Longhorns reach sexual maturity earlier than other breeds. In addition, they have remarkable reproductive longevity, with cows routinely continuing to calve at age twenty and older. One of E. H.'s cows had a calf at twenty-eight. When she died at thirty-three it wasn't of old age. "We found her in a bog hole. She didn't die a natural death," E. H. said. Neither did "John Garner," a favorite brindle steer. Old John got in the rice field one fall and ate himself to death, at twenty-six.[13]

E. H. seldom sold a Longhorn for beef. Like retired racehorses who have earned a rest, LH7 Longhorns roamed the ranch undisturbed until they died of old age—or mired in a bog. Though they might be pets, they were never pampered. E. H. had no use for cattle that had to be mollycoddled. He complained that "There is something always going wrong with these classy cattle," and joked about ranchers who brought blue-blooded types onto Gulf Coast ranges and had fans blowing on them all summer to keep them from dying in the heat. "The only kind of a fan the old Longhorn had was that tail. He would fan that at you and go to the brush. And once he'd git in there you couldn't git him out."[14]

Distilling years of Longhorn-watching into a concise assessment of characteristics that set the breed apart, E. H. concluded that "Longhorns are unique for hardiness, thriftiness, lots of constitution and the will to live." Like an indulgent father who forgives the hijinks of his spirited offspring, he added that "They're the toughest cattle in the world, and a Longhorn bull can lick any other bull living. The brindles seem to be the toughest of all. Bought my first brindle bull from Peeler [Graves Peeler, former Texas Ranger and early-day Longhorn breeder] for twenty-five dollars. He tore up everything."[15]

More precisely, the bull tore up his reproductive organs. Attempting to jump a fence, the brindle suffered such damage that he rendered himself useless as a sire. Consequently, the Peeler Longhorn bloodline was never introduced into the Marks herd.[16]

In selecting cattle for his Longhorn herd, E. H. was careful to choose animals that carried the breed's characteristic traits. It took a good eye and ruthless culling; on ranges where the Longhorn type could still be found, bloodlines often were so diluted as to be nearly valueless. Determined to have an outstanding herd, E. H. concentrated on building and maintaining a pure line of old-style Texas cattle. He judged Longhorns with confidence. Based on many years' experience with the breed, he knew what he was looking for:

> Longhorns have a wide skull, are lanky in the leg for walking, have short ears and a big nostril. They come in all colors and combinations of colors. About 75 percent are mealy mouthed [showing a light ring around the nose above the mouth, as though the animal had stuck its mouth in a bucket of meal and come away with some around its nose]. There is no mistaking the sound of a Longhorn. Throaty.
>
> Horns continue to grow as long as the animal is healthy. The horns always have a twist. Ordinarily they do not begin to develop the traditional twist until the cattle are about five years old. If the cow's or steer's horns do not twist by the time they are five or six, they are not true Texas Longhorns. Cattle in the coastal country develop better horns. Horns in the north are stubbier and heavier. Bull horns are thicker, forward and back for fighting.
>
> Whenever I buy cows, I don't look at the papers. I look at the cows. Having been in the cow business all my life, I place my judgment on a cow's age and condition. A cow ought to have some bloom on her, just like a peach when it is ripe.[17]

The soundness of E. H.'s approach to cattle breeding became evident as he developed a widely renowned Marks line of Texas Longhorns. J. Frank Dobie, historian and author, included photographs of Marks cattle in his 1941 landmark study, *The Longhorns*. Commented Maudeen: "My father was a good cattleman, and bought Texas Longhorns only when he could find what he knew were true examples of the breed. As a result, he ended up with cattle that had the true Texas Longhorn features and genetics and they performed accordingly.

"A lot of people ask why E. H. wasn't mentioned more in Dobie's book. Dobie didn't know about him," Maudeen explained. "I came home from Houston to find E. H. and another man leaning against a fence and engrossed in conversation. I did not want to interrupt but finally moved in slowly and heard the man say, 'Mr. Marks, I apologize. I should have come to you first, but I didn't know about you. And the book is at the printers.' He added, 'But I can still get those pictures in.' Then E. H. introduced me to J. Frank Dobie."[18]

For all its exceptional qualities, the old Texas Longhorn that established the cattle industry in the Southwest seemed very much out of step with the cow business of the twentieth century. After Travis Marks enrolled in the Agricultural and Mechanical College of Texas to study animal husbandry, he had the painful duty of informing his father that Longhorns were obsolete, old-fashioned, and virtually worthless, according to modern cattle breeding philosophies.

"My father was a great believer in a cow that would produce," Travis said. "Since he had a lot of cows, Texas A&M thought that he should know something about cows, so their people come down one time and drove around and said, 'Now, Mr. Marks, show us a good cow.'

"So he said, 'Well, there's a good cow.'

"They said, 'Well now, why is that a good cow?'

"He said, 'Because she has a calf every year, and she's a good long-bodied cow and she can travel to water and feed, and she can utilize this pasture and go a long way out and graze, and then come back to water.'

"Being an A&M student at the time, I had to tell my dad that that was all wrong, that what they wanted was a compact, low-set cow. And he said, 'Well, I never did study about it, I don't guess I know anything about what we ought to have.' It's ironic that what he preached about then is exactly what they were looking for in a cow forty and fifty years later."

Privately, E. H. may have wondered what kind of an education Travis was getting at college. Recalling the herds of lanky Texas Longhorns he had driven across a vast unfenced prairie land, he complained that "You couldn't get a hundred miles with these cattle we got now." Casting a critical eye at the short, stocky beeves designed by modern animal science for life on smaller pastures, E. H. gibed that if cattle got much closer to the ground they would have no legs at all: "If they keep on, by golly, they'll have 'em crawling around like snakes."

Undaunted by the visiting professors' lack of enthusiasm for his Longhorns, E. H. continued to draw attention to his steadily growing herd. The scarcer they became elsewhere, the more fiercely he protected and promoted the LH7's Longhorns. "To say that he touted Longhorn cattle through all the lean years is the understatement of the day," Travis remarked. "Anyone who come to our ranch was there to see the Longhorns, whether they knew it or not. He did that in the twenties, the thirties, the forties, and the fifties, and in the early years of the sixties before the Texas Longhorn breed association was formed."[19]

The Marks/LH7 Ranch Rodeo, held almost annually from 1918 to 1950, became a showcase for E. H.'s colorful Longhorn herd. "We had rodeos for thirty years on our ranch," Travis said, "and if you saw my father's rodeo, you looked at Longhorn cattle. He always drove them through the arena, first thing after the Grand Entry. He was proud of them, way back there. Some people admired him for what he did, but some would say, 'My God, we've been trying to get rid of those things for a hundred years, and here he is driving those Longhorns through the rodeo arena.'"

E. H.'s showmanship produced the desired results. Each year, he welcomed the estimated fifteen hundred to two thousand visitors who traveled to the LH7 from Houston and around the world to see genuine Texas Longhorn cattle. As tourists gathered at the ranch for the Longhorn tour, E. H. took charge of the entertainment, plying them with cowboy songs and poetry. It was Travis's job, meanwhile, to load the pickup with cattle feed and go ahead of the crowd opening pasture gates. "I have loaded no-telling-how-many sacks of ear corn or bales of hay, and I've opened ten thousand gaps to let people go into a pasture so my dad could call the Longhorns together and show them the big steers and the bulls and the cows," he remembered. "So I did my penance, too, over a period of thirty years, promoting Longhorns."

Travis followed in his father's footsteps both as rancher and as ardent Longhorn supporter. Well-versed in Longhorn lore by the time he was old enough to sit a horse, he grasped the reason for his father's confidence in the breed while critics remained oblivious to its essential character. The true nature of the Longhorn, Travis realized, is expressed in its unsurpassed instinct for survival:

What a lot of people don't understand is this: The constitution and the will to live is what a Longhorn has. It doesn't mean that a Longhorn is bigger or more muscular. That's not constitution. Constitution is the will to live and the will to just keep going. And that's what a Longhorn will do. I've seen it many times in my lifetime. When we had a lot of cows and our cattle run over a big area, we didn't try to feed them. They stayed out there, through the winter, through thick and thin, and raised their calves. They would get down just to hide and a little muscle and bone, and that's all there was to them. But they'd live. And when good times come along, they'd pick up and come on and have their calves and raise them.

An animal with less constitution would just give up. That's the difference in Longhorns and some other types of cattle. They just don't give up. They'll keep rooting and digging and trying to grub out a living. During the wintertime I've seen these old cows get in there and hustle and just be grubbing around for something to eat—leaves or sticks or anything. Some of these other cattle would be piled up, dead. And you'd think that old Longhorn cow would be dead, too. But she's not, she's still going.

Longhorn cattle evolved out of a condition where no one drenched 'em, sprayed 'em, fed 'em, watered 'em, sheltered 'em, weaned their calves, assisted 'em with their calves, or helped 'em in times of sickness or in need of any kind. If they couldn't do it all by themselves, they died. And generation after generation of that treatment by nature is what made the Longhorn. That's the reason their blood is important to a lot of the breeds we have today. Every time an acre of land is plowed up to be put into intensive farming, it's always the best acre of land. They leave the sorriest land, the marginal land, for cattle. Consequently, you've got to have cattle that can make it on that land—which is the Longhorn. That's where the Longhorn is going to shine.

Travis was graduated from Texas A&M in 1937 with a bachelor's degree in animal husbandry and returned to the LH7 Ranch as E. H.'s business partner. It was a less than ideal time to launch a ranching career, with E. H. still struggling to recover from the economic disaster of the 1930s. "After the Depression he wasn't exactly broke, but he was badly bent, and he more or less had to start over in the cow business," Travis said.

In restoring the LH7 to profitability, father and son concentrated on breeding registered Brahman cattle, with E. H. maintaining his Longhorn herd more or less as a hobby. In a few years' time, Marks-bred Brahman cows and calves were winning prize ribbons at the Houston Fat Stock Show and the Tomball Fair. Taking charge of the Brahman purebreds, Travis developed a show herd and made the rounds of regional livestock exhibitions, promoting the quality registered Brahmans of the Barker ranch. Inevitably, Travis's Brahman concerns began to conflict with E. H.'s Longhorn interests.

"I'm sorry to say that my father and I had many battles and arguments," Travis admitted. "I never did mind him keeping the Longhorns, but he wouldn't sell any of them regardless of how old they got. I'd say, 'We ought to sell some of these old Longhorns.' And he'd say, 'Well, they wouldn't bring anything. Let's keep them, maybe they'll pick up. Then when they get fat we'll sell them.'

"But then, of course, when they'd get to looking good he'd say, 'That old cow is doing pretty good. Let's just keep her.' We had about 250 head of Longhorn cows then, and I remember distinctly, one time I counted up and we had forty-three Longhorn bulls, mature bulls. They'd break out and jump in with my registered Brahman cows, and at that time I was selling the registered Brahman calves real good. I wanted to get rid of some of those Longhorn bulls!"

E. H. temporized by moving his Longhorn herd across the bayou, to put more distance between them and the Brahmans. While Travis despaired of persuading his father to cut the herd to a more manageable size, E. H. did in fact sell numbers of Marks Longhorns all over the country, shipping them to buyers in Ohio, Wisconsin, Florida, and across Texas.

Occasionally, an animal would come up missing from the Longhorn herd. If rustlers were not to blame, then the probable culprit was homesickness. E. H. told one interviewer he had bought and shipped Longhorns to Barker only to see them drift as far as seventy miles back to their old range. Once he was riding through Trinity County, seventy miles north of Houston, and saw an old cow with the LH7 brand on its right hip. It was a Longhorn he had purchased the year before and brought to the open rangeland around Barker. "But," wrote the reporter, caught up in the pathos of a homesick bovine, "when the wind began to blow across the open prairie that old cow just started drifting back until it finally returned to the tree-sheltered country of Trinity County, where the Spanish moss draped in gray festoons to the ground."[20]

The long-legged Longhorn's traveling ability, amply demonstrated in 1932 when Tex McDaniel rode the steer Barker from the LH7 to New York City, was put to the test once more in 1940 by Uncle Jim Fairchild. The seventy-year-old fiddler and itinerant cowboy fulfilled a lifelong ambition by creaking down the Old Spanish Trail to St. Augustine, Florida, in a covered wagon drawn by Longhorns, to find the fabled "Fountain of Youth." The trip of 930 miles took a year, a month, and seven days.[21]

Uncle Jim was a fixture in Houston. No parade through city streets was complete without his lumbering wagon drawn by a yoke of Marks Longhorn steers named, predictably, Bald and Spot. For several years, E. H. gave the old-timer a home on the LH7 Ranch. When E. H. was furnishing South Texas rodeos many of their horses, bulldogging steers, and running calves, Uncle Jim would go along to these events with the LH7 outfit to drive the chuckwagon, cook for the cowboys, and "add color and romance."[22]

His lifetime ambition, Uncle Jim said, was to travel the Old Spanish Trail in an ox-drawn wagon as his pioneering ancestors had done. When old age forced a halt to his ranch work, he started preparing for the trip, replacing the high iron-bound wheels of his antique wagon with rubber automobile tires and accustoming his team of Longhorn steers to the jangle and roar of highway traffic. On 20 July 1940, he set out for the Atlantic Coast, traveling with a goat named Isham and a cross between a timber wolf and shepherd dog named Tige.

"The goat with a taste for well-worn gloves and cheviot suits, as an interviewer found, is the old Texan's pride and joy," read a news account from Jacksonville, Florida. "He has developed into an expert judge of traffic and does a split-second side-slip under one of the 1,000-pound oxen when danger threatens."[23]

Tige the timber wolf earned his keep as a highly effective watchdog during the prairie schooner's thirteen-month voyage. The beast "guards the neatly arranged interior of the well-stocked wagon and is quick to recognize and resent hitchhiker tactics," the reporter testified.[24]

Making about ten miles a day to the accompaniment of clashing trace chains and creaking wagon timbers, the odd party of travelers rolled leisurely from Barker across Louisiana, Mississippi, Alabama, and Florida, selling some thirteen thousand postcards along the way. Uncle Jim's patient steers ambled through busy Jacksonville, Florida, and crossed the St. Johns River bridge "without delay or mishap," then turned south to St. Augustine.

"Wearing the goatee and drooping mustache of the early plainsman, Uncle Jim's sun-toughened face creased into a smile when his age was mentioned," wrote the Florida reporter. "'Don't want to talk about that,' he drawled. 'I've been hearing about the Fountain of Youth and thought maybe I might take me on a life partner when I come to the end of the trail.'" Although Uncle Jim brought home no new bride from St. Augustine, he did eventually return to Houston with E. H.'s yoke of Longhorn steers. The cowboy died in Houston 17 February 1957, his age unknown but estimated at eighty-six.[25]

While Uncle Jim was away on his odyssey, America's sudden entry into World War II brought a barrage of problems for the LH7. Wartime shortages of cattle feed, hired hands, gasoline, and auto tires severely pinched the ranch's operations. One of the first casualties of war-imposed austerity was the prize-winning show herd Travis had built from the LH7's registered Brahmans. Shortages of fuel, rubber tires, and sufficient manpower to handle the animals kept cattle and buyers away from the regional stock shows. All unnecessary travel ground to a halt as civilians sacrificed to support the war effort.

Both Emory and Travis served with the U.S. Army during the war. The absence of both sons created a hardship for E. H. as he labored to keep the LH7 going. Unable by himself to manage all the ranch's traditional activities, he was forced in 1942 to discontinue the spring rodeo. Within two years, however, E. H. announced that ranch routine without Travis and Emory was well-enough adjusted for him to resume the shows, and so the 24th edition of the Marks Rodeo was held in early May 1944. Only two concessions were made to accommodate a nation at war: "This year War Bonds will be substituted for the silver trophies and there will be no barbecue," reported the *Houston Chronicle*, "but the rest of the program remains the same."[26]

The fighting continued into the spring of 1945, compelling E. H. once again to cancel the feast of barbecue that was to many rodeo-goers the highlight of the show. "The thousands of Houstonians who have looked forward to this event may be disappointed," wrote the *Houston Post*, "but they will understand it is because there is a war going on." Noting that some of the best-known riders in the sport of rodeo would be competing in the LH7 event, the newspaper added that "Another feature of the 1945 rodeo will be the annual roundup and parade of the LH-7 Longhorn herd, largest privately owned herd of its kind in the United States...." It was a major victory in E. H.'s private war to save the Longhorn that a substantial herd could be found in the mid-1940s outside of federally supported wildlife refuges.[27]

Overcoming economic crisis in the thirties and wartime upheaval in the forties, the LH7 Ranch was prospering, a credit to E. H.'s good management. According to Dan Clinton, Harris County agricultural agent, the Barker cattleman was always the first to take a progressive step. Recognizing, for instance, that grass and hay grown on Gulf Coast soils were severely deficient in phosphorus, a mineral essential in cattle nutrition, E. H. became the first rancher in Harris County to apply phosphate to his land.[28]

"Clinton retired in the late 1950s after twenty-five years as ag agent," Atha related. "At his retirement party he told of E. H. spreading the first phosphate. There was no such thing as a fertilizer spreader, so a wagon with cracks in the bed was used. Phosphate was dumped in and the wagon driven over rough ground, shaking the product through the cracks."[29]

Never satisfied with conditions as they were, when E. H. studied his land and cattle he looked at possibilities. On a visit to Texas A&M in the fall of 1945, he saw thousands of young pine trees growing in the college nursery. He immediately got an idea to plant pines as windbreaks on the LH7, creating man-made thickets on the bald prairie to protect cattle from winter winds.

The ranch had the usual hardwood trees growing in low places and along watercourses on the Gulf prairies. In summer, the hardwoods made shade trees, but in winter, shed their leaves. Bare limbed, they gave little protection from blizzards and freezing temperatures.

Pine trees, evergreens, would make ideal windbreaks. Obtaining some two thousand seedlings of the longleaf, slash, and loblolly varieties, E. H. planted them in dense thickets on the higher, treeless areas of the ranch. The longleaf pines did poorly and many died, but with E. H.'s encouragement the slash and loblolly took hold and "grew like weeds," reported E. L. Summers, agriculture editor of the *Houston Chronicle*. E. H. fenced the thickets to protect the seedlings from livestock and had his ranch foreman, John Warnasch, plow a firebreak around each oblong stand of trees. Visiting the ranch to see how E. H.'s idea was getting along, editor Summers found that the pines which were six to eight inches tall when planted had grown twelve to sixteen feet in five years.

"Mr. Marks is highly satisfied with the result of his experiment," Summers wrote, "and he believes he has pointed the way toward substantial relief from the cold spells which often are such a trial to herds and their owners."[30]

As a progressive cattleman, E. H. was glad to see younger generations of ranchers doing more with the land and applying modern methods of range management. "The youngsters are doing a good job," he acknowledged. "They're trying to raise ten blades of grass where the old-timers raised one." In his heart, though, he longed for the days of open range and wild Texas cattle. Praising "the youngsters" for raising more grass on fewer acres, he added this reminder: "Of course, in the early days we didn't have to worry about grass, we had millions and millions of acres."[31]

Grazing those unfenced acres, once, were great herds of Longhorns, self-reliant specialists in survival. The phosphorus treatments and pine tree thickets of the twentieth century had E. H.'s approval, but the old-fashioned Texas Longhorn had his admiration. Those cattle lived off the land, whether ranging free or carrying a rancher's brand. Of his own herd, E. H. declared: "I never have done anything to these Longhorns except give them grass."[32]

It might as easily be said that grass was all life ever gave E. H. Everything else he had was a product of his own work. Travis admiringly recalled his father's career as a self-made cattleman: "He came up the hard way. Nobody ever gave him anything, he made it on his own. He made a success out of the cow business. And that's what he based it on, an animal being able to take care of itself and raise a calf and do it primarily without man's assistance on what Nature put out there for it: grass."[33]

"Family tree" at the Marks family picnic grounds, 1950. Marks grandchildren, grandnieces and nephews perch on woody grapevines that have climbed into the tree. (*Photo courtesy Atha Marks Dimon.*)

Maud and Emil Marks with six of their seven grandchildren, just before starting a week of vacation together in 1953. Left to right: Blevins Bundick; Maud; Travis Marks, Jr.; Suzanne Marks; Stephen (Rusty) Marks; Jon E. Marks; Milo Marks; and E. H. Not pictured is Athene Bundick, who was at band practice at Katy High School but joined the group before they departed on the annual "Grandchildren Trip." In the background is the log cabin where E. H. stored his "collectibles." (*Photo courtesy Atha Marks Dimon.*)

11

IN THE CITY'S SHADOW: A CLASH OF TWO CULTURES

"One of the nicest things about this place is that the ranch lies in sight of the bright lights of Houston, and is close to one of the leading highways."[1]

If Maud and E. H. grieved at the thought of someday losing four offspring to marriages and families of their own, it was a groundless fear. When Marks children wed, spouses came to live on the LH7 Ranch. Many of Maud and E. H.'s seven grandchildren, born over a span of a dozen years from 1937 to 1949, took their first steps in the bunkhouse adjacent to the main house. First Atha, then Travis, then Emory made homes for their families in the barracks originally built for LH7 cowboys.

Family trips had become a habit with E. H. and Maud when their own children were young. When the seven grandkids (five boys and two girls) got big enough, they began to travel with them. E. H. exercised only nominal authority on these annual camping trips. Mostly, he left it to the youngsters to choose, by democratic vote, what they would see and do.

"All the children remember the fun they had camping with their grandparents, 'Gaga and E. H.,'" Atha said. "My son was the eldest, and Emory's third son was the youngest. One time they came home telling about how they had all wanted to do something except my son, who wanted to do something else, so he tried to persuade the youngest boy to vote with him. But the youngest one kept looking at his two bigger brothers and voted with them."[2]

With all of E. H. and Maud's married children raising their families on or near the ranch, evenings frequently found everyone gathered at the LH7. Members of the extended Marks family, including the Smiths from Maud's side of the clan, often met on the rodeo grounds for a picnic. They needed little reason, Atha said: "We were a great picnicking family. If there was half of an excuse, we had a picnic. All the relatives came out from Houston. Daddy had the tables and the benches down there for the rodeos, so we had the facilities."

Remaining single, Maudeen worked farther afield than her siblings. After graduation from Texas State College for Women in 1939, she moved to an apartment in Houston and made a career in radio and publicity. She got her start writing for the Houston Fat Stock Show. Irritated at the hayseed image of the livestock business spread by clumsy stock show publicity, Maudeen drew from personal experience to write a fifteen-minute radio program and spot announcements that reflected her own firsthand point of view. Smartly dressed in her best western shirt, trousers, and boots, she delivered the material to W. O. Cox, head of the agricultural department at the Houston Chamber of Commerce. Her proposed radio announcements had an authenticity that won him over immediately: "Mr. Cox read this stuff and he leaned across to me and said, 'Miss Marks, could you write one of these for each day of the stock show?' I thought, 'Could I do it?' but to him I said, 'Oh, yes sir!' I wasn't going to tell him no. I wanted to interpret my people to those town people. I wanted them to get it right."[3]

For four years, as an unpaid volunteer, Maudeen wrote advertisements for the stock show and took her material to the Giezendanner Agency for release to local radio stations. During those years she saw owner Charlie Giezendanner once—"fleetingly"—so it came as a bolt from the blue when he asked her to run the agency while he joined most of the young male population of Houston in military service during World War II. In addition to handling all radio publicity during the stock show's run, she decorated store windows on Houston's Main Street with bits, spurs, mounted steer horns, and other Western regalia, much of it borrowed from the LH7. The ranch defined her life even while she lived in Houston: "I really never left home. I just went about agriculture in a different fashion."

When Giezendanner came home from the war, Maudeen continued as radio director for the agency, writing scripts and producing several popular programs. As the Houston Livestock Show developed into a major account for the agency, she organized and ran a pressroom for the agricultural editors and writers who covered the event each February.

While Maudeen was getting her big break in public relations thanks to wartime obligations that called her boss away and left her in charge, her father, paradoxically, was learning that wartime obligations would cost him much of his beloved LH7 Ranch. The trouble lay in the ranch's location next to Texas's largest city. In the early part of the century, Houston and the LH7 had existed comfortably side by side in the social and economic mosaic that was Harris County. But completion of the Houston Ship Channel in 1914 and construction of refineries and other petroleum-related industries beginning during World War I laid the groundwork for the city to grow into an industrial giant. World War II accelerated the pace of change. With the city growing ever bigger and stronger, rural and urban interests were bound to collide.

It was a measure of E. H's regard for Houston that he had always thought of the city's proximity as an asset. Indeed, ready access to markets, financing, and a large urban population had played to the ranch's advantage for decades. But the tables turned in 1945 when, for flood control purposes along Buffalo

Bayou, the federal government condemned 134.8 acres of LH7 ranchland at Devil Springs. E. H. got $135 an acre for the land.[4]

The flood control program, sponsored by Houston and Harris County and carried out by the U.S. Army Corps of Engineers, was devised to protect the many war industries at Houston and the area's half-million people from damaging floods along Buffalo and White Oak bayous. As it continued acquiring land for the flood control works, the Corps asked E. H. for another 323.7 acres of Marks land, but E. H. was unwilling to relinquish the property for what the government termed "just compensation." He took the matter to federal court. After a legal battle that lasted years and cost him thousands in attorneys' fees, he received payment of $420 an acre for the disputed 323 acres.[5]

The government closed proceedings on acquisition of the land in January 1951, effectively closing the long-running Marks Rodeo as well. The condemned acreage included the site where, in the twenties, E. H. had built his rodeo arena, grandstand, and picnic area. In April 1951, E. H. announced the cancellation: There would be no 31st performance of the annual LH7 Ranch Rodeo because of the action of the government in taking the rodeo grounds.[6]

E. H. was not the only landowner to suffer the loss of his property. For construction of two flood control reservoirs on Buffalo Bayou and its feeder creeks, more than twenty-six thousand acres in the Addicks-Barker area were acquired through negotiations and by right of eminent domain. Many of the affected landowners complained bitterly that payment received from the federal government for their land was unreasonably low. After the dams were completed—Barker in 1945 and Addicks in 1948—the government permitted grazing and farming over the flood control areas but placed restrictions on use of the land that the original owners perceived as unreasonable and unjustifiable.[7]

The smoldering discontent flared anew when, years after completion of the dams, the City of Houston and Harris County proposed to lease from the federal government much of the Addicks-Barker flood control area and devote it to recreation instead of ranching. Announcement of the plan brought an angry response from E. H. The seventy-eight-year-old rancher fired off a letter to United States Senator Lyndon B. Johnson and to Congressmen Bob Casey and Albert Thomas, asking their help in having his property returned for the amount the government had paid for it, less attorneys' fees and income tax. A copy of E. H.'s letter was sent to the editor of the *Houston Press*, 2 June 1960:

> I see in today's newspaper that Washington is about to sell [sic] the Barker Dam to the City of Houston.
>
> We, the original owners of that land, want that land back. At least part of it.
>
> If the City of Houston can use this land for a park, then we can use it.
>
> It was condemned to protect Houston. Most of it was taken for less than $100 per acre. Others who went through court had to pay 25 percent in attorneys' fees and another 25 percent in income tax.
>
> In my own personal case, the attorneys' fees and witness fees amounted to $33,000, and the income tax amounted to $19,000.
>
> The people who owned these farm and ranch lands, most of whom were reared on them, were not treated fairly.
>
> Most of the land is now worth from $500 to $2000 per acre.
>
> We also know that the U.S. government is not in the real estate business.
>
> I, for one, helped feed and build our big city of Houston. I drove a pair of mules and wagon to Houston with produce to help feed its people and build that great city.
>
> None of us ever thought that the United States government would condemn our property and then let the City of Houston have it for a park.
>
> When the land was condemned, they said it was to keep flood waters off Houston. Now they are talking about putting in picnic areas, golf courses, tennis courts, swimming pools, etc.
>
> I at my age cannot move lock, stock and barrel and help build another city.
>
> I need the land for cattle grazing. 811 acres of the condemned land had been used by me and my son for six or seven years prior to the U.S. taking it. It was agreed that we should have the use of same for $1.50 per acre.[8]

E. H. enlisted the help of other unhappy Addicks-Barker landowners in his quest to have a portion of the flood control acreage returned. Nearly fifty people gathered in the Addicks school one night to protest the park proposition. E. H. conducted the meeting. "We think food and feed are more important than recreation," he blazed. "What we'd like back is what the government didn't need to begin with."[9]

Travis seconded his father's proposal to allow former landowners to redeem their property at the government's rate of valuation. "If the government wishes to give the excess land to Harris County for a park, we feel that the original owners, the ones who gave up their land under wartime necessity and federal condemnation of the land for flood control, should have the right to buy it back at the same prices we were paid," he argued.[10]

The tiny band of rural landowners was somewhat placated when the City of Houston lost interest in leasing the Barker Reservoir. Harris County, however, followed through on its proposal to turn part of the Addicks Reservoir into a county park. The 1,918-acre Bear Creek Park was established in 1965 on land leased behind the Addicks Dam. Satisfying the public need for attractive recreation sites as well as security from flood damage was seen as a higher and better use for the land than continuing to allow former owners to graze cattle on it.[11]

Concerned only with flood protection and recreation, the urban public gave little thought to how the loss of land and grazing would affect the area's ranchers. Atha recalled the reaction of a friend from college who had seen the LH7 rodeo arena and picnic grounds before the government took them and who then came for a visit after the land was condemned. What her girlfriend found disturbed her, Atha remembered:

"I belonged to the Louis H. Hubbard Literary Club, a small group of girls who had graduated from CIA [Texas Woman's University] from 1928 on. We had a picnic out here. They had been out here before, and then they came out after the land was condemned for flood control. I remember this Jackie Greer said, 'Well, they can't do that. We voted for it [i.e., approved a bond issue to finance the flood control works], but we didn't mean for them to do something like this. We didn't know they meant this.'

Sometimes we vote on these things," Atha gently admonished, "and we don't really know what we're voting on."

E. H. was deeply wounded by the loss of his ranchland and rodeo grounds. To lose what he had worked so long to build was as painful to her father as a physical injury, Atha knew: "He was so well established here, it was just like pulling your teeth. It was just part of him. Then, when he had to give up the rodeos, that was another thing that really hurt him, because they had been going on for so many years. It wasn't a very happy situation."

E. H. Marks leads off the Salt Grass Trail Ride in Wagon No. 1. (*Photo courtesy Atha Marks Dimon.*)

E. H. Marks, Reese Lockett and Atha Marks Bundick visit during a meeting of the Salt Grass Trail Association held in the woods on the LH7 Ranch. (*Photo courtesy Atha Marks Dimon.*)

Night camp on the Salt Grass Trail, Waller County Fairgrounds, 1957. Left to right: E. H. Marks, camp cook (unidentified), Suzanne Marks, Atha Marks Bundick, Stephen (Rusty) Marks, and Kay Marks. (*Photo courtesy E. M. Marks.*)

12

THE LAST TRAIL

"Herding cattle now isn't like it was forty years ago. We used to take 'em up the old trail traveling about forty miles a week and camping out at night. You had to rough it in those days. Sometimes we'd have to wait a week before we could cross a flooded stream. Today, most of the cattle are shipped over modern highways in modern trucks. It isn't half as much fun as it used to be."[1]

In the rush of traffic and the press of industry, postwar Houston seemed determined to forget its country beginnings. But there were still some who liked to remind the city of her early heritage in cattle, cotton, and timber. One enthusiastic promoter of country ways was Reese Lockett, mayor of nearby Brenham, who threatened in January 1952 to cease all travel except what could be done on horseback. It seems he flew to Florida for the Orange Bowl football game, and his return trip was grounded several days because of bad flying weather. "I'll never make another trip where I can't ride home on my horse," Lockett declared to a gathering of friends that included journalists, officials of the Houston Livestock Show and Rodeo, and Maudeen Marks' boss, publicist Charles Giezendanner. They quickly reminded Lockett he already had agreed to be arena director of the rodeo in February. His rash statement obligated him to cover the seventy miles from Brenham to Houston on horseback in time for the opening of the show.[2]

In his youth, Lockett had been a rancher who had driven cattle from Central Texas to winter on salt grass along the Gulf Coast. He boasted to the gathering that in his younger days he had made the trip from Brenham to Houston many times on horseback; now he would do so again to kick off the stock show and rodeo.

With the publicity stunt of the decade thus falling into owner Charlie G.'s lap, the Giezendanner Agency sprang into action. Maudeen called the *Houston Post* and asked for page-one coverage of Lockett's ride; managing editor Arthur Laro agreed to send a photographer. Giezendanner telephoned Jack Harris, manager of KPRC radio and TV, who had been among the most vocal in daring Lockett to make the ride. Harris assigned newsman Pat Flaherty to carry a tape recorder and cover the trip as official media representative.[3]

The event was nearly scrubbed when it came to light that Flaherty could not ride a horse. Maudeen rescued the stalled plan by offering her father's wagon and mule team. The trip was on again—until it was found Flaherty could not drive a wagon and mules. Once more Maudeen saved the day: She volunteered one of her father's ranch hands as wagon driver, with the knowledge and consent of neither E. H. nor the hand.

When Maudeen told her father of Lockett's ride and the role she had arranged for him, E. H. balked. He had plans to host his neighboring rancher friends to barbecue and a game of cards that evening. As she knew he would, however, E. H. soon gave in: "Well, okay," he agreed. "I'll do anything for Reese Lockett . . . and for you."[4]

Caught short by the spur-of-the-moment plan, E. H. had to do some fast organizing to rendezvous with Lockett the following morning, January 30. Ranch foreman John Warnasch was sent to round up the mules, who were kicking up their heels somewhere in the pasture. By the time Warnasch got the team up and the wagon stocked with provisions, it was after midnight. Loading wagon and mules into a trailer, he hauled them to the starting point, Dr. Guy Knolle's in Brenham. Early the next morning the trail riders were on their way to Houston, E. H. and Lockett on horseback and Flaherty toting his tape recorder in the wagon with Warnasch driving.[5]

The four soon had cause to regret the hasty organization of their trip. While crossing a creek, the wagoners inadvertently dumped all their provisions from the chuckbox into the water. The winter weather rapidly deteriorated from bad to terrible; as the trail riders neared Houston, they ran into a furious hailstorm. Visibility was so poor in the heavy rain and hail, the two horsemen were separated from the wagon. Marks and Lockett sought their own shelter from the cold pummeling while Warnasch and Flaherty took refuge in the yard of a small house. Two wide-eyed children beckoned to them to come inside, and there the wagoners stayed until the storm passed. Reunited, the intrepid four—soaked to the skin and shivering in the cold—pushed on into Houston to the facilities of television station KPRC, picking up another thirteen riders at Spring Branch.[6]

The route followed by Marks, Warnasch, Lockett, and Flaherty was roughly that of pioneer cattlemen who had driven their stock each winter to the rich salt grass pastures on the Gulf Coast. The tall, bunchy grass stayed green all year, growing along the Texas coast from Orange to Brownsville in a strip that extended about fifteen miles inland. Cattle that grazed the succulent salt grass grew fatter and sleeker than herds inland, a mystery to ranchmen before science revealed that the grass's high mineral content made it exceptionally nutritious.[7]

Steers thrived on the salt grass grazing, and sometimes cattlemen also sent cows and young calves down the trail. For a herd numbering seven hundred to eight hundred head, seven was the usual complement of outriders, plus wagon drivers. If the herd had many small calves, the owner might send along extra wagons to pick up tired youngsters that straggled behind.

It took from three days to a week to move cattle down to salt grass. After reaching the coast, two or three men stayed to ride herd, usually from November through February. Cattle carrying many different brands ran together on the lowlands, grazing undisturbed through the winter months. In early spring each ranch's cowboys cut their cattle from the common herd and headed for higher ground. They had to be out of the marshes by March to escape the bloodthirsty mosquitoes.[8]

The 1952 retracing of the old Salt Grass Trail gave birth to one of Houston's most enduring traditions, reenacted each February to kick off the Houston Livestock Show and Rodeo. From four riders originally, the trail ride grew to nearly one hundred participants in 1953 and eight hundred in 1954. In a few more years the event would draw thousands. Stretching single file for a mile or more, wagons and horses carried bankers, lawyers, oilmen, housewives, and politicians, as well as cattlemen, stock show officials, newspaper reporters, and television celebrities. Participants ranged in age from five years to past eighty.

The trail ride was neither easy nor comfortable; perhaps that was the attraction. Riders slept on the hard ground and bumped along on horseback for days, often in a cold rain. They suffered saddle sores, sunburns, windblown dust, and foul weather. They risked injury while riding on the highway shoulder. Reported the *Houston Post*'s John Moore in February 1954: "During the last two days the procession has been cut in two by several trains, riders have almost been run over by trucks and automobiles, wagons have broken down and there has been a great deal of general confusion." By the time it hit Houston, the parade of riders stretched for three miles and created a traffic tie-up.[9]

Cofounders Lockett and Marks, astonished but gratified at the response of those wanting to take part in the ride, returned to the Salt Grass Trail year after year. Though past seventy years old, E. H. rode horseback ahead of the LH7 chuckwagon and served as assistant to Trail Boss Lockett. Brenham's mayor had his hands full bringing order to the chaos of horses, wagons, and riders that annually assembled in his town to follow U.S. Highway 290 to Memorial Park in Houston.[10]

The modern trail ride gained authenticity from E. H. and other old-time cowmen who had trailed cattle to market in the nineteenth century. These veteran drovers knew the value of a hot meal at the end of a long day's ride; they made sure the chuckwagon was well provisioned at all times with food, water, firewood, and—most important—a good cook. Before the 1954 ride, ranchers Marks and Lockett and long-time Harris County Sheriff T. Binford displayed their cowboy cooking skills in Jane Christopher's television kitchen on Channel 2. E. H. demonstrated his recipe for Cowboy Steaks: "Cover bottom of iron skillet with salt and heat until lightly browned—meaning it's hot. Toss in a 3/4-inch round steak and keep turning until browned on both sides. Cover skillet and set off of fire. In 10 to 15 minutes dot with butter." He assured his audience the salt method of frying round steak produces tender meat with natural gravy that does not taste salty.

Described by *Post* columnist Moore as "that grand old man of the trail ride," E. H. was a stalwart of the Salt Grass Trail for fifteen years, leading Wagon No. 1 astride his bay gelding, Roy. He mingled with Western celebrities that included Duncan Renaldo and Leo Carrillo (the "Cisco Kid" and his sidekick "Pancho" from the 1950s television series), Roy Rogers and Dale Evans, and *Gunsmoke*'s James Arness. He regularly hosted the Salt Grass Trail Association annual meeting at the LH7 Ranch. The entire Marks clan caught his enthusiasm. Each February a mounted brigade of E. H.'s children, grandchildren, and in-laws joined him on the trail.[11]

Two generations of devoted descendants helped Maud and E. H. celebrate their golden wedding anniversary in 1957. E. H. found years of outdoor exercise and fresh air paying off in persistent good health. Never tiring of the chase, he continued to hunt bear and deer on trips to Colorado, New Mexico, Montana, and Wyoming, marking his seventy-ninth birthday with a deer hunt on the western slopes of the Colorado Rockies.

Self-sufficient as an old Longhorn and tough as rawhide, E. H. remained a forceful personality within his community and the cattle industry. News reporters interviewed him regularly for insights into the Harris County ranching economy, which still was a factor in Houston's financial prosperity despite the industrial expansion spurred by petroleum and World War II. As the *Houston Chronicle*'s Pete Gilpin reported in February 1958:

"Mighty Houston is ringed with ranches, the industry that first made Texas great. Just a 'hoot and a holler' from city ways is the Emil H. Marks spread—a working ranch that boasts not only Brahmans but a 146-head herd of genuine Texas Longhorns.

"Marks, and men like him, are the reason Harris County still ranks second in Texas cattle production, despite the industrial boom which has overshadowed the cowman in the past few decades."[12]

E. H. was respected both for his knowledge of the cattle business and for his lively wit. Those who sought his opinion could count on the veteran cowman to state his views candidly and emphatically. Talking with a *Houston Press* reporter about the influence of consumer demand on cattle prices, E. H. remarked: "Do you know there are a lot more cattle in Texas than there are Texans? There are 9,602,000 cattle in Texas. If there were that many Texans, there would be less taxes, fewer Yankees, and a better pair of shoes for the baby in a quarter of beef."[13] (The 1950 census put the state's human population at 7,711,194.)

E. H. never retired from ranching, although he had begun dropping hints to that effect about the time he turned fifty. "Mr. Marks states he is of the opinion this is his last year as the operator of a large ranch," one paper had reported as early as 1930. "'Things are changing. The open ranges are gone and then I feel I have done my share for the cattle industry of Harris County. I don't know, but I think I shall retire' . . . "[14]

It proved to be a bluff. Well past retirement age, E. H. was still working cattle on horseback, riding at a brisk pace, as active as a man twenty years younger. In a face furrowed and weathered by decades of exposure to sun and wind, his blue eyes remained bright, clear, and full of mischief. Attending a cattlemen's convention in Dallas in 1959, E. H. passed around a picture showing him riding a Longhorn steer named Smoky. This sparked a debate among his cattlemen colleagues over whether the fierce Brahman cattle popular on Texas ranches could be as easily broken to the saddle.[15]

A popular after-dinner speaker, E. H. accepted hundreds of invitations to share with city dwellers his nearly inexhaustible stock of jokes and riddles, cattle lore, and cowboy poetry. As rural communities increasingly were absorbed into the Houston metropolitan area, E. H.'s urban audiences came to know him as their last link to a disappearing way of life.

"He was a live wire," Travis remembered. "He wanted to be in the middle of people. He talked to every Rotary, Lions Club and historical society within a hundred and fifty miles of Houston, and loved to give them old-time tales and cowboy poetry."[16]

An avid traveler since the days of the Model T touring car, E. H. used his out-of-state hunting and sightseeing trips to build his reputation as a storyteller. By the late 1950s he was averaging more than one hundred talks a year throughout the country. Everything audiences expected of the quintessential Texas rancher—that was E. H. Speaking once at a New York Rotary Club meeting, E. H. denied that Texans are a boastful lot, then offered to summarize his state's modest virtues: "All I told 'em was that Texas has got the biggest size, the brightest moon, the hottest sun, the fastest horses and the prettiest women on earth. We native Texans do not brag. We only state facts."[17]

These "facts," however, could take the form of utter lies. A respectable Texas liar never exaggerated, E. H. explained, but told outright lies: "They are straight, honest-to-goodness lies. We Texans never stretch an untruth for effect." He theorized it was the "converts" to Texas, not the natives, who gave the state its disturbing reputation for boasting. "You get a man comes here from Kansas or someplace, he might tell you Texas is pure heaven. Now that man's bragging. Texas ain't all that pure."[18]

E. H. had no monopoly on Marks wit and vitality. Also past seventy, Maud remained active in affairs of home, family, and community. Only a stranger could doubt the benevolence of "Mrs. M," gentle mistress of the LH7. But even those with the best of intentions could be misunderstood, as suggested by an item in George Fuermann's *Houston Post* column, August 1958:

Mrs. M. is a septuagenarian and a gentlewoman. But living in the country, where it is sometimes necessary to shoot a snake in the chicken yard or to kill a wounded animal as an act of mercy, she has her own gun.

It is a .45 Colt revolver, with which she has been known to shoot the head off a guinea hen that wandered too close to the ranch house when the pot was boiling. Her granddaughter is Athene Bundick, a University of Texas co-ed who likes to go barefooted when she is at home in the summer. Athene recently drove to the LH7 to take Mrs. Marks to the Bundick home, in Barker, for the week end.

Not wanting to leave a gun around the house while she was gone, Mrs. M. gave her barefoot granddaughter the pistol to carry while she followed with an overnight bag. Just as the pistol-toting Athene and Mrs. Marks stepped into the yard a car with New York license plates stopped at the gate. The occupants of the car, perhaps having come to see Longhorn cattle, got an eyeful of the womenfolk, one barefoot and carrying a big revolver.

The car circled hastily and sped back to the highway. By now, no doubt, the occupants are telling other New Yorkers about the narrow escape from two Texas wild women.[19]

The highway that carried off the alarmed New Yorkers, U.S. 90 from Houston to Katy, had long been a major artery through West Harris County. As early as 1930, E. H. had been promising "good road" all the way for visitors coming to see his Longhorn herd. The road cleaved a landscape of pastures, fields, and hay meadows; few businesses had yet built out from Houston along the route. Not until the construction in the 1960s of Interstate Highway 10 along an edge of the LH7 would the open land around Barker begin to fill with gas stations and commercial clutter.[20]

Filmmakers seeking Old West atmosphere combined with modern urban convenience found the ranch on Houston's uncrowded western fringe the perfect setting. A crew from "Walt Disney's Wonderful World of Color" picked the LH7 to begin filming *Sancho, The Homing Steer*. Based on a story by J. Frank Dobie and narrated by Rex Allen, *Sancho* aired on national television in January 1962 as a two-part Disney presentation and also was released in Europe as a feature film.[21]

The producers leased several LH7 Longhorns, marked alike but of different ages, to play the title character from calfhood to maturity. Filming went badly from the start. To the director's annoyance, the cattle refused to stand up, form ranks, and bed down on command. "Now get 'em lined up in a long, straight line," he instructed E. H. "I had to let him know that these here Longhorns aren't automobiles," E. H. quipped. "They all decided to lie down at once and the movie fellows got all excited, wanted to take pictures of 'em all bedded down," he remembered. "Naturally, with them running all over the place, the cattle all stood up right away to see what was going on." Blind to the futility of his command, the director ordered E. H. to make the herd lie down again.[22]

The Texas weather proved as uncooperative as the Longhorns. Filming was barely under way when a rare Gulf Coast snowstorm stopped the action. Emory described the one scene completed on location at the LH7: "The picture starts out with the small calf in a mud hole, and this fellow picks him up out of the mud hole and puts him on the saddle. That's as far as they got at Barker because of the snow. That stuff doesn't come down there but about every twenty or thirty years, and there it was. The snow was two-foot deep. They couldn't finish the picture, so finally they moved to Colorado."[23]

The film company used two nearly identical Marks Longhorn steers to play the part of the adult Sancho. Disney bought one steer outright to retain promotional rights to the animal. The other was returned to the LH7, but with the stipulation he be called "Sancho's Double."[24]

At age eighty-four, E. H. rode in the 1966 Texas Longhorn Centennial Trail Drive, a commemorative event sponsored by the Texas Longhorn Breeders Association of America to retrace the old cattle trail from San Antonio, Texas, to Dodge City, Kansas, a century after the first drives had gone up the trail. The ride brought E. H. close to the father he had lost seventy-five years before: "In 1866, my daddy went up the trail. Then in 1966 we went up the trail. I furnished fifteen Longhorn steers to put in that herd and we drove them to Dodge City." Altogether, 100 Longhorns and 120 cowboys participated.[25]

For the occasion, E. H. dressed to the hilt in cowboy fashion: "I guess I was the most typical old-time cowboy along that trail," he said. "I had a rawhide vest and the old boots that come up to your knee and some of the old steel spurs that they wore in the early days. They didn't have silver-mounted spurs. In those early days spurs had two little bells that would hit together while we walked down the street. You could hear them ring.... But [in 1966] I didn't have bells in my spurs. They were lost and I couldn't find them.

"Anyhow, I had the spurs and a big hat. A lot of fellows were dressed pretty good, they had on suspenders. I had on a rawhide vest that I'd had for years. It hasn't got any buttons, it just has leather straps to tie together, 'cause you couldn't lose a button in those early days. You didn't have a thread and a needle to sew on another one." A blue chambray shirt and leather chaps completed E. H.'s authentic cowboy attire.[26]

Steers from several ranches were gathered in San Antonio to begin the drive. Suspicious of each other, the cattle refused to herd together. Younger drovers, mindful of E. H.'s long experience with Texas Longhorns, turned to the veteran rancher for advice: "They asked me, 'Marks, what can we do? These cattle don't want to stay together.' I said, 'Well, that's easy. When we go to a picnic we get acquainted with people. We can't get acquainted by staying separate. So put these cattle in a pen tonight... maybe ten, fifteen acres, and let them get acquainted. Tomorrow morning by nine o'clock turn them out and hold them together, make them graze together.' It worked out pretty good. They held together fine."

As the drovers moved the cattle out of San Antonio on the first leg of the drive, they discovered that herding cattle in the Space Age posed problems never encountered by cowboys of the 1860s. "We had a little trouble at first because the airplanes dodged down so close to take pictures," spooking the herd, E. H. said.

With the asphalt and concrete of modern America covering much of the old trail, grass for grazing was scarce along the route. "In the early days those old steers got fat going up the trail but these didn't have the free grass that we had," E. H. noted. In places, however, the landscape was green and open and the steers got a taste of life as their predecessors had lived it: "We had some pretty good spots along the road where the road was wide and there was a lot of Johnson grass."

If cowboys on the Centennial Trail Drive faced problems unknown to their nineteenth-century counterparts, they also enjoyed conveniences undreamed of in the 1860s. The modern drovers took along portable, collapsible steel pens to hold the herd after dark, relieving the night riders. Where trail drivers once had relied on the Longhorn's strong legs and stamina to get a herd to market, the 1960s' cowboys had stock trailers. E. H. seemed to find no incongruity in mingling past and present to create the illusion of an old-time trail drive: "When we got on up the line we would drive the cattle within five miles of some town. Then we would drive them through that town and the pens would be put up on the other side. Then we hauled them to the next town."

E. H. made few concessions to age. When the Texas Longhorn Breeders Association of America was organized in September 1964, the octogenarian was elected to the first board of directors and served for five years. Only months after riding cross-country in the 1966 trail drive, E. H. was ready to head west for his annual hunting trip. A frequent companion on these expeditions was his son Travis, also his partner in the cattle and rice businesses for three decades. In describing times with his father, Travis profiled a man who found life an unending adventure:

> Over a period of 32 years we made a lot of hunting trips to West Texas, Montana, Colorado, and New Mexico. We also made two or three fishing trips to Laguna Madre, staying at Port Isabel each year.
>
> E. H. was an optimist and ready to meet the world everyday. These trips were the catalyst that kept me going, however, when the going was rough in the cow business or maybe the rice crop did not pan out due to a Gulf storm blowing it down. I could always tell myself that as soon as the northers started blowing we would be on our way somewhere on a hunting trip. E. H. always said when business interfered with hunting, cut out business.

E. H. loved hunting and was a very good shot with shotgun or rifle. He was an exceptional quail shot on the wing. His rule when hunting quail was to give his guests the first shot. If they did not drop the quail, then when it seemed the quail was out of range he would shoot and drop it.

In the 1950s and 1960s E. H. was getting up in years, but I never hesitated to take him hunting in Colorado or West Texas. Though there was always a possibility of a stroke or heart attack, I knew we were doing something he loved to do more than any other thing. Camping and hunting like his father was in his blood.

When we went to Colorado in 1966, E. H. was 85 years old. Things went smoothly at first, but out at deer camp at about 9,500 feet his heart developed some irregular beats. He and I agreed he had better go home to a lower altitude. The decision was made to drive to Denver and catch a plane.

E. H. had made up his mind years before not to ride an airplane any place, unless it was a dire emergency. We decided this emergency qualified. I did not want to seat him next to a window as it might not be a pleasant sight for him. On the way home he was joking and telling stories, when suddenly he leaned to see past me out the window. I said, "What is it?" He answered, "Oh, it looked like we just passed a bridge." I told him the pilot had just come on the P-A system and told us we were flying at 37,000 feet and the temperature outside was 35 degrees below zero. He said, "For gosh sakes, don't anyone open the window."

I had phoned ahead and told the family I was bringing E. H. home. We were met by the whole family—they expected him to be in a wheelchair or on a stretcher, but down the corridor we came with E. H. puffing on his cigar as usual. A big smile spread across everyone's face when they saw E. H. his usual self. This ended E. H.'s Colorado hunting trips.[27]

Life's minor trials and major disasters: E. H. met them all with humor and grit. He kept his spirits high and his wits sharp until the end of his days. "You can always tell a joke about something that happened if you have been around like I have," he maintained. "I've shipped cattle to Kansas and I've hunted in Colorado and New Mexico and I've killed my elk in Montana. Folks, I have enjoyed living the life that I have."[28]

E. H. died in Houston's Hermann Hospital on the night of 15 September 1969, a few weeks before his eighty-eighth birthday. Maud followed him seven months and a day later, dying at her home on the LH7 Ranch 16 April 1970. She was eighty-three.

In memory of the old-time Texas cowman, one of the last of his breed, Mayor Louie Welch and the Houston City Council passed the following resolution 17 September 1969:

> WHEREAS, only too rarely are we privileged to have among us a man whose life is a testimonial to the spirit of our region and whose activities and actions are a reflection of the best of human traits; and
>
> WHEREAS, Mr. Emil Henry Marks was such a man, rising with little formal education from relative obscurity to ownership of the largest herd of Longhorn cattle in the world; and
>
> WHEREAS, Mr. Marks became both respected and beloved for his enterprise and his vast store of knowledge of the Texas frontier and its stories and poems; and
>
> WHEREAS, Mr. Marks this week, at the age of eighty-seven, was taken from us by death;
>
> NOW, THEREFORE, BE IT RESOLVED by the City Council of the City of Houston that the deep sorrow of the people be expressed to the family of Emil Henry Marks. He will be missed.[29]

Epilogue

Following an early start in ranching, the restaurant business, and the army, Emory Marks became a banker with Houston National Bank, fulfilling his ambition of a career without cattle. After retiring in the 1960s, he lived in Santa Fe, New Mexico, a favorite vacation town of the Marks family when he was a boy. On 1 April 1970, back at Barker, he married Nova Bryant Dickson, a former missionary home to the States after thirty years in Bolivia. The couple settled in Kerrville, Texas, in 1979. Emory died there at his home on the 25th of October 1989, aged eighty-one.

By his first wife, Dorothy Katherine "Kay" Diederich Marks, Emory had three sons: Milo Val, Jon Emil, and Stephen Austin. As the oldest son of E. H. Marks's oldest son, Milo Marks inherited the Wet Hat brand registered in Harris County in 1851 by Godhilf Marks. He represents the fifth generation to continue the Texas ranching tradition of the Marks family.

Atha Marks Dimon, a retired Spring Branch teacher, and her second husband, the late Richard de Huquenelle Dimon (1908-1990), remained at Barker, near the original LH7 Ranch. As a young-married, Atha had made her home in the old Katy Railroad passenger station Maud Marks bought in the 1930s for two dollars. The Barker Home Demonstration Club met there until about 1936, when a small twister took the building off its blocks and set it down on land belonging to Atha and her first husband. They bought the former railroad station for fifty dollars and transformed it into the living room of their first house. Atha raised two children in the remodeled station house: Blevins Bundick and Athene Bundick Vaughan.

Atha was a favorite niece of August Marks, E. H.'s brother. When August died childless in 1964, she was one of the Marks family to inherit his property on the Katy Freeway. In 1972, developers negotiated with seven West Harris County families for four hundred adjoining acres in what became the Park Ten business center at the intersection of Highway 6 and Interstate 10. Six of the families sold their land for cash outright; the Markses agreed to a ninety-nine-year lease.

Between 1952 and 1988, Atha rode in every Salt Grass Trail Ride except the first—twice by wagon and other years horseback. In 1988, at age seventy-seven, she received an award as the oldest lady to make the entire ride horseback. She also was honored as the outstanding trail rider that year.

During the late 1980s, Atha became active with Friends of the Maud Marks Library, a support group for a Harris County branch library to be named for her mother. Plans called for a twelve thousand-square-foot facility with capacity for seventy thousand to eighty thousand volumes. The collection would reflect the interests of the Bear Creek–Katy area of western Harris County.

In 1973, Travis Marks moved his cattle operation from the home ranch at Barker to the rolling hills of Fannin, Texas. He purchased 1,466 acres popularly known in the area as the "old Boyd place." After the move, Travis and Maudeen Marks shared the LH7 brand for their separate herds of purebred Texas Longhorns.

The LH7 Fannin Ranch was established about fifty miles inland from the site of old Indianola, the original port for which Godhilf and Sophia Marks were bound when they left Germany in the 1840s. This was land that might have been settled by the Marks family 130 years earlier, but for a yellow fever epidemic that turned away the arriving ship of immigrants.

In May 1976, to celebrate the nation's Bicentennial, a four-day trail drive sponsored by the Texas Longhorn Breeders Association of America led off from the LH7 Fannin Ranch with Travis as trail boss. Some 175 volunteer drovers moved a herd of more than a hundred Longhorns along the shoulder of U.S. 59 from Fannin to Goliad. As the riders tried to herd the steers into position for a parade around the Goliad town square, the cattle spooked and stampeded through downtown. Cowboys on horseback raced across the courthouse lawn, jumping their horses over flowerbeds and park benches as they tried to slow the runaways circling the square. It was over almost as suddenly as it began, bringing a quick conclusion to the Bicentennial activities. Travis observed, with customary composure, that the stampede gave Goliad the record for the fastest parade in history.

Travis grew interested in training Longhorn steers as saddle mounts after breaking the steer that Tex McDaniel rode from the LH7 to New York City in 1932. About 1960, Travis selected a gentle, showy, red and white brindle named Ranger who had the temperament and intelligence to be a good riding steer. By the time Ranger died in 1985 at age twenty-six, Travis had exhibited the straight Marks-bred Longhorn in more than seventy-five public appearances.

By his first wife, Jeanne Houghton, Travis had two children, Travis S. Marks, Jr., and Suzanne Steffens. He remarried in 1984, to Linda Enke.

Upon division of the parental estate in 1970, Maudeen Marks inherited three Longhorn steers, a couple of old cows, seven heifers, and the LH7 homeplace at Barker. Travis offered her the use of a pure Marks bull to breed her first seven heifers. From that foundation, she built a nationally recognized herd of some 150 registered Texas Longhorns. Squeezed out by urban sprawl, she later moved most of her cattle operation to the LH7 Ranch and Resort, a 1,162-acre Texas Hill Country spread near Bandera that she acquired in 1981.

After inheriting the original LH7 at Barker, Maudeen strove to protect and preserve the historically significant ranch. For years she stood as one woman alone, resisting the pressure tactics of land developers. Then she found allies in county and state historical societies. In January 1985, the Texas Historical Commission designated the LH7 a State Archeological Landmark. SAL status gave Maudeen leverage in her fight to save the homeplace.

"People have had great designs on it," she said. "The president of one corporation, a big outfit, wanted to talk to me about selling the land. They were going to come in and bulldoze the place down, and I didn't want that to happen. I said, 'How can I make you understand that I love this land and I want to be here. I was born here and it's important for me to be here.' He said, 'I don't understand it. When you look out there all you can see is cattle. When I look out there all I can see is buildings.'"

Afraid that continued development of the area might force her off the land, and aware also that deep emotional ties to the LH7 made it impossible for her to objectively gauge the ranch's historical value, Maudeen sought an outside opinion: "I asked the people out from the Harris County Heritage Society and showed them the old dipping vat, the old slaughterhouse, and other things. I told them to assess it for me and tell me very bluntly if I had overvalued the place as something that should be preserved. If it were of any historical value, now was the time to do something about it."

As the only old ranch headquarters in Harris County to survive intact, the LH7 aroused the Heritage Society's immediate interest. The central headquarters area included not only the main house and cowboys' bunkhouse, but also the slaughterhouse; the restored log cabin in which E. H. kept his antiques and "curiosities"; a washhouse equipped with brick furnace and iron pot; the hay and horse barn; the dipping vat, long unused and filled with earth; and the wagon scale.

Intervention of the Harris County Heritage Society and the Texas Antiquities Committee saved the LH7 from imminent destruction. Still, the ranch's future remained uncertain. By the late 1980s, office buildings and parking garages crowded uncomfortably close. Working with the Heritage Society, Maudeen sought to provide for the long-term protection and maintenance of the property. The LH7's best chance of survival might lie in a plan to turn the headquarters complex into a museum to recreate a part of Houston's cattle heritage, teach the ranching tradition, and carry on the work of preservation begun by E. H. Marks at his ranch in the city's shadow.

Notes

1
August Texas

1. E. H. Marks as quoted by Leon Hale, "Good Way To Spend an Afternoon," *Houston Post*, 3 April 1967.
2. Maudeen Marks, notes taken during conversations with E. H. Marks, in Marks Family Papers, LH7 Ranch, Barker, Texas; Annette M. Parker, ed., "The Marks-Schulz Family," researched by E. Maxine Sullivan and Atha Marks Dimon, Marks Family Papers; Atha Marks Dimon, letter to author, 8 April 1988. The birthdate of August Texas Marks, 15 August 1843, is the family tradition. Any records that may have existed in passenger lists at Galveston were destroyed in the 1900 storm.
3. Maudeen Marks, notes; Parker, "The Marks-Schulz Family."
4. Emory Marks, interview with author, Kerrville, Texas, 3–4 December 1984; Joe Adcock, "Longhorn Man," *Houston Chronicle, Texas Magazine*, 27 February 1966, reprinted in *Texas Longhorn Magazine*, September 1967, 15; Maudeen Marks, notes.
5. E. H. Marks, questionnaire on the history of the LH7 brand, Marks Family Papers.
6. Emory Marks, interview; Maudeen Marks, notes.
7. Signed agreement between William Anders and Christian Striepe, Harris County, 23 May 1853, original document in Marks Family Papers.
8. Maudeen Marks, notes; Maudeen Marks, letter to author, 14 July 1987.
9. "3 Prize Guns Stolen From Ranch Exhibit," *Houston Press*, 28 November 1956.
10. Copy of signed agreement between Sophia Striepe and Albert Marks, Harris County, 29 June 1874, Marks Family Papers.
11. "Desert Water Wagon Relic to Serve Picnic on Ranch at Barker," *Houston Chronicle*, 20 June 1947.
12. E. H. Marks, 1967 interview, transcript in Marks Family Papers.

13. Alan Hoyt, "History of the Texas Longhorns," *Texas Longhorn Journal*, Part IV, March/April 1983, 131; Part V, May/June 1983, 59; J. Frank Dobie, "For Their Hides and Tallow," *A Vaquero of the Brush Country* (Austin: University of Texas Press, 1981), 22.

14. George W. Saunders, "The Old Trail," *The Cattleman*, March 1918, 143–47.

15. E. H. Marks, 1967 interview; Adcock, "Longhorn Man."

16. Ibid.

17. Chas. Goodnight, "The Cattle Trail and its Effect on Finance and Civilization," *Pioneer Magazine of Texas*, December 1925, 6.

18. Adcock, "Longhorn Man."

19. Ibid.

20. Maudeen Marks, 1987 letter.

21. Tax receipts in possession of Atha Marks Dimon, Barker, Texas.

22. Mrs. Glen T. Bundick, "Oldest Buffalo Bayou Home Rich in History," *Houston Chronicle*, 13 February 1949.

23. Maudeen Marks, interview with author, Bandera, Texas, 25–28 July 1984; Bundick, "Oldest Buffalo Bayou Home."

24. Leon Hale, "I Don't Guess a Man Could Hardly Write Those Words Down," *Houston Post*, 4 April 1967; Maudeen Marks, 1987 letter.

25. E. H. Marks, 1967 interview.

26. Parker, "The Marks-Schulz Family."

27. E. H. Marks, 1967 interview.

28. Parker, "The Marks-Schulz Family."

29. Travis Marks, letter to author, 24 July 1986.

30. Court order, Harris County, 5 March 1891, copy in possession of Atha Marks Dimon, Barker, Texas; Parker, "The Marks-Schulz Family."

31. Bundick, "Oldest Buffalo Bayou Home."

32. Hale, "Good Way To Spend an Afternoon."

33. Samuel F. Reaves, untitled newspaper clipping, 17 September 1950, in Marks Family Papers.

34. Hale, "Good Way To Spend an Afternoon."

35. Parker, "The Marks-Schulz Family."

36. E. H. Marks, 1967 interview; E. H. Marks, *Ranch Poetry and Stories*, sound recording made in Houston, Texas, December 1968, record album in possession of Atha Marks Dimon, Barker, Texas.

2

Prairie Poetry

1. E. H. Marks, 1967 interview, transcript in Marks Family Papers, LH7 Ranch, Barker, Texas. Unless otherwise noted, subsequent quoted material is from this transcript.

2. Bob Gray, "Longhorn Raiser Emil Marks Likes Poems and 'Facts,'" unidentified newspaper clipping, 1956, Marks Family Papers.

3. Leon Hale, "I Don't Guess a Man Could Hardly Write Those Words Down," *Houston Post,* 4 April 1967; E. H. Marks, *Ranch Poetry and Stories,* sound recording made in Houston, Texas, December 1968, record album in possession of Atha Marks Dimon, Barker, Texas.

4. E. H. Marks, 1967 interview transcript; E. H. Marks, *Ranch Poetry.*

5. A similar song titled "The Texas Cowboy" appears in John A. Lomax, *Cowboy Songs and Other Frontier Ballads* (New York: Macmillan, 1910).

6. The lines are from "The Old Chisholm Trail"—"Of all songs, the most universally sung by the cowboy"—Lomax, *Cowboy Songs.*

7. Cf. "The Outlaw" by Charles B. Clark, Jr., in J. A. Lomax, *Songs of the Cattle Trail and Cow Camp* (New York: Macmillan, 1927).

8. Cf. "Texas Rangers" in Lomax, *Cowboy Songs.*

9. The fifth stanza, beginning "Brandy is brandy," is similar to the ending of "The Texian Boys," in Lomax, *Cowboy Songs.*

10. E. H. Marks, *Ranch Poetry.* Cf. "Way Out West," in Lomax, *Cowboy Songs;* also "The Old Cow-man" by Charles B. Clark, Jr., in Mary Whatley Clarke, *A Century Of Cow Business* (Fort Worth: Texas and Southwestern Cattle Raisers Association, 1976), 73.

11. Leon Hale, "Good Way To Spend an Afternoon," *Houston Post,* 3 April 1967.

12. E. H. Marks, *Ranch Poetry.*

13. Maudeen Marks, "Marks LH7 Fannin Ranch," in C. R. Faupel, ed., *The History and Heritage of Six Famous Ranches* (n.p., n.d.); Travis Marks, interview with author, Fannin, Texas, 20 September 1982; Emory Marks, interview with author, Kerrville, Texas, 3–4 December 1984.

14. Gray, "Longhorn Raiser Emil Marks Likes Poems and 'Facts.'"

15. Maudeen Marks, notes taken during conversations with E. H. Marks, in Marks Family Papers, LH7 Ranch, Barker, Texas.

16. E. H. Marks, *Ranch Poetry;* "Ranch Owner Longs For Past Rough and Ready Range Days," unidentified newspaper clipping in Marks Family Papers.

17. E. H. Marks as told to Bob Gray, "Toughest Horse I Ever Rode!" *Texas and Southwestern Horseman,* May 1965, 27; E. H. Marks, 1967 interview transcript; Joe Adcock, "Longhorn Man," *Houston Chronicle, Texas Magazine,* 27 February 1966, reprinted in *Texas Longhorn Magazine,* September 1967, 15.

18. "E. H.'s Jokes," handwritten notes in possession of Atha Marks Dimon, Barker, Texas.

3
The Addicks Years

1. E. H. Marks, 1967 interview, transcript in Marks Family Papers, LH7 Ranch, Barker, Texas.
2. Ibid.; Maudeen Marks, notes taken during conversations with E. H. Marks, in Marks Family Papers.
3. Maudeen Marks, notes; Maudeen Marks, "Marks LH7 Fannin Ranch," C. R. Faupel, ed., *The History and Heritage of Six Famous Ranches* (n.p., n.d.); Joe Adcock, "Longhorn Man," *Houston Chronicle, Texas Magazine*, 27 February 1966, reprinted in *Texas Longhorn Magazine*, September 1967, 15.
4. Travis Marks, letter to author, 24 July 1986.
5. Maudeen Marks, notes; Annette M. Parker, ed., "The Marks-Schulz Family," researched by E. Maxine Sullivan and Atha Marks Dimon, in Marks Family Papers.
6. Atha Marks Dimon, interview with author, Barker, Texas, 30 May–2 June 1985.
7. Maudeen Marks, interview with author, Kerrville, Texas, 3 December 1984.
8. Leon Hale, "Good Way To Spend an Afternoon," *Houston Post*, 3 April 1967; Adcock, "Longhorn Man."
9. Travis Marks, letter to author, 24 July 1986.
10. Maudeen Marks, Kerrville interview.
11. Inez Franz, "The LH7 Ranch," *Junior Historian*, November 1950, 13–14; Maudeen Marks, notes.
12. Emory Marks, interview with author, Kerrville, Texas, 3–4 December 1984; Atha Marks Dimon, 1985 interview.
13. Emory Marks, 1984 interview. Unless otherwise noted, subsequent quotes from Emory Marks are from this interview.
14. Emory Marks recalled that E. H. competed in rodeo roping matches riding Billy without a bridle (letter to author, 24 June 1987).
15. The closest medical help was Dr. James M. Stewart in Katy (Maudeen Marks, letter to author, 14 July 1987).
16. E. H. Marks as told to Bob Gray, "Toughest Horse I Ever Rode!" *Texas and Southwestern Horseman*, May 1965, 27–29. Used by permission.
17. Emory Marks, 1984 interview.
18. "Gates Swing Wide at LH7," *Party Line*, Houston Farm and Ranch Club, September 1958, in Marks Family Papers; Bob Gray, "Longhorn Raiser Emil Marks Likes Poems and 'Facts,'" unidentified newspaper clipping, 1956, in Marks Family Papers.
19. "Annual LH7 Ranch Rodeo to be Held Saturday and Sunday," *Houston Chronicle*, 29 May 1934; Sigman Byrd, "The Old West Rides Again in Houston's Back Yard," *Houston Press*, 11 May 1950.

20. Travis Marks, letter to author, 24 July 1986.
21. Atha Marks Dimon, letter to author, 13 June 1987.
22. Atha Marks Dimon, 1985 interview.
23. Emory Marks, 1984 interview.
24. E. H. Marks, *Ranch Poetry and Stories*, sound recording made in Houston, Texas, December 1968, record album in possession of Atha Marks Dimon, Barker, Texas.
25. Travis Marks, letter to author, 24 July 1986.
26. P. Ann Kaupp, Department of Anthropology, Smithsonian Institution, Washington, D.C., letter to author, 25 July 1988.

4

Barker Rancher

1. E. H. Marks as quoted by Marge Crumbaker, "Rustlin' Days Not Over Yet—Ask Any Cattleman," *Houston Press*, 16 January 1964.
2. Joyce Harlow, ed., "Land and Change: Park Ten's Prophetic Past," *Park Ten Community Association Bulletin*, Summer 1982.
3. Atha Marks Dimon, interview with author, Barker, Texas, 30 May–2 June 1985. Unless otherwise noted, subsequent quotes from Atha are from this interview.
4. Maudeen Marks, letter to author, 14 July 1987.
5. E. H. Marks, 1967 interview, transcript in Marks Family Papers, LH7 Ranch, Barker, Texas.
6. Ibid.
7. Maudeen Marks, 1987 letter.
8. Maudeen Marks, "The Slaughter House," typescript (n.d.), Marks Family Papers; Mike Hocutt, "Texas Longhorns Coming Back," *Houston West Side Reporter*, 19 June 1975.
9. Travis Marks, interview with author, Fannin, Texas, 20 September 1982; E. H. Marks, 1967 interview.
10. Emory Marks, interview with author, Kerrville, Texas, 3–4 December 1984; Maudeen Marks, 1987 letter. Unless otherwise noted, subsequent quotes from Emory are from the 1984 interview.
11. "Brahman Cattle Play Role in New Agriculture Era," *Houston Chronicle*, 5 February 1941; "Brahman Breeders Follow 100-Year-Old Tradition," *Houston Chronicle*, 11 February 1944.
12. Mary Whatley Clarke, *A Century of Cow Business* (Fort Worth: Texas and Southwestern Cattle Raisers Association, 1976), 241–42; "Brahman Breeders," *Houston Chronicle*.
13. Emory Marks and Maudeen Marks, interviews with author, Kerrville, Texas, 3 December 1984.
14. Bob Gray, "Longhorn Raiser Emil Marks Likes Poems and 'Facts,'" unidentified newspaper clipping, 1956, Marks Family Papers.

15. "Ranching Within Sight of City Lights," *The Cattleman*, November 1933, 24.
16. Maudeen Marks, interview with author, Bandera, Texas, 25–28 July 1984.
17. Maudeen Marks, 1984 Kerrville interview.
18. Maudeen Marks, 1987 letter.
19. Ruby Robinson, "Ranch life . . . Barker resident listens to steers, opera," *Katy Times*, 9 October 1980.
20. Maudeen Marks, from an unidentified newspaper clipping, Marks Family Papers.
21. "Student Rides, Brands and Throws 'Em Out On the Woolly Texas Plains Where Men Are Cowboys and Not Yodelers," *The Lass-O*, Texas State College for Women (n.d.), Marks Family Papers.
22. Emory Marks, letter to author, 14 August 1986.
23. Atha Marks Dimon, 1985 interview; Robinson, "Ranch life," *Katy Times*.
24. Emory Marks, letters to author, 6 March 1985 and 17 March 1986.
25. Travis Marks, 1982 interview.
26. Emory Marks, 1984 interview and letter to author, 17 March 1986.
27. Emory Marks, 1984 interview and 1986 letter.
28. "Filming 'North of 36,'" *Pioneer Magazine of Texas*, August–September 1924, 24; "Harris County Rancher Has Herd of Rare Longhorns," unidentified newspaper clipping, Marks Family Papers.
29. Atha Marks Dimon, handwritten note on flyleaf of *North of 36* (New York: Grosset & Dunlap, 1923), in Mrs. Dimon's possession, Barker, Texas.
30. John Warnasch, interview with author, Barker, Texas, 1 June 1985; Maudeen Marks, 1984 Bandera interview; Atha Marks Dimon, 1985 interview.
31. Maudeen Marks, 1984 Kerrville interview.
32. "South Texas, Southern Region's biggest and fastest growing market," *Dairymen's Digest*, Southern Region Edition, August 1984, 7–9; E. H. Marks, 1967 interview transcript.

5

BRAUHAUSER AND HENRY FORD

1. E. H. Marks as quoted in "Mein Herr, Vas Upmixed?" *Houston Chronicle*, 18 March 1956.
2. Emory Marks, interview with author, Kerrville, Texas, 3–4 December 1984. Unless otherwise noted, subsequent quotes from Emory are from this interview.
3. Maudeen Marks, interview with author, Kerrville, Texas, 3 December 1984.
4. Ibid.

5. Atha Marks Dimon, interview with author, Barker, Texas, 30 May–2 June 1985. Unless otherwise noted, subsequent quotes from Atha are from this interview.
6. Emory Marks, letter to author, 24 June 1987.
7. Emory Marks, 1984 interview and 1987 letter.
8. Atha Marks Dimon, 1985 interview and letter to author, 23 May 1988.
9. Ruby Robinson, "A. O. Miller looks back," *Katy Times*, 10 April 1983.
10. Maudeen Marks, 1984 Kerrville interview.
11. Travis Marks, letter to author, 24 July 1986.
12. Maudeen Marks, interview with author, Bandera, Texas, 25–28 July 1984; Emory Marks, 1984 interview.
13. Maudeen Marks, 1984 Bandera interview.
14. Foghorn Clancy, "Memory Trail," *Hoofs and Horns*, April 1945; "E. H. Marks of Barker Has Many Hobbies, From Longhorns to Old Bottles," unidentified newspaper clipping, Marks Family Papers, LH7 Ranch, Barker, Texas.
15. E. H. Marks, 1967 interview, transcript in Marks Family Papers; "E. H. Marks of Barker Has Many Hobbies," clipping.
16. E. H. Marks, 1967 interview transcript.

6

Maud

1. E. H. Marks, 1967 interview, transcript in Marks Family Papers, LH7 Ranch, Barker, Texas.
2. Fred Henry Smith, "Memorandum—Genealogy and Comments on Kindred Subjects," notebook in possession of Atha Marks Dimon, Barker, Texas.
3. Emory Marks and Maudeen Marks, interviews with author, Kerrville, Texas, 3 December 1984. Unless otherwise noted, subsequent quotes from Emory are from this interview.
4. Annette M. Parker, ed., "The Marks-Schulz Family," researched by E. Maxine Sullivan and Atha Marks Dimon, Marks Family Papers.
5. Maudeen Marks, 1984 Kerrville interview and letter to author, 14 July 1987.
6. Maudeen Marks, 1984 Kerrville interview.
7. Ibid.
8. "Service Held for Mrs. E. H. Marks," obituary, reproduced in Parker, "The Marks-Schulz Family."
9. E. H. Marks, 1967 interview transcript.
10. Atha Marks Dimon, interview with author, Barker, Texas, 30 May–2 June 1985. Unless otherwise noted, subsequent quotes from Atha are from this interview.

11. Emory Marks, 1984 interview.
12. "Service Held for Mrs. E. H. Marks," in Parker.
13. Travis Marks, letter to author, 24 July 1986; Emory Marks, letter to author, 17 March 1986.
14. Maudeen Marks, 1987 letter.
15. Maudeen Marks, interview with author, Bandera, Texas, 25–28 July 1984; 1987 letter.
16. Atha Marks Dimon, 1985 interview.
17. Atha Marks Dimon, letter to the *Longhorn Scene*, 26 January 1983.
18. Travis Marks, letter to author, 24 July 1986.
19. As quoted by Stan Redding, unidentified newspaper clipping, 17 June 1973, Marks Family Papers.
20. Emory Marks, letter to author, 17 March 1986; Ruby Robinson, "Ranch life... Barker resident listens to steers, opera," *Katy Times*, 9 October 1980.
21. Atha Marks Dimon, 1985 interview.
22. Maudeen Marks, 1984 Kerrville interview.
23. Ibid. and 1987 letter.
24. Maudeen Marks, 1987 letter.
25. Maudeen Marks, 1984 Kerrville interview.
26. Ibid.
27. Emory Marks, 1984 interview and letter to author, 14 August 1986.
28. Smith, "Memorandum—Genealogy and Comments on Kindred Subjects."

7
Real Cowboys and Rodeos

1. E. H. Marks, *Ranch Poetry and Stories*, sound recording made in Houston, Texas, December 1968, record album in possession of Atha Marks Dimon, Barker, Texas. The lines are from E. H.'s slightly altered version of "Cowboys for Sure" by S. Omar Barker, in *Songs of the Saddlemen* (Denver: Sage Books, 1954).
2. Atha Marks Dimon, interview with author, Barker, Texas, 30 May–2 June 1985. Unless otherwise noted, quotes from Atha are from this interview.
3. "Student Rides, Brands and Throws 'Em Out On the Woolly Texas Plains Where Men Are Cowboys and Not Yodelers," *The Lass-O*, Texas State College for Women (n.d.), Marks Family Papers, LH7 Ranch, Barker, Texas; E. H. Marks, 1967 interview, transcript in Marks Family Papers. Unless otherwise noted, subsequent quotes from E. H. are from this interview.
4. Wilhelmina Beane, "LH7 Ranch," in *Texas Thirties* (San Antonio: The Naylor Company, 1963), 14.

5. Emory Marks, interview with author, Kerrville, Texas, 3–4 December 1984. Unless otherwise noted, subsequent quotes from Emory are from this interview.
6. Maudeen Marks, interview with author, Kerrville, Texas, 3 December 1984.
7. Beane, "LH7 Ranch," 11.
8. E. H. Marks, 1967 interview transcript; S. Omar Barker, "Code of the Cow Country," in *Songs of the Saddlemen* (Denver: Sage Books, 1954).
9. E. H. Marks, 1967 interview transcript.
10. E. H. Marks, 1967 interview transcript; Maudeen Marks, "Uncle Rufe & Tanta Lula," typescript (n.d.), Marks Family Papers.
11. Beane, "LH7 Ranch," 12.
12. Travis Marks, letter to author, 24 July 1986.
13. Beane, "LH7 Ranch," 13.
14. "Picturesque Cowboys and Herds of Milling Cattle Found Near City," *Houston Chronicle*, 28 May 1930.
15. "Marks Ranch Rodeo to be Held May 6-7," *Houston Chronicle*, 16 April 1944.
16. John Moore, "Salt Grass Trail Folk Elect, Eat, Ban Liquor," *Houston Post*, 19 September 1955; "Gates Swing Wide at LH7," *Party Line*, Houston Farm and Ranch Club, September 1958; Marge Crumbaker, "Rustlin' Days Not Over Yet—Ask Any Cattleman," *Houston Press*, 16 January 1964.
17. "Two-Day Rodeo At LH-7 Ranch To Open Saturday," *Houston Post*, 2 May 1941.
18. Inez Franz, "The LH7 Ranch," *Junior Historian*, November 1950, 13–14.
19. "Rodeo and Barbecue at Barker Sunday," unidentified newspaper clipping in Marks Family Papers.
20. Beane, "LH7 Ranch," 18.
21. "Airplane Cowboy Is Injured in Fall From Rope Ladder," unidentified newspaper clipping in Marks Family Papers.
22. "Annual LH7 Ranch Rodeo to be Held Saturday and Sunday," *Houston Chronicle*, 29 May 1934.
23. Franz, "The LH7 Ranch."
24. Maudeen Marks, 1984 Kerrville interview.
25. Travis Marks, 1986 letter.
26. Maudeen Marks, 1984 Kerrville interview.

8

Danger on the Range

1. E. H. Marks as quoted by "Ranching Within Sight of City Lights," *The Cattleman*, November 1933, 24.

2. Emory Marks, interview with author, Kerrville, Texas, 3–4 December 1984. Unless otherwise noted, subsequent quotes from Emory are from this interview.

3. Maudeen Marks, interview with author, Kerrville, Texas, 3 December 1984. Unless otherwise noted, subsequent quotes from Maudeen are from this interview.

4. Atha Marks Dimon, interview with author, Barker, Texas, 30 May–2 June 1985. Unless otherwise noted, subsequent quotes from Atha are from this interview.

5. Emory Marks, letter to author, 28 March 1986.

6. "Objects of Prehistoric Origin Lie Under Springs in County, Rancher Thinks," newspaper clipping in Marks Family Papers, LH7 Ranch, Barker, Texas.

7. Ibid.

8. Ibid.

9. *The Handbook of Texas* (Austin: The Texas State Historical Association, 1952), s.v. "cattle tick"; Loretta Ewart, "'Texas' Fever Quarantine Nearly Fatal to Early Cattle Industry," *Independent Cattlemen*, June 1986, 9.

10. Mary Whatley Clarke, *A Century of Cow Business* (Fort Worth: Texas and Southwestern Cattle Raisers Association, 1976), 65–66.

11. Maudeen Marks, 1984 Kerrville interview.

12. Travis Marks, interview with author, Fannin, Texas, 20 September 1982; *The Handbook of Texas*.

13. Maudeen Marks and Emory Marks, 1984 Kerrville interviews.

14. Ibid.

15. Wilhelmina Beane, "LH7 Ranch," in *Texas Thirties* (San Antonio: The Naylor Company, 1963), 17.

16. E. H. Marks, 1967 interview, transcript in Marks Family Papers. Subsequent quotes from E. H. are from this interview.

17. Ruby Robinson, "Open prairies give way to Houston skyline," *Katy Times*, 10 April 1983; Atha Marks Dimon, 1985 interview.

9

DELIRIUM AND DEPRESSION

1. E. H. Marks as quoted in "Rancher Retains LH7 Cattle Brand," newspaper clipping in Marks Family Papers, LH7 Ranch, Barker, Texas.

2. "Picturesque Cowboys and Herds of Milling Cattle Found Near City," *Houston Chronicle*, 28 May 1930.

3. Travis Marks, interview with author, Fannin, Texas, 20 September 1982. Subsequent quotes from Travis are from this interview.

4. Travis Marks, letter to author, 24 July 1986.

5. "Comes In From West on Longhorned Bovine," newspaper clipping in Marks Family Papers.
6. "Police Chief Rivals Sheriff, Wears 12-Gallon Stetson and Rides Longhorn Steer," newspaper clipping in Marks Family Papers.
7. "Tex and Steer in Town," newspaper clipping in Marks Family Papers.
8. "Texas Cowboy on Steer Here, Washington Bound," newspaper clipping in Marks Family Papers; "Tex and Steer in Town," clipping.
9. "Cowboy Riding Pet Steer Brings Wild West to City," newspaper clipping in Marks Family Papers.
10. Emory Marks, letter to author, 15 July 1986.
11. "State Police Shelter Steer-Mounted Texan," *Wilmington* (Del.) *Morning News*, 1 May 1933; Robert Donaldson, unidentified newspaper clipping in Marks Family Papers.
12. Maudeen Marks, "This Is No Bull" (typescript), June 1987, Marks Family Papers.
13. Maudeen Marks, interview with author, Kerrville, Texas, 3 December 1984. Unless otherwise noted, subsequent quotes from Maudeen are from this interview.
14. Emory Marks, interview with author, Kerrville, Texas, 3–4 December 1984. Unless otherwise noted, subsequent quotes from Emory are from this interview.
15. Emory Marks, 1984 interview.
16. Maudeen Marks, "The Slaughter House" (typescript, n.d.), Marks Family Papers.
17. Maudeen Marks, letter to author, 14 July 1987.
18. Atha Marks Dimon, interview with author, Barker, Texas, 30 May–2 June 1985. Unless otherwise noted, subsequent quotes from Atha are from this interview.
19. Wilhelmina Beane, "LH7 Ranch," in *Texas Thirties* (San Antonio: The Naylor Company, 1963), 11, 18.
20. Maudeen Marks, interview with author, Bandera, Texas, 25–28 July 1984 and 1987 letter.
21. Maudeen Marks, 1984 Bandera interview.
22. Maudeen Marks, 1984 Kerrville interview and 1987 letter.
23. "Passing of LH7 Ranch Looms as Paddock-Marks Partnership Is Dissolved," newspaper clipping, 17 January 1936, in Marks Family Papers; "Gossip of the Livestock Realm," *The Cattleman*, February 1936, 31.
24. Maudeen Marks, 1984 Kerrville interview.
25. "Rancher Retains LH7 Cattle Brand," clipping; "Passing of LH7 Ranch Looms," clipping; "Gossip of the Livestock Realm," *The Cattleman*.
26. "San Jacinto Ceremony to be Broadcast," *Houston Chronicle*, 24 March 1936.
27. Emory Marks, letter to author, 17 March 1986.
28. Emory Marks, 1984 interview and 1986 letter.

29. "LH7 Rodeo at Barker Draws 7,000 Persons," *Houston Chronicle*, 4 May 1936.

30. E. H. Marks, 1967 interview, transcript in Marks Family Papers; Anne Nelson, "Tale of a Rancher—Emil H. Marks," *Junior Historian*, November 1966, 30–32.

31. Atha Marks Dimon, 1985 interview; Emory Marks, 1984 interview.

10

LH7 LONGHORNS

1. E. H. Marks as quoted in "E. H. Marks of Barker Has Many Hobbies, From Longhorns to Old Bottles," newspaper clipping in Marks Family Papers, LH7 Ranch, Barker, Texas.

2. E. H. Marks, 1967 interview, transcript in Marks Family Papers. Unless otherwise noted, subsequent quotes from E. H. are from this transcript.

3. Travis Marks, interview with author, Fannin, Texas, 20 September 1982. Unless otherwise noted, subsequent quotes from Travis are from this interview.

4. Maudeen Marks, interview with author, Bandera, Texas, 25–28 July 1984.

5. "E. H. Marks Has Many Hobbies," clipping; Maudeen Marks, letter to author, 14 July 1987.

6. "Harris County Rancher Has Herd of Rare Longhorns," newspaper clipping in Marks Family Papers.

7. Joe Adcock, "Longhorn Man," *Houston Chronicle, Texas Magazine*, 27 February 1966; reprinted in *Texas Longhorn Magazine*, September 1967, 15.

8. "E. H. Said," 1969, notes by Maudeen Marks reproduced in "The Marks-Schulz Family," Annette M. Parker, ed., Marks Family Papers. ("During the months before his death, September 1969, I sat at my father's bedside and wrote down his observations on Texas Longhorn cattle. These are excerpts from those notes."—M. Marks.)

9. Ibid.

10. Ibid. and E. H. Marks, 1967 interview transcript.

11. "E. H. Said"; Adcock, "Longhorn Man."

12. "E. H. Said."

13. "E. H. Said"; E. H. Marks, 1967 interview transcript.

14. Ibid.

15. "E. H. Said"; "No Longhorns? Take That Back," *Houston Press,* 18 January 1955.

16. Maudeen Marks, 1987 letter.

17. "E. H. Said."

18. Maudeen Marks, 1984 Bandera interview and 1987 letter.

19. The Texas Longhorn Breeders Association of America was established in San Antonio in 1964 to recognize the Longhorn as a distinct breed of cattle, protect the breed's heritage, preserve its history, encourage breeding practices that would promote Longhorn purity, and create a greater public awareness of the cattle. The TLBAA relocated to Fort Worth in 1981. Distinguished for its purity, the Marks LH7 Longhorn bloodline is one of the seven foundation "families" of the TLBAA registry.

20. "Harris County Rancher Has Herd of Rare Longhorns," newspaper clipping.

21. Foghorn Clancy, "Memory Trail," *Hoofs and Horns,* April 1945.

22. "Uncle Jim Fairchild Sticks to His Covered Wagon, Finds It Good," newspaper clipping, 7 November 1937, in Marks Family Papers.

23. "Covered Wagon Arrives Here From Far West," *Southside News Notes,* (Jacksonville, Florida) newspaper clipping in Marks Family Papers.

24. Ibid.

25. Ibid. and "Uncle Jimmy, Fiddler Champion, Is Buried," *Houston Post,* 21 February 1957.

26. "Marks Ranch Rodeo to be Held May 6–7," *Houston Chronicle,* 16 April 1944.

27. "Cowboys Set for Annual Rodeo Opening Saturday at Barker," *Houston Post,* 29 April 1945.

28. E. L. Summers, "Emil Marks Is Honored by Area Dairymen," newspaper clipping in Marks Family Papers.

29. Atha Marks Dimon, letter to author, 13 June 1987.

30. E. L. Summers, "Rancher's Pine Thickets Pay Off as Shelter for Cattle," *Houston Chronicle,* 28 January 1951.

31. E. H. Marks, 1967 interview transcript.

32. Ibid.

33. Travis Marks, 1982 interview.

11

In The City's Shadow: A Clash of Two Cultures

1. E. H. Marks as quoted in "Ranching Within Sight of City Lights," *The Cattleman,* November 1933, 24.

2. Atha Marks Dimon, interview with author, Barker, Texas, 30 May—2 June 1985. Unless otherwise noted, subsequent quotes from Atha are from this interview.

3. Maudeen Marks, interview with author, Bandera, Texas, 25—28 July 1984. Unless otherwise noted, subsequent quotes from Maudeen are from this interview.

4. "Ex-owners Want Park Land Back," *Houston Post,* 4 June 1960; Hugh Berry, telephone interview with author, 9 September 1987.

5. "Three Dams to End Houston Floods," *Engineering News-Record*, August 13, 1942, 107-8; "Ex-Owners Want Park Land Back," *Houston Post*.
6. "Marks Ranch Rodeo Canceled," *Houston Chronicle*, 15 April 1951.
7. Hugh Berry, 1987 telephone interview; "Flood Protection for Houston," *Engineering News-Record,* 26 August 1948, 8; "Addicks-Barker Citizens Argue for Return of Land," *Houston Post*, 14 June 1960.
8. E. H. Marks, letter to the editor, *Houston Press*, 2 June 1960, copy in Marks Family Papers, LH7 Ranch, Barker, Texas.
9. "Addicks-Barker Citizens Argue for Return of Land," *Houston Post*.
10. Ibid.
11. "Houston citizens approve record city bond issue," *Engineering News-Record*, 23 October 1941, 78.

12
The Last Trail

1. E. H. Marks as quoted in "Ranch Owner Longs for Past Rough and Ready Range Days," newspaper clipping in Marks Family Papers, LH7 Ranch, Barker, Texas.
2. George Fuermann, *Houston: Land of the Big Rich* (Garden City, N.Y.: Doubleday, 1951), 143; "Saga of the Salt Grass Trail," Circle S Association, 15 February 1964, booklet in possession of Atha Marks Dimon, Barker, Texas.
3. Maudeen Marks, letter to author, 14 July 1987.
4. Ibid.
5. John Warnasch, interview with author, Barker, Texas, 1 June 1985.
6. Ibid. and Maudeen Marks, 1987 letter.
7. "Saga of the Salt Grass Trail."
8. "Saga of the Salt Grass Trail"; Joe Adcock, "Longhorn Man," *Houston Chronicle, Texas Magazine,* 27 February 1966, reprinted in *Texas Longhorn Magazine,* September 1967, 15.
9. John Moore, "Riders Strike Tall Salt Grass," *Houston Post*, 2 February 1954.
10. "1000 Riders A-Headin' to Houston!" *Houston Press,* 1 January 1954.
11. John Moore, "No Better Spot For A Salt Grass Session," *Houston Post,* 26 August 1955.
12. Pete Gilpin, "Houston Boasts Industry, But Ranches Helped Make It Great," *Houston Chronicle, Texas Magazine,* 16 February 1958.
13. Louis Blackburn, "Big-Time Ranchers Expect Good Year," *Houston Press,* 2 February 1954.
14. "Picturesque Cowboys and Herds of Milling Cattle Found Near City," *Houston Chronicle,* 28 May 1930.
15. Frank X. Tolbert, "Texas," *Dallas Morning News,* 23 March 1959.
16. Travis Marks, letter to author, 7 December 1982.

17. Irwin Frank, "Texas Talk Dead Serious With Oldtime Cattleman," *Sedalia* (Mo.) *Democrat*, 23 February 1958; Bob Gray, "Longhorn Raiser Emil Marks Likes Poems and 'Facts,'" newspaper clipping, 1956, in Marks Family Papers.

18. Phyllis Battelle, "Emil Marks Sets the Record Straight," *Houston Chronicle,* 19 March 1956.

19. George Fuermann, "Post Card," *Houston Post,* 28 August 1958. Used by permission.

20. John Warnasch, 1985 interview; Atha Marks Dimon, interview with author, Barker, Texas, 30 May–2 June 1985.

21. Leonard Maltin, *The Disney Films* (New York: Crown Publishers, 1984).

22. Adcock, "Longhorn Man."

23. Emory Marks, interview with author, Kerrville, Texas, 3–4 December 1984.

24. Maudeen Marks, 1987 letter.

25. E. H. Marks, *Ranch Poetry and Stories*, sound recording made in Houston, Texas, December 1968, record album in possession of Atha Marks Dimon, Barker, Texas.

26. E. H. Marks, 1967 interview, transcript in Marks Family Papers. Unless otherwise noted, subsequent quotes from E. H. are from this transcript.

27. Travis Marks, letter to author, 24 July 1986.

28. E. H. Marks, *Ranch Poetry and Stories*.

29. "A Resolution," passed and approved by unanimous vote of the Houston City Council, 17 September 1969, reproduced in "The Marks-Schulz Family," Annette M. Parker, ed., Marks Family Papers.

BIBLIOGRAPHY

Unpublished Material

Dimon, Atha Marks. Letters to author, 13 June 1987; 8 April 1988; 23 May 1988.
Kaupp, P. Ann. Letter to author, 25 July 1988.
Marks, Emil H. *Ranch Poetry and Stories*. December 1968. Sound recording in possession of Atha Marks Dimon. Barker, Texas.
Marks, Emory. Letters to author, 6 March 1985; 17 March 1986; 28 March 1986; 15 July 1986; 14 August 1986; 24 June 1987.
Marks, Maudeen. Letters to author, 14 July 1987; 29 July 1987.
———. "The Slaughter House." n.d. (typescript).
———. "This Is No Bull." June 1987 (typescript).
———. "Uncle Rufe & Tanta Lula." n.d. (typescript).
Marks, Travis. Letters to author, 7 December 1982; 24 July 1986.
Marks Family Papers. In possession of Maudeen Marks and Atha Marks Dimon. Barker, Texas.
Parker, Annette M., ed. "The Marks-Schulz Family." Researched by E. Maxine Sullivan and Atha Marks Dimon. Barker, Texas.
"Saga of the Salt Grass Trail." Circle S Association. 15 February 1964. Booklet in possession of Atha Marks Dimon. Barker, Texas.
Smith, Fred Henry. "Memorandum—Genealogy and Comments on Kindred Subjects." Notebook in possession of Atha Marks Dimon. Barker, Texas.

Interviews

Berry, Hugh. Telephone conversations with author, 9 September 1987; 18 September 1987.
Dimon, Atha Marks. Interview with author. Barker, Texas, 30 May–2 June 1985.
Marks, Emil H. Interview with unidentifed Houston-area journalists. Barker, Texas, 1967. Typed transcript in Marks Family Papers.
Marks, Emory. Interview with author. Kerrville, Texas, 3–4 December 1984.
Marks, Maudeen. Interviews with author. Bandera, Texas, 25–28 July 1984; Kerrville, Texas, 3 December 1984; Bandera, Texas, 31 August 1987.
Marks, Travis. Interview with author. Fannin, Texas, 20 September 1982.
Warnasch, John. Interview with author. Barker, Texas, 1 June 1985.

Newspapers

Dallas Morning News
Houston Chronicle
Houston Chronicle, Texas Magazine
Houston Post
Houston Press
Houston West Side Reporter
Katy Times (Katy, Texas)
Sedalia Democrat (Sedalia, Mo.)
Wilmington Morning News (Wilmington, Del.)

Articles

Adcock, Joe. "The Longhorn Man." *Texas Longhorn Magazine*, September 1967: 14–16.

Arnold, Darrell. "Marks Longhorns: Best of the Texas Tradition." *Texas Longhorn Journal*, March/April 1985: 108–12.

Chadwick, Susan. "The Trail Ride." *Texas Monthly,* March 1985: 144.

Clancy, Foghorn. "Memory Trail." *Hoofs and Horns*, April 1945.

Ewart, Loretta. "'Texas' Fever Quarantine Nearly Fatal to Early Cattle Industry." *Independent Cattlemen*, June 1986: 8–9.

"Filming 'North of 36.'" *Pioneer Magazine of Texas*, August–September 1924: 24.

"Flood Protection for Houston." *Engineering News-Record*, August 26, 1948: 8.

Franz, Inez. "The LH7 Ranch." *Junior Historian*, November 1950: 13–14.

Goodnight, Chas. "The Cattle Trail and its Effect on Finance and Civilization." *Pioneer Magazine of Texas*, December 1925: 6.

"Gossip of the Livestock Realm." *The Cattleman*, February 1936: 31.

Harlow, Joyce, ed. "Land and Change: Park Ten's Prophetic Past." *Park Ten Community Association Bulletin*, Summer 1982: 3.

———. "Wolff, Morgan and Company: Footprints for the Future." *Park Ten Community Association Bulletin*, Summer 1982: 2.

"Houston citizens approve record city bond issue." *Engineering News-Record*, October 23, 1941: 78.

Hoyt, Alan. "History of the Texas Longhorns." *Texas Longhorn Journal*, March/April 1983, May/June 1983.

Marks, Emil. As told to Bob Gray. "Toughest Horse I Ever Rode!" *Texas and Southwestern Horseman*, May 1965: 27–29.

Marks, Maudeen. "Marks LH7 Fannin Ranch." *The History and Heritage of Six Famous Ranches*, C. R. Faupel, ed. (n.d.)

Morris, Eleanor. "The LH7–Ranch for a Lady." *Texas Highways*, September 1985: 4–9.

Nelson, Anne. "Tale of a Rancher–Emil H. Marks." *Junior Historian*, November 1966: 30–32.

Nicholas, William H. "America's 'Meat on the Hoof.'" *National Geographic*, January 1952: 65.
"Ranching Within Sight of City Lights." *The Cattleman*, November 1933: 24.
Saunders, George W. "The Old Trail." *The Cattleman*, March 1918: 143–47.
Sizemore, Deborah. "Emil H. Marks—Longhorn resurrectionist of long ago." *Longhorn Scene*, February 1983: 40–44.
———. "Milby Butler, 1889–1971. The Butler Longhorns Live On." *Longhorn Scene*, October 1983: 85-88.
"South Texas, Southern Region's biggest and fastest growing market." *Dairymen's Digest*, Southern Region Edition, August 1984: 7–9.
"A Tradition of Preserving the True Longhorn." *Texas Longhorn Journal*, November/December 1982: 116–17.
"Three Dams to End Houston Floods." *Engineering News-Record*, August 13, 1942: 107–8.
Weigard, Tim. "Ranger: Travis Marks' Remarkable Riding Steer Is Captured in Bronze." *Longhorn Scene*, April 1985: 65–68.

Books

Barker, S. Omar. *Songs of the Saddlemen*. Denver: Sage Books, 1954.
Beane, Wilhelmina. *Texas Thirties*. San Antonio: The Naylor Company, 1963.
Clancy, Foghorn. *My Fifty Years in Rodeo: Living With Cowboys, Horses and Danger*. San Antonio: The Naylor Company, 1952.
Clarke, Mary Whatley. *A Century of Cow Business*. Fort Worth: Texas and Southwestern Cattle Raisers Association, 1976.
Dobie, J. Frank. *A Vaquero of the Brush Country*. Austin: University of Texas Press, 1981.
Fuermann, George. *Houston: Land of the Big Rich*. Garden City, New York: Doubleday, 1951.
Hough, Emerson. *North of 36*. New York: Grosset & Dunlap, 1923.
Lomax, John A. *Songs of the Cattle Trail and Cow Camp*. New York: Macmillan, 1927.
Lomax, John A., and Alan Lomax. *Cowboy Songs and Other Frontier Ballads*. New York: Macmillan, 1910.
Maltin, Leonard. *The Disney Films*. New York: Crown Publishers, 1984.

INDEX

Abilene, Texas, 92
Addicks Reservoir, 46, 176
Addicks, Texas, 2, 4, 7, 10, 32–34, 35, 36, 37, 39, 42, 43, 50, 52, 69, 95, 97, 99, 112, 122, 126–27, 139, 149
Addicks-Barker flood control area, 174–76
Adkins, Eleanor, 58
Adkins, Milburn, 121–22
Agricultural and Mechanical College of Texas. *See* Texas A&M University
Allen, Rex, 186
American Brahman Breeders Association (ABBA), 54
Anders, William, 3
Anderson, Eric, 113
Anderson, John Wesley, 34–35
Anderson Ranch, 128, 151
Angus cattle, 78, 153
armadillos, 44
Arness, James, 183
Arnold, Frank, 112
Atlantic Coast, 165
Atlas (bull), 53
Ayr, Scotland, 86
Baca, Elfego, 148
Baker, Mason, 10
Bald (steer), 148, 164
Bandera, Texas, 195
Baptist Sunday School, 92
Baraboo, Wisconsin, 85
Barker, Ed, 10, 49
Barker (steer), 138–41, 164
Barker, Texas, 44, 49, 50, 52, 56, 57, 59, 65, 76, 88–89, 111, 117, 130, 131–32, 137, 146, 148, 163, 186–87, 193, 195

Barker Dam, 175
Barker Home Demonstration Club, 88, 193
Barker Reservoir, 126, 176
Barker Rural Telephone Company, 134
Barker School, 97
Barker Store, 138
Barrow, Clyde, 130–31
Beane, Wilhelmina, 111
Bear Creek, Texas, 2, 3, 4, 5, 9, 10, 71, 151, 194
Bear Creek community hall, 68, 69, 70–71, 72
Bear Creek Park, 176
Beaumont, Texas, 32
Beebe, Doctor, 91
Beery, Noah, 61, 62
Belew, Tom, 110
Ben (horse), 115
Big Feast, 71, 72
Big Freeze (December 1924), 121
Big Thicket, 21, 32
Billy (horse), 36, 37–39, 57
Binford, Thomas Abner (T. A), 77, 112, 139, 181
Blakely, Bassett, 61, 62, 63
Blakely ranch, 61, 62, 132
Bleick, Henrietta, 7–8
Bleik, Mrs., 35
Blue Earth, Minnesota, 85
Bodak, Katy, 135
Bojan (bull), 53
Bonner, Mr., 143
Borden, Abel Pierce (A. P.), 53
Bos indicus, 54
Bowallopers (steer), 62
Brahman cattle, 53–54, 76, 78, 113, 138, 155, 163, 165, 184–85

217

Brandt, Adolph, 7
Brandt, Emma, 7
Brandt family, 3
Bray's Bayou Slough, Texas, 8
Brazos River, 9, 11, 39
Brenham, Texas, 179, 181
Brinks Security, 129
Brookshire, Texas, 37, 42
Buffalo, New York, 140
Buffalo Bayou, 2, 4, 7, 46, 64, 65, 122, 125, 130, 173–74
Bundick, Athene, 86, 186, 193
Bundick, Blevins, 193
Burro Alley, Santa Fe, N. M., 79–80
Burton, Mose, 59, 61, 104, 106, 115, 131–32, 144
Butler, "Old" or "Boss," 17–18
Captain of the Great Lakes. *See* Smith, Myron Thaddeus
Carrillo, Leo ("Cisco Kid"), 183
Carter, "Old Man," 39, 92
Casey, Bob, 175
Cattleman, 54
Center, Texas, 59
Central Texas, 6, 180
Chicago, Illinois, 55
Christmas, 50, 65, 100
Christopher, Jane, 183
Cisco Kid. *See* Carrillo, Leo
Civil War, 4, 5, 6, 7, 9, 10, 81
Clancy, Foghorn, 58
Clark, Martha Elizabeth. *See* Smith, Martha Clark
Clinton, Dan, 89, 166
Clodine, Texas, 57, 88, 130, 132
Coca-Cola Company, 116–17
Coleman County, Texas, 92
College of Industrial Arts. *See* Texas Woman's University
College Station, Texas, 89
Colorado River, 5, 21
Colorado Springs, Colorado, 77
Columbus, Christopher, 14
Confederacy, 4
Coon, Leiber, 27–28
Coon's Bayou, Texas, 3
Corpus Christi, Texas, 5
County Donegal, Ireland, 86
Cowboy life—
 branding time, 111–13
 meals, 24–26
 pay, 22, 24
 poetry and songs, 13–28
 rodeos, 103–19
 typical day, 110
Cox, W. O., 172
Crawford, Mr., 27–28
Cypress community hall, 68, 69
Cypress, Texas, 117
Cypress Creek, 3
Dan Moody (bull), 53
Davis sisters, 131
Delco electric system, 51, 89
Denton, Texas, 144
Depression, 139, 141, 143, 145, 162
Devil Springs, 125, 146, 174
Dickson, Nova Bryant, 193
Dimon, Atha Marks. *See* Marks, Atha
Dimon, Richard de Huquenelle, 193
Dix, Richard, 62
Dobie, J. Frank, 159–60, 186
Dodge City, Kansas, 187
Dodge Straight Eight (automobile), 78
Dodge Victory Six (automobile), 51, 78, 81, 82
Dollar (a drifter), 77
Double Trouble (bull), 113
Draemer, Louise, 58, 130
du Pont gunpowder factory, 3
"Duck Ranch," 151
Durham cattle, 153
Dutchmen, 69
Dying Swan, The, 96
Eagle (horse), 107–08
Earhart, Amelia, 80
East Texas, 22, 32, 59, 60, 153–54
East-West Narrow Gauge Railroad, 8
Easter, 139
Eastern Air Lines, 115
Ehlert, Helena Matzke, 134
Elmore family, 92
Embry, Henry, 111
Emerson (a horsethief), 27–28
Enke, Linda. *See* Marks, Linda

Evans, Dale, 183
Fairbanks, Texas, 34, 36, 52, 59, 87, 146
Fairchild, Uncle Jim, 164–65
Fannin, Texas, 194
Farmer's Cooperative Market, 65
Flaherty, Pat, 180–81
Ford, Henry, 71, 81, 143
Ford automobile, 43, 50, 71, 76, 77, 78, 79, 81, 90, 93–94, 97–98, 109, 118–19, 143, 185
Fort Bend County, Texas, 53
Fort Worth, Texas, 56
Fountain of Youth, 165
4-H Club, 88, 145
Frederick William IV, 2
Frenchie (horse), 62
Friends of the Maud Marks Library, 194
From the Plains to the Pulpit, 35
Frost, J. M. (Milo), 45–46
Frost, J. M., Sr., 53
Fuermann, George, 185
Galli–Curci, Amelita, 96
Galveston, Texas, 1, 3, 5
Galveston Bay, 33, 74
Galveston hurricane (1915), 44
Galveston Island, 44
Galveston Storm (Great) (1900), 33
Garner, John Nance "Cactus Jack," 138, 141
Garner, Mrs., 141
Gastman family, 71
German community, 72
German community halls. *See* Bear Creek, Cypress, Spring Branch, White Oak
German language, 67–68, 87
German Methodists, 2
Gertrude (housekeeper), 88
Giezendanner, Charles, 173, 180
Giezendanner Agency, 173, 180
Gilpin, Pete, 184
Goliad, Texas, 194
Goose Creek, Texas, 82
Gorman, Bill, 103, 109, 111, 128, 147
Grand Prize Beer, 116
Granger, Dorothy, 75
Great Plains, 55
Greer, Jackie, 176
Grisbee, Charlie, 104
Groeschke, George, 149–50
Groeschke, Henry, 32–33
Groeschke, Laurence, 50
Groeschke family, 1, 3
Gulf Building, 137
Gulf Coast, 121, 124, 126, 129, 166, 180–81, 187
Gulf Coast ranches, 53, 54, 154, 158
Gulf of Mexico, 1, 5, 33
Gunsmoke, 183
Habermacher, Johnny, 46
Habermacher, Mason, 112, 141
Habermacher, W. J., Sr., 7–8
Habermacher Crossing, 8
Habermacher family, 3
Habermacher House, 7–8
Habermacher Station, 8
Hamilton, Raymond, 131
Hammond, Asher, 46
Happy Hawkins (horse), 88
Harris, Jack, 180
Harris, T. J., 74
Harris County, Texas, 2, 3, 5, 7, 31, 43, 56, 61, 62, 67, 68, 71, 77, 88–89, 111, 113, 127–28, 131, 166, 173–74, 176, 183–84, 186, 193, 194, 196
Harris County Court, 9
Harris County Heritage Society, 196
Harvard Elementary, 98
Heard, Percy F., 139
Heights Hospital, 129
Hempstead, Texas, 24
Henke and Pillot, 36, 52
Hereford cattle, 78, 153, 155
Herklotz, Jim, 103
Hermann, George, 21
Hermann Hospital, 191
Hermann Park, 21–22
Hicks, Tommy, 75
High Plains, 78
Hillendahl, "Old Man," 73
Hillendahl, Willibald, 10
Hillendahl place, 36
Hockley, Texas, 37, 57

Hodges, Uncle Ben, 104
Hollywood, 61
Holt, Jack, 61
Hoover, Buck, 114
Hot Wells, Texas, 117
Hough, Emerson, 61
Houghton, Jeanne, 195
Houston, Andrew Jackson, 148
Houston, Sam, 35, 148
Houston, Texas, 2, 7, 8, 10, 27, 33, 35, 36, 39, 40, 49, 53, 54, 57, 59, 64, 67, 74, 76, 77, 81, 87, 89–90, 91, 94, 96–98, 111, 113–14, 118–19, 121–22, 127, 132, 133, 137, 139, 142, 144, 147–48, 150, 161, 163–64, 172, 173–75, 181–83, 184–85, 186
Houston Chamber of Commerce, 172
Houston Chronicle, 137, 148, 166–67, 183
Houston City Council, 191
Houston City Hall Square, 65
Houston Fat Stock Show, 163, 172–73, 180, 182
Houston Livestock Show. See Houston Fat Stock Show
Houston National Bank, 142, 193
Houston Post, 166, 183–85
Houston Press, 175, 182, 184
Houston Ship Channel, 173
Houston Symphony, 97
Humble Oil Club, 115
Huntsville, Texas, 59, 60, 75
Impossible (bull), 113
Indian territory, 6
Indianola, Texas, 2, 5, 194
Indians, 7
Isham (goat), 164
Jacksonville, Florida, 164
James Hogg Junior High, 98
Jennings, Al, 148
John Garner (steer), 155
Johnson, Lyndon B., 175
Jones, Charley, 104
Jones, Thelmore, 104
Jones, "Uncle" Aaron, 113
Jordan, Mrs. Armaderry "Fairy," 144
Kane, Bebe. See Granger, Dorothy

Katy, Texas, 37, 39, 43, 51, 56, 65, 75, 76, 186, 194
Katy Railroad, 10, 88, 193
Kerrville, Texas, 193
Khedive (bull), 53
Kiefer, A. H., 64
Knolle, Doctor Guy, 181
Kobs, Fritz, 68
Koennecke, Fritz, 6
Koy, Dick, 128
KPRC radio and TV, 180–81
La Porte, Texas, 74
Langham Creek, 46
Laro, Arthur, 180
Lauder, Sir Harry, 96
Laurel and Hardy, 34
Leo (employee), 107
Letitia, Texas, 2, 11
Lewis's Oyster Parlor, 144
LH7 brand, 31, 147
LH7 Peach, 51
LH7 Ranch, 35, 51, 59, 62, 88, 93–94, 117, 122, 127
LH7 Ranch and Resort, 195
LH7 Ranch Rodeo, 113–17, 129, 139, 149, 161, 166, 174
Liberty Bonds, 76
Lions Club, 185
Lockett, Reese, 179–82
Loma Linda nightclub, 62
Lomax, Claude, 37
Lomax, Mr., 37
Long Beach, California, 81
Longhorn cattle, 6, 7, 13, 16, 35, 52, 61, 62, 63, 78, 96, 104, 126, 138, 139, 148, 149, 153–68, 184, 186–87, 194, 195
Longhorns, The, 159
Lou (horse), 36
Louis H. Hubbard Literary Club, 176
Louisiana Purchase Exposition, 33
Lubbock, Francis R., Governor, 4
Lucius B. ("Old Lucius"), 42–43
Lyons meat market, 52
McAdams, J. F., 75–76
McCormack, John, 96
McDaniel, Samuel Franklin "Tex," 138–41, 164, 195

McFarland's Auto Sales, 43
McMasters, Dan, 61
Madison Square Garden, 114
Marks, Adolf, 3
Marks, Adolph, 5
Marks, Albert, 1, 4, 5
Marks, Albert, Jr., 5
Marks, Atha, 33, 50, 52, 58, 61–62, 64, 69, 70, 71, 72, 73, 74, 75, 78, 89–90, 92–100, 106–07, 110–13, 116, 123, 130, 134–35, 144, 151, 166, 171, 172, 176, 177, 193–94
Marks, Anna Marie Elizabeth, 7, 9
Marks, August E., 10, 33, 43, 194
Marks, August Texas, 1–11, 151
Marks, August Texas "A. T.," 6–7, 8, 9, 27
Marks, Carl, 3
Marks, Clara, 5
Marks, Emil Henry (E. H.)—
  at Barker, 49–65
  beginning cattleman career, 11, 14
  and Billy, 36–39
  boyhood, 8–9, 11, 13
  cattle career, 14–28, 31, 39–41
  courtship and marriage, 34–35
  crossbreeding Brahmans, 53–54
  crossbreeding shorthorns, 52
  culture, 96–97
  Depression, 141–43, 146–48
  family trips, 71–72, 77, 189–90
  first car, 43–44
  flood control, 173–77
  Houston Fat Stock Show, 163, 180–82
  longhorns, 6–7, 153–68
  poetry and cattle songs, 13–28
  raising poultry, 65
  ranching career, 103–12
  rice, growing, 64
  rodeos, 112–17, 121–29
  St. Louis, trip, 33–34
  Salt Grass Trail, 180–83
  schoolboy, 14–15
  Texas Longhorn Breeders Association of America, 189

Texas Longhorn Centennial Trail Drive, 187–89
Marks, Emory Myron, 35, 36, 38, 39, 43, 44, 45, 50, 55, 56, 58, 59, 60, 61, 62, 63, 65, 68, 72, 73, 74, 75, 77, 79, 80, 90, 95–99, 109, 114, 115, 116–19, 121–24, 127–29, 130–31, 140–43, 148, 165–66, 171, 172, 193
Marks, Godhilf, 1, 2, 3, 4, 193, 194
Marks, Hattie, 5
Marks, Hilf, 5
Marks, 'Hilf, 1, 4
Marks, Hulda, 10
Marks, Jeanne. *See* Houghton, Jeanne
Marks, Jon Emil, 193
Marks, Dorothy Catherine "Kay" Diederich, 193
Marks, Laura, 5
Marks, Linda, 195
Marks, Maud May, 34, 36, 50, 58, 69, 78, 79, 80, 81, 85–100, 111, 116, 124, 129–30, 142–47, 151, 171, 172, 185, 191, 193
Marks, Maudeen Martha, 50, 54, 56, 57, 58, 63–64, 68, 75, 78, 87, 91–93, 96, 97–98, 106, 115–17, 123, 130–31, 141–47, 154–56, 159, 172, 173, 180, 184, 195
Marks, Milo, 46, 193
Marks, Minnie, 5
Marks, Sophia, 1, 2, 3, 4, 151, 194
Marks, Sophie, 10
Marks, Stephen Austin, 193
Marks, Suzanne, 195
Marks, Travis Smith, 32, 40, 44, 50, 58, 59, 90, 94, 97–98, 111, 117, 123, 127, 138–39, 144, 149, 154, 160–61, 163, 165–66, 168, 171, 175, 185, 189, 194–95
Marks, Travis S., Jr., 195
Marks, Willie, 10, 35, 44, 108, 128–29
Marks family, 2, 5, 69, 74
Marks Rodeo. *See* LH7 Ranch Rodeo
Masonic Lodge, 92
Matagorda County, Texas, 133
Matzke, Albert, Mrs., 134

Matzke family, 134
Maxwell (automobile), 75
Mayde Creek, 46
Meyer family, 1
Midwest, 6
Miller, Arthur, 75
Miller family, 75
Miller, Ollie, 75
Milton, Jeff Davis, 87
Miss Eva (teacher), 14
Missouri City, Texas, 62
Missouri-Kansas-Texas Railroad (MKT), 10, 49, 88
Montgomery Ward, 110
Moore, John, 182–83
Muske, Louise "Tanta Lula," 9, 10, 11, 13, 76
Muske, Rufus "Uncle Rufe," 9, 10, 11, 13, 76, 110
Neuman, Gussie Matzke, 134
New Orleans, Louisiana, 62
New Year's, 100
New York City, New York, 82, 138–40, 164
North of 36, 61
North Texas Agricultural College. See University of Texas at Arlington
Oil money
Oklahoma City, Oklahoma, 56
Old Boyd Place, 194
"Old Chisholm Trail, The," 103
Old Pioneers Association, 148
Old Spanish Trail, 164
Old West, 137
Orange Bowl, 179
Oregon's Pendleton Roundup, 114
Owens, Jack, 19
Paddock, W. A., 54–55, 77, 111, 146–47, 149
Paddock-Marks Partnership, 146
Paige, Texas, 121
Painted Desert, Arizona, 81
"Pancho," 183
Parker, Baldwin, 149
Parker, Bonnie, 130–31
Parker, Gus, 128
Parker, Quanah, 149
Pattison, Texas, 11, 13, 24, 76
Pavlova, Anna, 96

Pawnee Bill, 148
Peek, Elmer, 104
Peeler, Graves, 158
Pennyhill station, 141
Petrick, Jessie Matzke, 134
Pierce, "Shanghai," 21, 53
Pierce Estate, 53
Pillot, Chris, 111
Piney Point, Texas, 59
Poison Ivy (bull), 113
Port of New Orleans, 5
Prohibition, 73, 99, 116–17
Querfurt, Prussia, 1
Ralston, Esther, 62
Ranger (steer), 195
Raton Pass, New Mexico, 79
Rawhide, Texas, 2
Reagan High School, 98, 143–44
"Red River Valley," 103
Renaldo, Duncan, 183
Republic of Texas, 2
Revolutionary War, 81
Rice Hotel, 109
Rice University, 32
Richard III (bull), 53
Richmond, Texas, 62
Rickenbacker, Eddie, 115
Ringling Brothers Circus, 85
Rinkel, John, 4
Rio Grande, 53
River Oaks (Houston) Texas, 39
Roberts, Rube, 58
Roberts, Rudy, 58
Rodeos. See Marks/LH7 Ranch
Roebuck
Rogers, Roy, 183
Romack, Ed, 51
Roosevelt, Franklin D., 138, 141, 148
Rotary Club, 82, 185
Rouff, Melvin, 142–43
Roy (horse), 183
Rubinstein, Arthur, 96
St. Augustine, Florida, 164–65
St. Johns River bridge
St. Joseph's Infirmary, 114
St. Lawrence County, New York, 99
St. Louis, Missouri, 33–34
Salt Grass, 181–82

Salt Grass Trail, 182–83, 194
Salt Grass Trail Association, 183
Salt Grass Trail Route, 181–82
San Antonio, Texas, 187–88
San Felipe, Texas, 8
San Jacinto Battleground, 148
San Jacinto Memorial, 148
San Jacinto River, 60
Sancho, The Homing Steer, 186
Sancho's Double (steer), 187
Santa Anna, Texas, 92
Santa Anna Mountains, 81, 93
Santa Fe, New Mexico, 79, 193
Sauer, Dick, 14
Saums, Mr., 134
Sayso, 70
Scardina's, 55
Schmidt, John, 126
Schotts Bakery, 43
Schuetzenfests, 69
Schulz, Anna Marie Elizabeth. *See* Marks, Anne Marie Elizabeth
Schulz, Johann Joachim Friedrich, 9, 10, 33
Schulz, Louise. *See* Muske, Louise
Schulz, Marie Emilie, 33
Schulz, Sophie, 9, 10, 33
Schulz, Wilhelm "Uncle Billy," 7, 9, 10, 43
Schulz family, 9, 35
Scott family, 132
Sears, 110
Shorthorns, 52, 155
Shriners, 115
Shudde's Hat Company, 76
Silliman, Mrs., 7
Sills, Joe, 45
Simonton, Texas, 111
Simpson, Boots, 129
Simpson, Judd, 10, 44, 50, 52
Simpson, Sophie, 44, 50
Smith, Ada, 86–87
Smith, Fred Henry, 51, 86, 86–87, 90
Smith, Freda, 73
Smith, Martha Clark, 85, 86
Smith, Maud May. See Marks, Maud May
Smith, Myron Thaddeus, 99

Smith, "Old Man," 42
Smith, Reed, 72–73
Smith, Stafford, 22
Smith, Thad, 38–39, 59
Smith family, 36, 52, 172
Smith hotel, 85–86
Smithsonian Institution, 46
Smoky (steer), 184
Snakey, Mabel, 36
Sour Lake oil field, 32
South Texas, 6, 54, 60, 126, 164
South Texas Commercial National Bank, 143
South Texas Producers Association, 64
Southeast Texas, 21, 32, 153
Southern Pacific Railroad, 132, 144
Spindletop oil field, 32
Spot (steer), 148, 155, 164
Spring Branch, Texas, 36, 181
Spring Branch community hall, 68
Stafford, Texas, 62
Stallones, B. E., 64
State Archeological Landmark (SAL), 195
Steffens, Suzanne, 195
Stetson hat, 15
Stevens, Buck, 104
Straack's mill, 67
Striepe, Christian, 3–4
Striepe, Sophia, 4
Sugar Land, Texas, 33, 130
Sullivan, Moon, 104
Summers, E. L., 167
Sussex County, England, 86
Sylvan Beach, 74, 75
Syracuse, New York, 140
telephone girls, 134
Texas A&M University, 51, 88, 145, 160, 162, 167
Texas and Southwestern Cattle Raisers Association, 133
Texas and Southwestern Horseman, 37
Texas Antiquities Committee, 196
Texas Centennial (1936), 148, 149
Texas City, Texas, 32
Texas coast, 5
Texas fever, 126

Texas Hill Country, 195
Texas Historical Commission, 195
Texas Longhorn Breeder Association, 187, 189, 194
Texas Longhorn Centennial Trail Drive, 187, 189
Texas Prison Commission, 54
Texas Revolution, 35
Texas State College for Women. *See* Texas Woman's University
Texas Woman's University, 144–45, 172, 176
Thanksgiving, 65
Thomas, Albert, 175
Thornton, Otto, 104
Tige (wolf-dog), 164–65
"Tin Hall." *See* Cypress community hall
Tomball, Texas, 64, 67
Tomball Fair, 163
Trinity County, Texas, 163
Turner, Doctor, 100
U. S. Army, 165–66
U. S. Army Corps of Engineers, 174
United Cigar stores, 109
University of Texas, 186
University of Texas at Arlington, 143
Vallee, Rudy, 75
Vandre, Gerhardt, 104
Vaughan, Athene Bundick. *See* Bundick, Athene
Vicksburg campaign, 4
Waco, Texas, 10, 56
Waggoner, Silas, 46
Waggoner family, 134
Wagner, Richard, 97
Waldorf-Astoria Hotel, 140
Walker County roundup, 60
Waller, Texas, 37
Walt Disney's Wonderful World of Color, 186
Walter, Mina S., 5
War Bonds, 166
Ward, Sam, 19, 103
Warnasch, John, 106, 167, 180–81
Warneke, Ed, 104
Warwick Hotel, 22
Washington, D. C., 140, 175

Watkins products, 95
Weiman, Albert, 51
Welch, Mayor Louie, 191
Wendling family, 44
West Texas, 92
"Wet Hat" brand, 3, 193
Wharton County, Texas, 53
White House, 138, 141
White Oak Bayou, 174
White Oak community hall, 68, 72, 87
Wild West days, 14, 141
Wilkins, George, 64
Wilmington, Delaware, 141
Wilmington Morning News, 141
Wilson, Lois, 61
Wolf Creek, 112
Womanhandled, 62
World War I, 71, 76, 112, 115, 173
World War II, 165, 173, 184
Yellowstone National Park, 78, 79

About the Author

Native Texan Deborah Lightfoot Sizemore has written extensively on the cattle industry and Texas and Western history and biography. Her work has appeared in *The Cattleman, Persimmon Hill*, the *Longhorn Scene, Simbrah World, Lone Star Horse Report*, and other magazines. She is an active member of Western Writers of America, has served as a Spur Awards judge, and is a professional member of the National Writers Club. A summa cum laude graduate of Texas A&M University with a bachelor of science in agricultural journalism, she is listed in *Who's Who in the South and Southwest* and *Who's Who of American Women*. *The LH7 Ranch: In Houston's Shadow*, while still in unfinished manuscript, was a prize winner in the 1988 Texas-Wide Writers' Competition and a finalist in the 1989 C. L. Sonnichsen Book Award competition.

She is researching a biography of Texas trail driver and cattleman George W. Saunders. Her own grandfather, George Winfield Lightfoot, cowboyed on the Panhandle-South Plains around the turn of the century; her grandmother, Fannie Tennessee Watts Lightfoot, is on the Honor Roll of Texas Quilters.

Deborah and her husband Gene Sizemore live and work in the country south of Fort Worth in a self-designed and self-built house.

www.ingramcontent.com/pod-product-compliance
Lightning Source LLC
Chambersburg PA
CBHW030315080526
44584CB00012B/578